Casino and Gaming Resort Investigations

Casino and Gaming Resort Investigations addresses the continued and growing need for gaming security professionals to properly and successfully investigate the increasing and unique types of crime they will face in their careers. As the gaming industry has grown, so has the need for competent and highly skilled investigators who must be prepared to manage a case of employee theft one day and a sophisticated sports book scam the next.

This book provides the reader with the fundamental knowledge needed to understand how each gaming and non-gaming department functions and interacts within the overall gaming resort, allowing the investigator to determine and focus on the important elements of any investigation in any area. Each chapter delivers a background of a department or type of crime normally seen in the gaming environment, and then discusses what should be considered important or even critical for the investigator to know or determine in the course of the investigation. Likely scenarios, case histories and tips, as well as cautions for investigators to be aware of, are used throughout the book.

This book was written for and directed at gaming security and surveillance professionals, including gaming regulators, and tribal gaming authorities, who are almost daily confronted by the ingenious and the most common scams, theft, and frauds that are perpetrated in the gaming world.

Derk J. Boss is a gaming surveillance, security and loss prevention specialist. He has served in executive positions in security, surveillance and compliance capacities for American Casino and Entertainment Properties, Grand Casinos, Bally's, Aztar, Del E. Web, Corp., Palms, Tropicana Entertainment and MGM Resorts.

Alan W. Zajic is a Nevada licensed, Board Certified, independent security consultant specializing in gaming and nightclub environments. He has over forty years of practical hands-on experience in security and surveillance operations including Security Director for the Sahara Tahoe and High Sierra resorts in Lake Tahoe as well as corporate security for Del E. Web, Corp. in Nevada.

Casino and Gaming Resort Investigations

Derk J. Boss and Alan W. Zajic

Routledge
Taylor & Francis Group

NEW YORK AND LONDON

First published 2020
by Routledge
52 Vanderbilt Avenue, New York, NY 10017

and by Routledge
2 Park Square, Milton Park, Abingdon, Oxon, OX14 4RN

Routledge is an imprint of the Taylor & Francis Group, an informa business

© 2020 Taylor & Francis

Library of Congress Cataloging-in-Publication Data
Names: Boss, Derk J., author. | Zajic, Alan W., author.
Title: Casino security and gaming resort investigations / Derk J. Boss &
Alan W. Zajic.
Description: 1 Edition. | New York : Routledge, 2019. | Includes index.
Identifiers: LCCN 2019007296 (print) | LCCN 2019012036 (ebook) |
ISBN 9781315118734 (Ebook) | ISBN 9781482246360 (hardback) | ISBN
9780367259549 (pbk.)
Subjects: LCSH: Casinos–Security measures–Handbooks, manuals, etc. |
Electronic surveillance–Handbooks, manuals, etc. | Gambling–Corrupt
practices. | Criminal investigation.
Classification: LCC HV6711 (ebook) | LCC HV6711 .B672 2019 (print) |
DDC 795.068/4–dc23
LC record available at https://lccn.loc.gov/2019007296

ISBN: 978-1-4822-4636-0 (hbk)
ISBN: 978-0-367-25954-9 (pbk)
ISBN: 978-1-315-11873-4 (ebk)

Typeset in Bembo
by Swales & Willis, Exeter, Devon, UK

MIX
Paper from
responsible sources
FSC   FSC™ C013985
www.fsc.org

Printed in the United Kingdom
by Henry Ling Limited

This book is dedicated to those who make my happiness possible in so many ways,

To my beautiful Jen
My wife, my life, my love, my sail. You make it all possible! Thank you for coming into my life!

To Jason
Jason, my wonderful son. You've been a joy to me since the day you were born. I am very proud of you,
indeed!

And now there are John Lucas and Micaela to add to that joy.

To my family: Suzanne and Tim, Mike and Lori, and Zane and Benjamin: We have all always been there for each other!

To my new family: Katelyn, Kyle and Morgan, and Alynna: Thank you for welcoming me into your family and sharing your beautiful mother with me!

To Jacob
An amazing young man!

Derk J. Boss

I dedicate my portion of this book to my daughter Angie whose natural investigative mind continues to amaze and motivate me.

Alan W. Zajic, CPP, CSP

Contents

About the Authors

 **Derk** is a gaming surveillance, security and loss prevention specialist. He has served in executive positions in security, surveillance and compliance capacities for American Casino and Entertainment Properties, Grand Casinos, Bally's, Aztar, Del E. Web, Corp., Palms, Tropicana Entertainment and MGM Resorts.

Derk, as a director of security and later as a vice president of security and surveillance, has performed risk assessments and developed emergency response manuals for several different properties, as well as action plans for business recovery. Derk has prepared both security and surveillance teams to respond to emergency events through regular training and drills. He has hands-on experience in the assessment of threats and risks, and the handling of different types of critical events. He has served as a consultant for security and surveillance to Tribal Gaming properties and is a Raving Partner with Raving Consulting.

Derk is Board Certified as a security professional and possesses knowledge and proficiency in security principles and practices, business principles and practices, legal aspects of security, personnel security, physical security, information security, crisis management and investigation. The surveillance teams trained and led by Derk have a proven track record of success in the detection of cheating at gaming, advantage play, and internal and external theft and fraud.

Derk has earned professional certification as a Certified Fraud Examiner (CFE), as a Certified Protection Professional (CPP) and as a Certified Surveillance Professional (CSP). He is currently the President of the International Association of Certified Surveillance Professionals (IACSP) and is one of its founding members.

He co-authored *Casino Security and Gaming Surveillance* (2010) and is a respected author, instructor and speaker, specializing in the fields of surveillance training and methodology, gaming protection, loss prevention and the detection of internal and external theft and fraud.

He has appeared as an expert on several television networks, including the Travel Channel, and his technical articles have appeared in dozens of professional journals, including *Security Management* magazine, which is published by ASIS International. ASIS International is the largest organization for security professionals with more than 36,000 members worldwide. As a speaker, he has been featured at several international conferences, including the Global Gaming Exposition (G2E), World Gaming Protection Conference and ASIS International seminars and programs.

Derk is currently Director of Surveillance for the Angel of the Winds Casino Resort in Marysville, WA where he resides with his beautiful wife, Jen.

 **Alan W. Zajic** is a Nevada licensed, Board Certified, independent security consultant specializing in gaming and nightclub environments. He has over forty years of practical hands-on experience in security and surveillance operations including Security Director for the Sahara Tahoe and High Sierra resorts in Lake Tahoe as well as corporate security for Del E. Web, Corp. in Nevada.

Alan is a member of ASIS International where he holds the certification of Certified Protection Professional (CPP) and is a long-standing member of the Gaming and Wagering Protection Council including past chairman. He is also a past chairman of the Hospitality Entertainment and Tourism Security Council and is a past Council Vice President for ASIS International. He is actively involved in the Northern Nevada and Las Vegas Chapters as well as the international security community. He was awarded the ASIS International "Outstanding Council Chairman of the Year" for 2010.

He is a member of the International Association of Certified Surveillance Professionals (IACSP) where he holds the designation of Certified Surveillance Professional (CSP) and is a member of the International Association of Professional Security Consultants (IAPSC). Additionally he is a member of the International Society of Crime Prevention Practitioners (ISCPP) and holds their designation of International Crime Prevention Specialist (ICPS).

Alan is an instructor for the University of Nevada at Reno in the Gaming Management Program and for the International Gaming Institute at UNLV as an instructor in casino security and surveillance applications. He is frequently requested to present sessions at international security conferences and for various organizations throughout the country including ASIS International, IAPSC, International Security Conferences (ISC), World Game Protection Conference, National Indian Gaming Association Conference, Southern California Surveillance Symposium, Minnesota Casino Intelligence Unit, Table Games Conference, Nightclub and Bar Conference, and others.

He is co-author of the book *Casino Security and Gaming Surveillance* (2010), has written numerous professional articles and has been media interviewed internationally on various security and surveillance topics. In addition he is frequently requested to perform the services of a forensic security consultant (expert witness) in gaming, hospitality, retail, bars, nightclubs and multi-unit housing environments and has testified in various jurisdictions nationally.

His practice areas include forensic consulting, management consulting, major incident management, and policy and procedure development, and he conducts tailored training programs for gaming operations.

Foreword

It was a Wednesday afternoon and the casino was quiet. The weekend crowds were still a few days away.

The surveillance room was quiet too. Two of the three on-duty surveillance agents were patrolling the pit and the slot departments looking for suspicious activity or bad guys.

The third agent, Jerry, was assigned to an audit. He was observing pit floor persons as they rated players, often a point for fraud. The more time a player was shown playing large wagers the more comps or cash back he could obtain. If a player was tight with a floor person, he could easily obtain more than he deserved. People knew this and ratings were frequently inflated. Thus, the reason for the audit.

Jerry, growing tired of watching the on-duty floor personnel, moved his camera into the center of the pit and looked over the shoulder of the pit clerk as she entered information into her terminal. Suddenly, Jerry sat straight up and hollered for David, his supervisor. "David, can you come over and look at this, it's weird." David, a surveillance veteran of fifteen years, sprang over. "What'd you got, Jer?"

"Carrie is doing weird things with these accounts, check it out." David took one look at what Carrie was doing and knew immediately something was wrong. He picked up the phone and called me. "Boss, you need to check this out!"

When I walked out to the room and looked at the monitors displaying the cameras focused on Carrie and her computer, I didn't know that I was looking at a case that would ultimately result in the identification of over $100,000 of loss to our property and the arrest of Carrie (and her fiancé and their roommate) for embezzlement and computer fraud, or that this case would expose a fatal weakness in slot clubs, one that continues to this day.

This case is among the many I've been involved with over my thirty years in surveillance. It's funny to me, looking back over the years, the way my gaming career has changed and how surveillance has changed in that time span also. When I began my casino career I never thought I would end up in surveillance or that I would spend much of my time investigating casino crime, especially employee crime.

When I started in surveillance I was trained to look for card counters. That was our major effort at the time. We didn't spend much time looking at much else. Craps, slots, keno, or race and sports were rarely looked at. Employees in those areas, almost never. It was always the twenty-one pit and those notorious card counters.

As I got better at my job I began realizing that there was more out there. I started not only looking at other areas, I also began small investigations of my own, looking at reasons for employee cash variances, watching for credit claimers and monitoring bartenders, to name a few. I also realized that I had no training in investigations and really didn't know much about handling a case. What I did have on my side was that I was unafraid to ask questions of others, and ask I did. I was fortunate at that time to know two individuals who provided their wisdom and guidance. The first, Greg Spendlove, was a Nevada gaming enforcement agent assigned to the Laughlin, Nevada area where I worked at the time. He gave me many tips on how criminals operate. The second is my co-author Al Zajic. He has, over the years, given generously of his time, wisdom and vast casino experience. Without either of these two gentlemen I would never have been able to perform successful investigations.

This case is just one of the hundreds of cases I've dealt with over the years. During that time I was taught, or learned the hard way, investigative techniques that I could apply to my work in surveillance and in the casino world. I believe that these techniques can be learned by anyone and when used properly are usually successful. In today's gaming environment, a surveillance director must be able to investigate anything and everything, from a bartender stealing from his drawer, to collusion between players and table games staff.

Gaming crime is not going away. You would think with all of the new technology being developed that our ability to detect crime would get better. It has, but it is also apparent that the bad guys are benefiting from technology too. As I write this, three properties in Las Vegas were hit by a sophisticated gang of Asians who used a hidden camera on baccarat to cheat each of these properties of a considerable amount of money!

Besides the outside threat, there is always the internal threat. It has always been my contention that we (gaming properties) lose more to our own employees than we do to cheats and advantage players. That may surprise some of you but I believe it sincerely. I say this not to take away from the criticality of the outside threat but to stress that the insider is just as, if not more, dangerous.

My gaming career started in the early 1980s in Lake Tahoe, Nevada. My first job was as a change person in the slot department on the graveyard shift at the Sahara Tahoe. I had moved from the San Francisco Bay Area because

I loved the snow and the mountains. It was going to be a temporary thing; have some fun, make some money, meet new people. Little did I know then that my life would be changed forever by gaming and that I would never return home to the Bay Area.

Working in a casino was and still is fun. Even though I worked graveyard, things were always happening. The lounges were open with great acts! I saw lots of performers and bands starting out, hypnotists, comedians. It was fantastic and exciting! There were lots of people my age, girls everywhere and everyone was partying and having a good time. For a twenty-two year old it was heaven.

The casino got into my blood. I was always a hard worker and I loved a great time: perfect for the casino world. I worked hard, had a good attitude and did what I was told. I began to move up. First as a booth cashier (I wish I had pictures of those old slot booths; they were huge!), then a slot floor person. When a position for an assistant slot shift supervisor opened up I applied even though I didn't have as much experience as the other applicants. Well, they saw something in me I didn't know I had and gave me the job.

I worked hard. I was all over the floor, helping everyone I could and learning my new job. I loved it! Eventually, I was promoted to a slot shift supervisor and began honing my leadership skills. I think that because of my positive attitude and willingness to work as hard as everyone else, my shift always got more done than the other shifts and had more fun doing it!

As I progressed through my slot career, one thing became very apparent; I was good at spotting things or people out of place or acting unusually. These were the days of slugs in slot machines, handle popping and mechanical progressive slot machines that were, at that time, being hit by slot cheat teams.

It was their behavior that caught my eye. These kinds of people acted differently than the players I saw every day. Looking around (rubbernecking); one or more people standing around while another played a single slot machine; I've even been approached by some of these people with questions (to get me away from the area).

Rather than divert my attention, their behavior made me even more suspicious. I usually wasted no time in reporting my suspicions to the surveillance department. We made a number of good busts that way.

Eventually, my ability got noticed by the surveillance director and he asked me if I was interested in taking a job as a surveillance agent in Laughlin, Nevada. I agreed and the rest, as they say, is history.

This book is about my career in surveillance, as a trainee and as I progressed through the ranks. But, more importantly, it is about what I learned about surveillance operations and investigations, and how to protect a casino hotel resort. I know when I started in surveillance the training was virtually nonexistent. It is not much better today. Surveillance directors can't afford to learn the hard way anymore (by getting cheated or taken advantage of), it is too costly! Nowadays, we'd all be out of a job before we learned everything we need to know.

So, contained herein are the short cuts and techniques I learned and used over a still continuing career (into its third decade) to investigate casino and hotel crime.

I hope these thoughts and techniques help you in your career and guide you in the protection of your property.

Derk J. Boss, CFE, CPP, CSP
Las Vegas, Nevada
December 24, 2018

Foreword

This book was written to assist all of the security and surveillance professionals that enter, work in and help solve the mysteries surrounding internal theft, undesirable behavior and criminal actions in the gaming environments. Most investigators in our industry must start with little guidance outside of the management oversight and with sometimes only a curious mind and a sincere desire to solve mysteries. This book is designed to help those willing to learn and grow.

This book can be used as a basic guide to conducting professional investigations within the walls of a casino resort, riverboat, racino or other establishment that houses gaming. In every environment where there is constant exchange and handling of cash or chips, there is the potential for theft regardless whether it is a tribal casino or mega resort. In every environment where people are charged with dealing with patrons, employees or cash, there is potential for regulatory infractions, violations of protocol and procedure, or criminal activity.

We have inserted many instances of career success involving investigations but have not always included those failures every investigator faces during their career. We made mistakes during our investigations and learned from them every time, which may be hidden as lessons learned within each chapter throughout this book.

This book is designed to be a desk reference for the investigator to stimulate their minds, give them ideas for solving those mysteries and increase their professionalism as an investigator. This book is for those who want to learn and grow and not for those who believe they know everything about investigating. We ask that you always continue to learn and improve your investigation skills with an open mind, with professionalism and in an ethical manner.

Alan W. Zajic, CPP, CSP

Foreword

Part I

The Process of Investigation

Chapter 1

The Art of Investigations

> The true investigator continuously learns and improves as each investigation is worked on, solved or closed, and hopefully brought to a satisfactory conclusion.
>
> Alan W. Zajic

There is an art to conducting investigations that requires knowledge, skill, expertise and experience. To be successful the investigator must also have a strong fundamental understanding of the industry he/she works within and the issue being investigated. The gaming industry poses a unique challenge to investigators due to the scope of potential issues and types of losses that may occur. In gaming, the investigator may investigate a case of retail theft one day, a case of cheating at gambling the next, and at the end of the week be involved in the review of a potential conflict of interest involving an executive. In this chapter we discuss the components of a properly conducted investigation.

An important part of any professional security, surveillance or compliance entity is conducting investigations. The necessity of having a competent, professional investigator who can communicate in writing cannot be over-emphasized when dealing in gaming environments with complex regulatory conditions and a diversified employee population. Conducting comprehensive investigations is an art that every investigator learns as they work on a particular case and subsequent cases throughout their career. Although certain training is valuable for the investigator most security professionals believe that trial and error, through experience, is the best teacher. Fundamental investigative practices can be improved for areas such as interviewing through professional courses or study, yet experience is considered the most important tool for the investigator in gaming environments.

Part of any security and surveillance officer's job function is to conduct investigations. These investigations will vary widely in scope and type from the initial field investigation by a uniformed security officer or incident observation by a surveillance employee to the more formal and structured one conducted by a full-time investigator.

The true investigator continuously learns and improves as each investigation is worked on, solved or closed, and hopefully brought to a satisfactory conclusion. There is no magic cookie-cutter list of tasks or items an investigator uses that will solve a particular inquiry where assets, reputation, intellectual property or criminal acts are the focus. There are however consistent items and processes that will guide the investigation process to ensure it is conducted in a thorough and fair manner.

A routine process in all gaming environments is the daunting task of ensuring that compliance to rules, regulations and those self-imposed standards (policies and procedures) designed to protect people and assets within a gaming facility are accomplished and enforced. Compliance investigations are important to casinos to ensure that appropriate follow-up and follow-through occur when a breakdown of the established safeguards creates an opportunity for internal theft.

Any experienced gaming investigator or manager knows that with a loss there is typically a breach of policy or procedure that created an opportunity for that loss. Those breaches are typically an evolved process as a result of inadequate management and oversight of the employees performing various functions. Over time, employees become aware of those failures of supervisors in making sure that proper procedure is followed, which creates the motivation and more importantly the opportunity for internal theft.

Internal theft investigations are consistently presented to be solved in gaming environments. Anything from a company tool, to large amounts of cash, to steaks and lobster for a personal BBQ will be the focus of investigation. Internal theft will be the most emphasized investigation by executive-level management due to principle issues and retention of profits to a property. Internal theft will affect operations in every department of a gaming facility and no entity or department is immune from internal and external theft.

As in any business environment, when profits and company assets are preserved it has a direct impact on the bottom line of the enterprise. We can use the following basic formula: if the process of investigation results in the recovery of $100,000 over a period of one year, the enterprise must make $1 million to compensate for that loss (if you utilize a basic 10 percent profit margin). In other words, if employees steal the equivalent of $100,000, business volumes must be increased by $1 million to re-make that profit. The same goes for when expenses are made in any department. Creating a mechanism to reduce internal theft will positively impact profits or the bottom line of an organization.

There will also be management investigations that will involve many different types of incidents from sexual harassment to embezzlement, collusion to theft, or receiving favors from vendors in return for substantial contracts for goods or services. These investigations require careful analysis and implementation in that the risk of litigation is higher from management-level employees and the potential of the future employment or future financial implications of the intended suspect can be affected. There may also be employment contractual limitations for executive-level employees that must be considered.

Team member or employee investigations also can be sensitive and can affect morale and operations if not handled in the proper fashion. There could be an array of incidents that require some form of investigation including altercations, narcotics, discrimination or other social issues. Internal theft is the most significant risk for loss to an enterprise, which ultimately comes down to employees stealing services, time, inventory, cash or any other thing of value whether obviously negotiable or not.

The simple process that creates revenue itself is compromised routinely by employees. A food server who does not charge for drinks or desserts is essentially stealing from the company, especially if they are doing it to increase gratuities in a restaurant. A dealer can make "mistakes" to the benefit of the customer for the same reason. Ghost employees or punching someone in who is not at work are also theft and should be investigated and prosecuted if proven.

Gaming environments are unique in that they include numerous working parts that must be considered by the investigator. The first consideration should be the specific regulatory environment that governs the gaming operation and whether it is applicable to the target environment. The regulatory environment is a critical part of any gaming facility and a clear understanding of the regulatory authority, processes and history will assist in the process of determining what occurred in any loss. In many environments the regulators will actually conduct internal theft investigations and request (or sometimes require) assistance from operational security or surveillance including staff investigators.

Gaming facilities' many parts include departments and operations that may be part of the primary casino management or may be an amenity or a leased operation of the facility. The details in the individual lease or management agreements may dictate the process of investigating within the four-wall agreement. There are circumstances where a regulator may be involved in a leased operation as part of an investigation even though they may not have a direct management oversight or regulatory oversight authority.

A good example of this would be in the state of Nevada where the Nevada Gaming Control Board has authority anywhere within the four walls of a licensed establishment even when they are within a leased premises. A nightclub, for example, could create criminal activity and cause the licensee to be fined or even lose their gaming license as a result of drugs, prostitution, underage drinking or other criminal acts. In recent years, several nightclubs in Nevada have caused the gaming operator to be the subject of an intense investigation and subsequent fines up to $1 million for not controlling activity inside the venues even though they have no direct control over the activities within the venue. Scrutiny of the regulations is essential to understand that most regulations include language that identifies certain conduct as that which negatively affects the integrity of gaming within the state. The state of Nevada imposed actual regulations involving nightclubs in 2016 even if the casino did not own or operate the leased spaces.

Gaming investigations can become more complex than in isolated environments such as a financial institution. A gaming facility, for example, has an internal department that is much the same as a financial institution, which includes the cashier's cage, sometimes credit operations and the supporting subcomponents, which may include soft and hard count departments, contracted services such as ATM management, accounting departments and others. These will often intersect with other departments or entities within a casino resort, which can include employee interpersonal relationships such as roommates or romantic relationships, friendship or social acquaintances. These relationships may involve illegal drug connections or other undesirable activities that may, and often do, intersect within an investigation. It is quite common for the same name to appear in a link chart as a witness or victim in different investigations.

As gaming facilities evolve in any jurisdiction, many revenue streams are created through operations that do not include gaming tables, machines, keno or bingo lounges, and sportsbooks. Food and beverage operations, retail operations and even movie theaters and bowling alleys are more and more a part of the typical casino complex with direct oversight. Wherever there is cash or credit cards, there is exposure to internal and external theft and therefore the need to monitor, investigate and retain those assets. The more revenue streams that are in place, the more potential for internal theft is present.

There has been a dramatic change in casino operations over the last twenty-five years that includes player incentive programs and additional cost centers. These were "given away" in prior times as an amenity rather than a revenue source, based on the older theories in casino marketing that subscribed to the theory that if you give away the buffet or other teaser, the customers would stay and gamble. This paradigm shift was in part a result of economic conditions in 2007 and 2008 when casinos had to do more with less and creative executives found sources of revenue that were taboo in earlier decades. It also created a reduction in oversight through reduced payrolls and operational changes to adjust to the economic trends in gaming environments.

The investigator's job is to retain the assets of the enterprise in an efficient and productive manner with minimal risk for litigation, negative morale or negative management perceptions. Their job is also to develop and recommend procedures and processes to reduce the risk of future internal theft and incidents based on their experience and details collected during investigations.

The investigation function must also demonstrate that the expense of investigation is a worthwhile investment. This is accomplished in proving that the end results can be easily quantified in dollars to the enterprise in deterrence, savings, recovery and proactive management. Many investigators fail to calculate the numbers, which rule operations in gaming environments, and justify the process.

Understanding where you have made a mistake and how it was made is always a learning tool that also should not be underestimated. There are many great books and publications on investigations and techniques for obtaining positive results in an investigation. This book is not designed to teach basic investigation skills but to enhance those that are already being done in a facility with gaming.

Key Takeaways

- Conducting investigations is a critical component of any professional security, surveillance or compliance entity.
- Having a professional and competent investigator is a necessity.
- Losses typically occur due to a breach or violation of controls, policies or procedures.
- Investigators who work in a gaming environment may investigate losses, issues or complaints arising from gaming and non-gaming areas, as well as regulatory compliance violations.
- In recent years player incentive programs such as "free play" issued by player's club has only added to the assets exposed to loss on a gaming property.

Best Practices

- Develop and maintain a robust investigative program that can be used in all areas and facets of the modern gaming facility.
- Ensure each of your investigators is prepared to investigate the issues that may arise.

Chapter 2

Field Investigations

> One of the critical functions of any investigation is the initial discovery and what is commonly referred to as the field investigation.
>
> Alan W. Zajic

Many investigations begin in the field with the first responders, who are typically security officers. It is this initial response that often determines the success of the investigation. The identification of witnesses and obtaining their statements, securing the crime scene, gathering and securing of evidence, and review of available video must happen to ensure the incident at hand can be investigated. It is at this point that investigations may begin to fail and never recover if the field investigation isn't performed properly. On the other hand, a thorough and well-documented field investigation immediately puts the investigation on track and normally contains the elements needed to solve crime or resolve the issue.

One of the critical functions of any investigation is the initial discovery and what is commonly referred to as the field investigation. In gaming environments, the vast majority of investigations will start with the field investigation by security personnel, surveillance officers, compliance officers or operational supervisors and managers. This will be the basis and primary understanding of the loss or incident, how it was discovered and by whom, employees with access, and the collection of evidence that may or oftentimes may not be critical in solving the loss.

In incident investigations it will start with the employee or customer reporting to an employee or manager. The importance of collecting all potential evidence immediately cannot be underestimated in that failure to retain simple documents, witness information or enough video data may decrease the solvability of the loss and could potentially cause liability and spoliation of evidence. All contacts should start with the collection of primary information, identity and contact information.

In surveillance investigations it is prudent to save large amounts of video data during this phase to ensure that there is sufficient video to conduct an investigation. A simple example may be a cashier cage robbery of an employee where video from a previous shift or day may show important facts such as the employee speaking to the robber, or the perpetrator conducting intelligence gathering prior to committing the robbery. This collection of many hours of digital media is a simple process that, if not completed, will be gone forever once the video is rewritten by the surveillance system. These many hours of video may also provide other valuable information such as bad cash habits, violations of internal controls or just inattention or sloppy work habits.

Many investigators will require notification when an event or loss occurs in order to start the direction of the investigation at hand. Certain triggers or *trip wires* will prompt the on-site management to notify the investigator who may choose to come in after normal working hours and take over the investigation from the staff member conducting the field investigation. This is a common practice and can be beneficial in most serious investigations. A dollar amount is identified regarding a loss or shortage with a mandate for notification of the investigator and certain protocols are implemented immediately to prevent a potential suspect from destroying or changing evidence.

As a simple example in a hypothetical cage drawer shortage, important items to retain during the field investigation are the trash cans in the work area, which may yield many important clues and evidence. Multiple adding machine tapes used when attempting to balance a drawer, balance worksheets, currency straps, personal notes, and contraband such as evidence of alcohol or drugs are just a very few items that may prove productive in the course of the investigation. The trash will also yield a chronology of information that may prove beneficial to retrace and compare to the video evidence collected. People throw away things they no longer need and believe psychologically that if they throw it away it is gone forever.

Any private investigator knows that if you collect the trash from a targeted person under investigation it will always yield details of the person who disposed of it. Our trash contains many clues of our lifestyle, eating habits, bad habits and even criminal activity. It is much easier to collect and bag the trash and throw it away later than to try and recover something from it when it is long gone.

Another perishable item is the exact condition of the immediate environment when the loss or incident occurred. This is typically taken as still shots from video and actual photographs by the field investigator to document conditions, placement of items and condition of the area overall. A good practice is to also slowly pan, in detail, the area of the loss as soon after as possible, which will also document the changes in the environment post-loss for comparison to the review coverage. A purse or backpack located close to the loss location may prove beneficial if it is there before the loss and is removed shortly after the loss.

Still photography from the video should be taken on all investigations from all angles of coverage. These still pictures will become a great resource and reference during the course of the investigation. Pictures taken from video can aid during interviews and even assist the investigator in completing the report by inserting a digital photo into the report to help illustrate with drawn symbols, arrows or text boxes.

Additional items that should not be perishable such as access control records by the employee, meal punch times and other tracking may be automatically purged after a short period of time. These perishable evidentiary items are critical to retain during the field investigation. If the investigator gets in a habit of collecting all of the potential evidence the process will become automatic and much easier over time.

In some environments there are personnel assigned to work a shift with the sole purpose of conducting preliminary investigations as losses or incidents are discovered or as they occur on the casino floor. For example, many tribal gaming operations have compliance officers who perform these tasks on a routine basis during their work shift. Some of these officers often lack a fundamental understanding of how to conduct an investigation and how to document it for further follow-up for satisfactory conclusion. Although most investigators will have a desire and believe that they are competently conducting an investigation, they often lack the training and experience to obtain critical information and evidence when it is fresh and most valuable. Much of the evidence in gaming investigations is perishable in that over time it loses its value or it may even disappear. These same inexperienced investigators will tend to offer opinions and conclusions counterproductive to the investigation in their written reports.

It would be productive to supply these compliance investigators or any other security or surveillance employee who performs the initial field investigation with written guidelines or bullet points for the most common types of investigations they will come across in daily activities. A written checklist of items the field investigator or initiator should be looking for and collecting is always helpful in the evolved on-the-job training of the operational or compliance staff.

In the hypothetical cage loss, the following example checklist may be provided to the field investigator:

- Retain trash cans marked, sealed and identified by location.
- Retain all shift paperwork, coordinate with accounting for entire shift and all employees.
- Pull adding machine tapes not located in trash, marked by location.
- Request full video retention for review of all cameras inside and outside of the cage that may view employees or customers.
- Retain a copy of the work schedule for the day and any break schedules.

- Document all employees working for twenty-four hours before and twenty-four hours after discovery of loss.
- Pull supervisor logs or daily reports for all shifts for twenty-four hours before and twenty-four hours after loss.
- Determine if any employee took an "early out" and left mid-shift or early.
- Pull access control records if applicable and any evidence of access by non-cage personnel.
- Identify CRT or computer terminals utilized by primary employee and other employees.
- Pull all paid out documents, TITO (ticket in ticket out) manual payout reports and any other department processes.
- Request the over/short reports for employees with access for a period of time.
- Interview the immediate supervisor for any information on unusual changes in behavior or conditions.

The basic guide can be modified to the environment and will prove valuable once the full-time investigator comes in to start their formal investigation. A guide should be made for what are the common losses or incidents that would involve a field investigation. Working with the risk manager to help develop these field investigation guides would also be suggested as they deal with the claim process and would have valuable input.

Physical security officers will also often conduct a field investigation when first responding to an incident or a *call for service*. These security personnel are typically also not trained investigators and do not always ask or document the much-needed details or causes for a particular incident or loss. It is also important to work with these security officers to help develop their field investigation skills and not to openly criticize them if they failed to collect information you would have wanted. The professional investigator is also a teacher to the first responder to an incident in that they can train security personnel in the methods to collect information, evidence, witness contact information and sufficient detail at the scene where the evidence and opportunities are perishable and will be gone or forgotten in a short period of time.

We have found that if the investigator conducts infrequent classes on conducting field investigations the quality of reporting and overall investigations will improve including recovery and other successful outcomes. Physical security personnel actually enjoy training that allows them to be creative and assist in the investigation process.

Security personnel will typically take the easiest way out when responding and reporting a loss or incident unless directed by supervision otherwise. In rare exceptions, there will be that security officer that will outshine others and demonstrate investigative abilities. Because they are service-call driven, security personnel will not always pay close attention to the detail needed in an investigation. Not only is a good working relationship with the security officers recommended, more importantly a solid working relationship with each and every security and surveillance shift manager or supervisor will prove beneficial in long-term solvability of cases.

Complimenting security officers when they conduct good field investigations will go a long way in the ultimate goal of obtaining initial information during the field investigation. Controlling the quality of information collected initially will make the process easier and less stressful in the long run. In short, use good management skills in working with the initial field investigator.

Key Takeaways

- Field investigations are a critical function of an investigation.
- Identifying sources and witnesses, and collecting and securing evidence should be done during the field investigation.
- Officers who first respond to incidents or calls for service should be trained to obtain and document necessary information.

Best Practices

- Conducting a thorough field investigation provides the necessary components for a professional and complete investigation.
- Train first responders to gather necessary information and secure evidence.

Chapter 3

Marketing Considerations and Investigations

> Marketing promotions can create opportunities for fraud, conversion and internal theft.
>
> Alan W. Zajic

A much-misunderstood function by security, surveillance and compliance officers is the marketing function in a gaming facility. Marketing is a dynamic, constantly changing condition that has far-reaching ramifications to the security and surveillance function in protection of assets. The simple and basic player incentive program management is typically managed by a marketing department that has a vested interest in proving that they have accomplished the task of generating revenues through volumes of customers with incentives and gimmicks. The importance of marketing in the investigation function should not be underestimated.

The marketing that occurs in gaming environments is constant, creative and permeates every department and function within a casino. Marketing programs are designed to get customers in the doors and then capture those customers with incentives or processes that entice them to spend money and attempt to make them a loyal return customer. They also count on human behavior to keep the customers once they have drawn them into the casino and ultimately spend more disposable income gambling, eating, drinking or making other retail purchases. Marketing programs will be the subject, motivator and cause of many internal and external theft investigations. The need to be well informed on marketing programs is important to adequately perform well and investigate thoroughly.

Marketing programs frequently offer cash back or other negotiable instrument incentives to the dishonest employee and the opportunity for conversion to cash for their own use at the expense of the property. These programs often offer cash back, additional premium player points, two for one discount coupons, discounts for food and beverages, and many others. The fact is that every promotion will have some *scam factor* involved and will have internal theft associated with it. The question will be how much money will be involved and what scams will be found, and if the scam factor is high or low. Think of it in a risk assessment form whenever a new promotion is contemplated or initiated. Knowing the vulnerabilities in a marketing program will quicken the investigation process and assist in design of future promotions.

By conducting a risk assessment of the promotion, identifying the potential risks involved and including the potential financial gains the program will produce, the security professional can develop a plan ahead of time to deal with scams before they hit, or mitigate the potential losses by implementing strategies that will limit opportunity by local abusers or others. The only way this will work is if you have a good working relationship with the marketing department and have an opportunity to be involved in the planning and implementation phases before the program is deployed. This also involves buy-in from the general manager (GM) or chief operational officer (COO).

In most environments where casinos are located there is a segment of the undesirable population, which includes the homeless or indigent persons who will work hard to obtain access to the marketing promotions to obtain food, cash or even clothing. These people often have nicknames that they are given and communicate with each other regularly on the latest way to get something from a casino. In the Lake Tahoe market they were referred to as "tree trolls", in Laughlin, Nevada they were referred to as "river rats" and in Louisiana as "swamp rats". The investigator should stay away from these nicknames during the interview processes and be very familiar with these groups as they tend to drive the abuse methods, which can be very creative.

These groups of undesirables are much like bands of outlaw gypsies who will prey on a property and vulnerabilities in marketing programs. These are much different than the organized retail gangs (ORG) who will be able to penetrate your facility and in a short period of time will commit theft, pickpocketing, shortchanging and many other distraction crimes or scams and be gone before the first loss is reported. Imagine if a group of twenty-five people comes into your property, all well versed in the art of shortchanging employees, and each comes out with $100 within a fifteen-minute period. It would also be when a *flash-rob* occurs. Again, imagine your retail operation being flooded with people who take items and leave all at once with the lone clerk watching helplessly, or the pit floor man when the same group each takes a handful of chips at the same time on a bust night.

Most contemporary gaming operations employ someone within the marketing department to monitor the World Wide Web and social media for negative and positive postings regarding the facility and take action to mitigate or remove the negative ones. Rarely do they actually use this person for detection of scams, theft or just looking for that person selling an item on eBay that belongs to the enterprise. Some gaming operations are employing social media investigators that can assist in internal theft or external planning of organized theft using social media that the perpetrator thinks no one can see. In larger more sophisticated operations these same investigators who monitor social media also complete the process of *data mining* to watch for anomalies in hold percentages, machine abnormalities, revenue reports, cash over/short reports and other accounting records.

The basic communication and full knowledge of all marketing programs including player incentive and tracking programs will aid in the quest to solve internal theft, conversion and collusion and will save the investigator time and effort in case management. As a minimum a monthly lunch meeting with the marketing department would be beneficial and very productive to assist in hardening the promotion. The scam factors we always identified and rated in the marketing program used low, medium, high or "are you out of your mind" categories.

The other important marketing concern is the player tracking or incentive programs, which are covered in depth later in this book. We would strongly recommend that the investigator have access to and be thoroughly trained in the program to include software training, password control, merging and closing reports, and exception reports. This access will prove very beneficial in link charting people involved internally and externally during an investigation either directly or indirectly. The investigator must also clearly understand the sensitivity of the customer personal data and not release it even when involving law enforcement or executives and only on a need-to-know basis.

In a good working relationship with marketing, the head of marketing would often notify the security director of their scam factor rating before even getting notified formally. The objective is always to make them think of potential holes and therefore losses before they propose it to the GM. The investigator again is a teacher to marketing executives. It also eventually will become mandatory that appropriate management and the investigator are copied on all proposals and internal memos on promotions. It can be surprising how marketing will intertwine in most casino investigations.

The following are some examples of questions the investigator should ask and consider when evaluating a marketing promotion:

- Is there a direct cash payment involved in the promotion where a customer gets cash or other negotiable items such as casino chips?
- Is there a mechanism to control "2 for 1" purchase promotions?
- Can conversion to negotiable benefits or cash be accomplished easily?
- Are there limitations clearly printed and posted on abuse and restrictions?
- Does marketing have and use a master eviction or exclusion list to prevent direct mail or abuse and use by barred patrons?
- Does marketing have a database of winners checked regularly for abuses?
- Do player incentive points have clear restrictions and controls to prevent abuse and internal theft by employees?
- Are exception reports taken from the data and actually analyzed to include unusual point transfers or bulk point distributions?

And finally, the investigator and supervisors should review the program and meet to check the vulnerability of the particular program and brainstorm the possible ways that employees or undesirable patrons can scam it and perpetrate an internal theft. This knowledge drawn for the discovery of other losses and experience will also prove productive in hardening the marketing promotion from abuse. The investigator must always keep in mind that the marketing function is to maintain and increase business and customer volumes and they do not necessarily consider scams and impacts to the operation or crimes that may occur as a result.

Key Takeaways

- Poorly designed and monitored marketing programs and promotions can pose a significant risk of loss for a gaming property.
- There should be review and involvement of security and surveillance departments prior to implementing any marketing promotion.

Best Practices

- Conduct a risk assessment of each marketing program or promotion prior to its implementation to identify potential vulnerabilities.

Chapter 4

Objective and Impartial Investigations

Investigations must be conducted objectively and impartially, always and in every case.

Alan W. Zajic

In this chapter we discuss the importance of conducting an objective and impartial investigation. In the gaming environment as well as many others there can be many distractions, pressures and motivations to solve a case including the investigator's own thoughts and beliefs. It is necessary for investigators to understand and even expect such pressure and distractions, and to remain impartial. It is also easy to become too focused on one theory or individual based on initial information and investigate based on that premise alone. Investigators should always consider the potential for confirmation bias.

Investigators should always approach any investigation with open eyes and without any preconceived thoughts on the cause and/or potential suspect. Many investigations will take twists and turns that will dictate the roadmap for the investigator to ultimately solve the investigation. It is very important that the investigator approach the task in an objective and impartial manner and leave open the many possibilities.

An objective and impartial investigation is crucial for many different reasons. Investigators in gaming environments have a tendency to gravitate to the most likely suspect and focus too much valuable time on that perceived suspect at the expense of other potential suspects or perpetrators. An example might be at our hypothetical cash loss in a cage cashier drawer within a particular shift. An investigator should avoid concluding that the person responsible for the drawer is the most likely suspect and not focus all of their attention on that one person.

The phenomenon known as *confirmation bias* is also a concern for investigators including surveillance agents. A confirmation bias is the tendency to interpret new evidence as confirmation of one's existing beliefs or theories. If an investigator has a known result when they start an investigation, they will tend to conduct the investigation in a narrow fashion to their precon-ceived result rather than be objective to consider all factors and potential suspects. They will tend to focus intently on the known result and conclude that a particular person or circumstance caused the incident or loss. They then do not investigate or confirm all other factors, and miss potential crit-ical evidence. When a confirmation bias is maintained at the very start of the investigation it will typically steer the investigation towards that bias at the expense of other critical information or evidence. It also may place an unfair bias or suspicion on an employee.

In the very famous case in Lake Tahoe where eleven-year-old Jaycee Lee Dugard was abducted as a child and held captive for thirteen years, the law enforcement community focused almost solely on the stepfather as the sus-pect and conducted interviews and continued a steady stream of investiga-tion on him for decades. As it turned out he was not the abductor and the bias involved was unfair and life changing for him.

An example might be in a *dram shop* or intoxication incident where a patron left a casino drunk and got into an accident causing serious injury or death. When the police come to the property and ask surveillance to review video to track the victim, care should be made to not have a confirmation bias during the review and objectively look at the video to determine if the person's motor skills were truly affected and displayed to floor personnel. With a confirmation bias the investigator may interpret a simple move to be a stagger or a person touching a slot stool as stumbling when the known serious injury was the end result. An objective look at each and every factor and piece of evidence will help mitigate any confirm-ation bias as well as management oversight over the investigator.

Objective investigations will not be easy especially in light of all the fac-tors and persons involved in a gaming environment. It is however important to always take a step back and ask yourself if you are being objective or if you are taking the easiest path to close the file. It is most effective when the investigator errs on the side of objectivity and clearly establishes the evi-dence. The evidence will always take you where you should go and attempting to steer the evidence in a desired direction will not only end in credibility issues involving the investigator, it could also drastically change the professional life of a perceived suspect.

As in any investigation the first twenty-four hours and sometimes the eight-hour shift involved will typically be the most productive time to inves-tigate while the information and evidence is fresh. If an investigator focuses on what they think is the obvious answer and not on the whole picture or all persons with access, the chances of solving the incident will decrease as time passes, especially if that *perishable evidence* is lost or not retained.

In the case of a hypothetical cage drawer loss the first critical task is the initial video review of the drawer to "follow the money". The surveillance review must be done first to establish a timeline of when the drawer was confirmed to be accurately accounted for, each and every transaction during the shift, assurance of only the assigned cashier's access, and the end of shift count where a loss was discovered. It is often found that there actually is not a loss and there are errors in the counting process, strapped cash, chip denominations, shared banks or simple mathematical errors.

If the initial video review of the affected cash drawer does not result in solving the loss, then the previous shift activity should be reviewed. In many cases where internal theft has occurred a loss actually occurs on a previous shift and the loss is hidden creatively during the drawer count. This also can occur when a theft has occurred many days prior and was not discovered based on inadequate countdown and inventory at the beginning and end of every shift. Cashiers who handle volumes of cash and chips on a regular basis do not consider the high value important, and consider the process involved more important.

In these cases where a loss has the potential of having occurred several shifts or days prior, the investigator should request the *video retention period* be saved for all cameras in the subject location where the loss occurred and not just the drawer suspected of being involved. The video retention is the period of time video is maintained on the system before being written over on the servers and is typically governed by the regulatory authority. A diligent inquiry may even prove that the video system actually retained more than the mandated retention period based on video recording settings, which could prove helpful. In most jurisdictions there is a seven-day mandated retention period for digital video.

It is very important that each and every employee with potential access, regardless how remote, be interviewed and eliminated. Included in that access is anyone who accesses the area including cleaning personnel, maintenance, outside vendors and security officers. This also gives the investigator an opportunity to ask general questions of those employees with access about any suspicions the person being interviewed has of co-workers or any social relationships they may have that may be helpful in the current investigation as well as past and future investigations. It also allows the investigator to query each employee's knowledge of the applicable policies, procedures and controls, and compliance to them. Conducting single interviews without regard to other employees that have indirect access to cash and shortages should be avoided. Demonstrating thorough interviews will demonstrate a fair process.

Use of Anonymous Hotlines

In most major gaming corporations, the use of the anonymous hotline has proven very effective in gaining leads to solve crimes and other violations. Certain laws involving the implementation of ethics hotlines have emerged over time including *Sarbanes Oxley*. These laws were essentially designed to allow employees to report ethical violations of employees and managers in an anonymous manner in corporate environments and publicly traded organizations.

The anonymous hotline is a tool that has always yielded results in the reporting of internal theft and providing clues to an ongoing investigation. It will quickly become an investigator's valuable resource. Many employees want to report an observation or what they heard in a conversation that is part of an investigation or to simply report a loss that was not caught by management, security or surveillance. Employees also do not want it known who they are and what they reported for fear of reprisals from co-workers or the perpetrator and therefore are more willing to report anonymously.

With the increase in workplace violence and *active shooter* incidents these phone lines also allow employees to report suspicious behavior of co-workers who may have the ability, motive and resources to carry out a mass shooting or other harmful workplace act. These hotlines allow the concerned employee to report other employees who brag about buying an AR-15 or cases of ammunition and in the same breath complain strongly about their manager or make a threat.

Decades ago the common application was to have that big red phone in surveillance, which was an extension off the Private Automatic Branch Exchange (PABX) or company telephone switchboard that any employee could call while at work or call from the outside through the switchboard operator or automated answering system. Because this involved untrained personnel in collecting the information and leaks in the information collected, these generally vanished over time. It also was possible to recognize an employee's voice and therefore was not truly anonymous and not trusted by the employee population.

In today's casino environments many operations utilize companies that specifically manage a toll-free number where anyone can report anything in a truly anonymous manner. These companies train their employees on how to collect important information and how to tell the caller how to report changes or update additional information valuable for the enterprise.

They will typically have a pre-designated contact person with e-mail notification or by phone that will initially review the information provided and determine what, if any, action should be taken. The GM or high-level executive is typically the one chosen to then delegate the report out to the appropriate person or department for investigation or action. That primary executive can also make an evaluation of the report and have knowledge of property conditions and circumstances that lower-level executives or employees may not. Some corporate environments have multiple contacts for the distribution of the information collected to include internal audit, compliance, human resources and others to assure action.

There is basic initial information obtained that includes date, time of call, sex of caller, emotional characteristics of the person and content of what was told to the intake employee at the service. Terms of art are noted, which also gives the investigator clues of the knowledge of the caller and therefore the reliability of the information.

These hotlines become valuable in management investigations such as sexual harassment complaints or intimidation of employees by supervisors or managers. They also are the source to report that employee who is taking those steaks and lobsters from the walk-ins in the kitchen home for that BBQ or the food cashier who buys a $50,000 car without any legitimate source of other income.

These hotlines always prove to be interesting and even entertaining at times and care should be made when setting up the process and assigning the contact persons for the information from the hotline company. It would be recommended that the contact person not be the investigator or any security or surveillance manager or employee. It should be the highest level possible to allow for the anonymity and confidence of the employee population that it truly will be anonymous. The contact is typically the GM who can then determine how the information is used with assistance from others on the notification list.

The toll-free number is posted on employee bulletin boards and the process is explained to all new employees during new-hire orientation to ensure all employees are aware of the benefit and responsibility to report illegal or unethical behavior. The employee population will embrace the hotline once word spreads of an employee or manager who was caught because of its existence.

Regulations, Rules and Laws Involved

A key component of any investigation is the appropriate applicable laws, ordinances, rules, regulations, minimum internal controls (MICS) and any other document that lays the foundation for what you are attempting to prove or at least solve. If you are investigating a loss within a cashier's cage, for example, the professional investigator will know the local laws for larceny, what constitutes a felony and under what circumstances, what elements are required for the crime of embezzlement or what the details are of a particular gaming law or regulation.

Those documents should be at the fingertips of the investigator at all times throughout the process until it is closed. Any experienced prosecutor will tell you that one of the main reasons a case is not prosecuted is that the elements were not met in order to prove the violation of law. Once a report nears conclusion, the professional investigator should read the law, compare it to their written report and ensure that all elements have been met before submitting it for potential prosecution.

The regulatory documents are different in every jurisdiction. Because of evolution, legal processes, court decisions and government organization, these written regulations utilized are often not up to date or accurate to be relied upon for criminal prosecution or disciplinary actions. Care should always be exerted when reviewing and relying on a particular regulation and assurance should be sought that it is the most current, approved and up-to-date guiding document.

Additionally, all of the current pertinent cashiering policies and procedures and other internal controls should be copied and placed in the file for later interviewing use. Using the actual laws or regulations as part of the report will ease in the process for all who review or use your report. Once again you will find that a consistent cause for loss is the failure to follow established internal controls or procedures. The existence and purpose of internal controls is to prevent losses from occurring and a breakdown is typically involved in any loss or infraction. These should be memorized and thoroughly known inside and out by the investigator before the first interview, which will assist in the questions asked of parties.

Rules governing employee or team member behavior are typically found in every organization. They are also typically managed by the human resources department and are called various things including Standards of Behavior, Employee Rules and Regulations, Rules of Conduct, etc. These behavior standards that are established by the organization are an investigator's valuable tool and can be used very effectively in an investigation during various interviews.

Conduct rules should always include sanctions for theft or misappropriation, undesirable conduct, intoxication and drug use. Additionally, this is the ideal place to include the following:

- Failure to cooperate in a company investigation.
- ' Failure to report a known violation of rules of conduct.
- Failure to report the theft of company property to a supervisor.
- Failure to report a violation of law.

The investigator should work with human resources to develop reasonable and enforceable rules to govern employee behavior before, during and after an internal investigation. These rules should not be arbitrarily used and should be a tool to illicit cooperation.

All of these documents are crucial in order to prove the elements of the infraction or violation of law. Again, the elements are basically what constitute a violation and without them the hard work may end up in a refusal to prosecute. The written reports, statements and evidence must also clearly prove what violations occurred and in sufficient detail to prosecute or take appropriate action. The most simplistic method to assure complete documentation is to take each sentence or bullet in the law, regulation or rule and make sure it is well covered in the body of the investigator's written report and is proven by the evidence collected.

The most common basic mistake made by either criminal investigators or internal investigators is not meeting the elements of a crime, violation of policy or procedure or regulation. Another reason is that witnesses are not available to testify and as a result the prosecutor determines this will create a failure to prove the case in court. Retired police officers will typically understand this based on their Peace Officer's Standards Training and experience with the courts in criminal cases. A gaming investigator who has not had the benefit of training and exposure to the elements of the crime will not always understand and will not document them in the written report for prosecution. This is the leading cause for lack of prosecution in most jurisdictions in that the report does not provide evidence that the crime was committed, by whom and what specific things occurred to establish the person committed the offense.

A suggestion would be to always prepare an outline of what the elements are for a violation to occur, which is the focus of the investigation. This is not a difficult task and takes little time to prepare. It also will teach the investigator, through repeated similar incidents, of the elements required and most importantly how to document them effectively for action in the case at hand.

The elements are very basic in that the outline should contain each and every item or condition that must be present for proving or disproving a violation. For example, in embezzlement investigations the outline will include specifics of the local law to include amounts, number of occurrences, valuation and periods of time for the crime of embezzlement to occur. It also includes the entrustment and control of assets by the potential suspect. All of this should always be documented regardless of how obvious it may be to the investigator or if it is deemed a *common-sense* factor. This will be necessary to prosecute or discipline without criticism by human resources, management or potential union representatives.

The elements, even the basic ones such as documenting the person (the subject or suspect), must be established in the written report for successful outcomes, along with dates, times and other very simple but often missed details. This will hold true for any investigation including employee or management ones where there are employee rules of conduct or other oversight self-imposed standards for behavior that human resources would have in place.

The same goes for MICS, policies and procedures, and rules and regulations that evolve internally in any gaming environment. Care should also be made in this area based on the typical disconnect from what is written as policy, procedure or regulation to what is actually practiced by the department employees. These are typically known as "shortcuts" or "work-arounds".

It is not fair to discipline a single employee for something that all employees are doing through ineffective management or a manager's disregard for written protocols. The written procedural document should be the baseline and if these shortcut conditions exist, the investigation should pause and a meeting with appropriate stakeholders is then in order. The elements may fall apart and disciplinary action may not be possible if these common conditions exist where all employees are disregarding the established protocols.

The professional gaming investigator will also follow their investigation files all the way through to the final resolution including tracking down any employee and independent witnesses that are critical to proving that a person had committed an offense. Showing up at a trial or hearing on a criminal case is also recommended for final follow-up and case closure.

Many investigators make the mistake of not contacting the prosecutor before, during and after a trial or hearing to ensure they know the company's or tribe's desire for prosecution and restitution. Demand for restitution is covered later in this book.

Key Takeaways

- Investigations must be conducted objectively and impartially, always and in every case.
- Anonymous hotlines are an effective source of tips to identify potential and existing threats or losses.
- Rules, policies and procedures, controls statutes and laws serve as the foundation of your case.

Best Practices

- Implement a confidential employee hotline.
- Ensure your property develops, maintains and enforces controls, policies and procedures.

Chapter 5

Understanding the Scope of the Investigation

> The scope of the investigation will drive many different priorities and at times will impact operations in various ways.
>
> Alan W. Zajic

The investigator must fully understand the purpose of the investigation they have been assigned or are seeking approval to conduct. It is critical to fully understand what the company or tribal policy is regarding the investigation, any special conditions and where your authority starts and stops before starting on your mission. This will always save time, energy and misunderstandings by superiors and interested parties and will give a real direction to the assigned investigation.

The scope of an investigation should always be fully understood at the start of the process. This allows for executive oversight of the many processes and interviews to be conducted and provides a limitation, if any, for the investigator to follow. Without a clear understanding of the purpose or scope, an investigation can go off track and evolve into something different than the original mission. An example is how a simple internal theft investigation can turn into an illegal drug case involving other employees. For the purposes of documentation, the scope should not change from the original reason for the process. As the scope develops and changes, executive review should keep the investigation on track.

Which law enforcement agencies or regulators are required (or sometimes desired) to be involved in an investigation falls within this initial scope evaluation to ensure that all stakeholders are kept informed and copied as necessary in the event that status reports are required. In major investigations there can be local, state and federal agencies involved with very differing requirements and objectives.

In some environments the regulator is required to conduct and coordinate an investigation and the property-level investigator is assigned in a support role to provide information, audit reports, promotional materials or just assist in tracking down witnesses for interviews. This common role is important even though you may not be the lead investigator. The faster you can provide accurate information the faster the investigation can proceed and ultimately successfully close.

If the investigation becomes increasingly complex and time consuming your other work must not suffer, and priorities should be established regularly if not daily to ensure the scope is still the same as when you started the investigation. It is crucial that the investigator maintains the priority and scope throughout the assignment and is adaptable to the ever-changing dynamics of gaming operations.

The gaming investigator may have to manage several investigations at the same time and therefore must also have the ability to turn each one on and off like a light switch when necessary. When a project is stalled due to witness availability, the next one may need some report writing and yet a third may involve a meeting with internal audit on some follow-up that needs to be confirmed.

The scope of the investigation will drive many different priorities and at times will impact operations in various ways. Removing employees from their work stations or locations always has an impact on the operation to all other employees, managers and patrons. Requesting employees after or before their work shift will involve overtime payroll, scheduling and work displacement. These scheduled interviews, whether formal and in depth or informal and casual will have impacts on operations and the investigator must balance all of the operational factors rather than insist and demand interviews or materials needed for the investigation.

Once the scope of the investigation is clear, communication with the affected department managers is desirable to ease the departmental impacts and assist the investigator in the process by letting supervisors know to cooperate and support the process. If the investigator asks the department head what the best method is to accomplish the process, the department manager will then be more likely to support the process rather than impede it and use the excuse of impact to operations. This will also develop a better working relationship between the department head, supervision within that department and the investigator. It will also generate positive feedback to the executive level during normal day-to-day business discussions or staff meetings and will again foster a better working relationship overall.

The scope of the investigation is the basic outline of what the investigator will want to accomplish initially in order to obtain the basic information, evidence and interviews needed to solve the case or obtain as much information as possible to explain the causes for a loss or incident. This scope will always change as the investigation progresses and upward communication is required to keep the stakeholders in the loop as the scope increases or decreases.

Most investigators do not realize the full impact that they have on operations when they go about what they feel is their normal job. The faster a professional investigator realizes and considers this in determining the scope of the investigation the easier their job will become in deciding to investigate and then conducting an investigation.

The following are some items to consider when outlining the scope of the investigation:

- Which departments will be affected during the interview process and how many employees will be interviewed?
- Will the accounting department be required to pull information on point of sale (POS) systems, over and short reports, payrolls, accounts payables or receivables, or other financials such as hold reports or revenue breakdowns?
- Will the IT department be needed to determine log in and log out into computer systems used by employees in an effected area or other data information?
- Will surveillance be required to review, collect, log and organize video evidence?
- Will it be required for the investigator to meet with surveillance personnel reviewing video to explain the loss and potential areas for scrutiny?
- Will human resources be involved to pull employment files and disciplinary history of employees and supervisors?

The Decision to Investigate

There are many reasons for a company or tribal operation to conduct investigations in a gaming environment. There are some very basic items that need to be considered during the process of deciding if an investigation warrants the time, effort and costs associated. Management level employees will typically direct the decision to investigate and will also typically direct at least part of the scope of the investigation. It is the job of the investigator to advise and recommend the investigation course and scope.

The following questions should be answered before the formal investigation is started:

1   Is there really a loss?
2   Is the loss worth the time and expense to investigate?
3   Will there be a significant impact to operations?
4   Will a decision not to investigate create long-term issues?
5   Is there a regulation or local law that mandates an investigation?
6   Are there internal political issues that will impact the investigation?

The experienced investigator will always ask these questions first and determine if in fact there is a loss. The gaming facilities are a vast enterprise that includes sometimes thousands of employees, contractors, vendors and customers that cross and have an effect on an outcome. There are many different variables that will come into play when making the initial determination whether a loss has actually occurred. Ensuring that there is actually a loss and not an error or other factor will save time and energy and therefore costs to the enterprise.

The following are some examples of where an investigator may find the loss before spending an inordinate amount of time investigating:

- If equipment or tools are involved, have you checked to see what jobs were completed since the last time the item was known to have been there and could they be located somewhere on the facility property like in an attic, crawlspace, truck or rooftop and someone forgot to put them away?
- Is there an error somewhere in the paper trail or inventory that created the perception of a loss through human error?
- Was the item replaced by a newer version and it was not communicated?
- Is there a duplicate entry into an accounting spreadsheet or in the POS system that created an exaggerated loss?
- Did an executive or manager remove the item and did not communicate with staff?
- Did a vendor accidently remove the item thinking it was theirs?

Is There an Actual Monetary Loss and Is There a Desire to Locate and Take Action?

This is also a very basic assessment and should be included in the investigation summary of the final report. All direct and indirect costs should be considered and at least estimated in this initial process. If the loss has shipping or delivery costs involved, retail value vs. purchased value, other costs associated to the loss, and operational impact costs, they should all be evaluated and understood in the preliminary steps by the investigator before the actual collection of evidence or interviews are started.

There will be circumstances that present themselves to the investigator where there is no desire to waste time investigating a loss. An example may be an outside Christmas decoration that turns up missing. The inclination will be to just replace it and not spend a lot of time on the item even if it cost hundreds of dollars to purchase. At a minimum, the investigator may choose to have a video review done if there is coverage to determine when and how the item became missing. There may be no desire to spend time and money on some losses, which are considered a cost of doing business by executive management. Regardless, the investigator should still monitor these and do cursory documentation in the event it becomes chronic and a decision is made to review and investigate at a later time.

As an example, if an arc welder owned by the facility turns up missing, the investigator needs to obtain any asset information, to include original purchase price and the replacement cost in the event the asset is not located or found. Additionally, record any costs incurred if the company now has to hire an outside welder to complete jobs normally associated with the arc welder and facilities staff, and any other impacts. These are all cost considerations that should be evaluated, documented and reported.

The scope of the monetary loss may take some investigating itself and will be required for a comprehensive investigation. It may include speaking to the department head, purchasing, warehouse, accounting and even IT. A loss of an asset is rarely stand-alone and involves other loss or replacement. If it appears the loss may involve hundreds of dollars and loss of productivity, management will most likely want to pursue the investigation.

The final value should not be exaggerated and should be as accurate as possible. The final number should also be included in the annual spreadsheet by the investigator to show what losses were investigated and the cost to the organization. This number will be useful during restitution demands and in the event a determination is made to file a claim against the property or tribe's crime insurance policy.

Each property will typically purchase crime insurance annually and many gaming establishments do not file claims against this very valuable type of insurance. A major embezzlement case where money is taken from soft count can be recovered through crime insurance. A forensic accountant can also calculate losses not found directly by the investigator and can prove that the larceny was occurring for an extended period of time.

I was once involved in such a case where the surveillance staff were not watching the processes as required and a team of two soft count employees took large denomination bills from high limit drop boxes over an extended period of time. The very competent new surveillance director started his investigation and accurately documented the losses, which then resulted in the forensic accounting analysis that, based on the available information, the loss could be estimated at over $700,000. A claim was carefully filed and accepted with the result that a check for the loss was issued by the insurance carrier. The crime insurance carrier then civilly sued the perpetrators because the video retention only proved a loss of $40,000. A default judgement was filed and these two perpetrators' assets they accumulated were all seized and future wages or income was and is being attached.

Part of this primary initial decision to investigate may rest on the investigator's determination if there is a loss, if it is recoverable and at what cost to the organization. It is the job of the investigator to fully understand the value of the loss and assist in the decision to spend time and resources on investigating it and solving the cause of the loss.

Is There a Fundamental Company Philosophy Overall or in the Minds of the Executive Level above You that Compels You to Conduct the Investigation?

What is the company or tribal philosophy regarding asset misappropriation, are they willing to prosecute, are there any exceptions to arrest and prosecution, and what impacts will occur if the asset is recovered and the perpetrator is arrested? For instance, if the loss occurs in the tribal environment what political or environmental conditions exist and may involve tribal philosophy or registered tribal members? Political impacts may very well influence the decision to even investigate in the first place. The investigator must have thick skin in these instances and understand who they work for and that they serve at the pleasure of the typical autocratic environment in most casino operations.

Additionally, what exact employee rules and regulations can you rely on that are well established and enforceable should the result of your investigation lead to an employee suspect? If you do not have a written rule that says you cannot steal from the company and you cannot prove that an asset was owned by the enterprise, there will be little success in prosecuting or administering employee discipline. Investigators should have the most current rules and regulations and policies and procedures for every department that includes the latest revision dates on the documents.

Some operations believe that if someone takes assets belonging to that organization they will investigate and prosecute regardless of the amount, person responsible or type of loss. Although an optimum philosophy in a gaming environment to maintain some deterrence against internal theft, there is always a cost, political circumstance and human resources implication in any loss or incident investigation.

Some major retailers have a threshold amount for shoplifting or internal theft that mandates that prosecution or severe employee discipline be delivered only if the amount is over $25 or some other amount. These thresholds can be dangerous in that employees will routinely steal as long as the amounts are under the published threshold amount. The same holds true of casinos that develop thresholds of when to notify security, surveillance or the investigator directly.

In many gaming facilities, the threshold for notification of a cash loss for example is $100 before notifying an investigator or generating a report. Each operation will determine what that loss threshold should be. Care should be made when establishing any threshold where theft can occur even as a one time or infrequent occurrence where the perpetrator can use the threshold to their advantage.

The GM or operational chief executive will certainly have their own philosophy regarding losses and theft by entrusted employees. Most executives will want to investigate and prosecute absent extraordinary circumstances. Regardless of the decision, the investigator must always remember that they serve at the pleasure of their bosses and must ultimately comply with their directives.

In the event of an employee who is directly related to a tribal council member and is implicated in theft from the company, the immediate decision could very well be to stop the investigation and let the GM or tribal council deal with it. Although hard for rank and file investigators to accept, this will and often does occur in all gaming environments.

Regardless of what the operations loss thresholds are or what the philosophies are, the investigator must have a clear understanding of them before starting the formal process and of whether proceeding is appropriate and actually desired before wasting time and energy. Regardless the investigator should have some manner to document basic information in the event it is needed at a later time.

What Is the Estimated Cost of Investigation?

There is always a cost involved to investigate a loss or incident: not only the time and payroll involved with the actual investigator, but also the time of their supervisor or manager and anyone else who becomes involved in the investigation process. It must be understood that any time spent on an investigation should be calculated in what it costs the enterprise to have the investigator working on the case.

The investigator's time includes the hourly wage based on payroll or salary, all fringe benefits including payroll taxes, worker's compensation and other company paid expenses on payroll. This amount should be calculated and known by the investigator broken down hourly during the course of any investigation. The estimated time the investigation will take can then be applied and a direct cost be made.

Any other direct costs are also added to the mix and the investigation costs are then available. These figures will also become valuable during budget periods or requests for more investigators as to what the costs associated would be for additional staff.

If a loss of an item valued at $150 is reported and the time and effort involved in investigating the loss is well over $1,000 and there are not any enterprise or company philosophies or directives, the loss could very well not be investigated absent unusual circumstances. The decision should not be made by the investigator not to conduct one; their supervisor should make that decision. An investigator should automatically conduct investigations on losses or incidents, keep their direct supervisor informed and let that supervisor make final decisions not to conduct an investigation. This will always move the decision upward and develop a consistent process of property investigations.

The use of a control document with signatures for basic investigations can be helpful, which notes basic investigation tasks, including assignment and closure, with appropriate signatures. This will assist in control and overall management of the investigation process.

What Other Investigations or Work Will Suffer as a Result of the New Investigation?

Depending on the size of the operation, many investigations will be conducted at the same basic time. The priority of work will shift weekly, daily and sometimes even hourly back and forth between case investigations. Priorities are important to establish and communicate to supervisors to allow the smooth, methodical investigation process to proceed effectively. There may be times that the investigator cannot accomplish minor investigations as a result of multiple serious ones being presented to them. A common practice for investigators is the progress whiteboard.

The whiteboard is a wall board where markers are used to identify current investigations and the status of those investigations in general. This visual is a motivator to not only the investigator working a case; it can also be a motivator to another investigator, supervisor or director. Additionally, it can keep management visually informed of current investigations and any need to provide assistance to investigation personnel. Obviously, this whiteboard should be out of view of the general employee population.

Again, the decision not to investigate based on workload should be made by the supervisor of the investigator. That supervisor may be able to solicit a security or surveillance staff member to conduct a minor sub-investigation and possible develop an employee who desires to become an investigator. A log of all investigations conducted, who they were assigned to and if any management determination was made not to investigate will also be helpful in evaluating the investigation progress overall and track costs out and restitution in.

There are some sensitive investigations that it may not be appropriate to list and be visible to other staff in the organization on a whiteboard. These may include executive level investigations, internal affairs or other sensitive factors. In these cases, the investigator is typically instructed to report to only one executive-level employee and they will instruct on the precise methods and actions. These *need to know* reporting requirements are not common and may occur based on a myriad of reasons. The investigator must also keep their objectivity and ethics in check even under these unusual circumstances.

Key Takeaways

- The investigator must identify the purpose of the investigation to ensure the proper strategy and resources are applied within the scope of the investigator's directives.

- The scope of the investigation is the basic outline of what the investigator will want to accomplish initially in order to obtain the basic information, evidence and interviews needed to solve the case or obtain as much information as possible to explain the causes for a loss or incident.
- Management-level employees will typically direct the decision to investigate and will also typically direct at least part of the scope of the investigation. It is the job of the investigator to advise and recommend the investigation course and scope.

Best Practices

- Develop a plan for your investigation to include strategy, resources available, controls, policies, procedures, regulations, laws that were violated or broken, as well as time and funds necessary.
- Determine if there is a fundamental company philosophy overall or in the minds of the executive level above you that compels you to conduct the investigation.

Chapter 6

Starting the Investigation

Start with what you know.

Alan W. Zajic

There are numerous considerations that must be evaluated before an investigation can formally be started. Every organization will have their reporting relationships established for the investigator to include authority, updates, written reporting and distribution and financial approvals if needed.

In simplistic cases such as an immediate loss or incident there may not be many considerations and the field investigation will quickly evolve into a formal investigation based on the circumstances and obvious evidence presented initially. The following are all considerations that should be evaluated, if applicable, before starting a major and sometimes a minor investigation that may impact operations.

Start with What You Know

Any experienced investigator knows that they must start the process of investigation by listing out what they know at the start of the investigation. The very concept of making sure of what you know regarding the loss or infraction will guide the investigation forward and determine the next steps in the process. This is accomplished through outlines and organization of the intended processes, interviews and development of the case.

The information provided needs to be confirmed and it must be verified that it is accurate and is in fact the basis of the investigation. For example, if an arc welder is reported missing from the facilities department and the cost is $6,000 for replacement, you must first confirm that the welder is actually lost or missing. A diligent inquiry into the location it was last used or observed and of any management or supervisors who may have allowed a vendor or employee to use the equipment will certainly prevent unnecessary time and effort if it was lent to someone. Establishing that the arc welder is in fact missing is the first step.

Conducting an interview to confirm what is contained in the loss or theft report is the next step in confirming what you know. A line by line inquiry and interview of the person reporting the loss, determining if the equipment was permanently marked with company name, serial numbers, description, and even a picture from a brochure or internet searches will all establish what is missing and in fact if it is missing.

Many times, this process of interviewing employees will prompt a bad employee who is involved to return the item to a logical location and it is mysteriously "found" by another employee based on fear of being caught. In many instances, employees will temporarily place an item in a hidden location and see if anyone notices it is missing. If no one notices in a few days, the item is then removed from the property. This is often the case in theft from hotel rooms by employees.

A check with security or surveillance to request a video review of the time element from when the item was last known to be in a particular location can produce results if the time frame is not an extended period of time, like days or weeks, where it would be a major task to do a 24/7 video review.

Start with a Case Outline

It should be obvious by now that outlines will assist in planning and executing an investigation. Any investigator who has a basic plan of attack by religiously preparing an outline prior to any interview to make sure that he asks all of the questions will be successful in making fewer mistakes or not forgetting to ask questions during an interview. This lessens the need to conduct second follow-up interviews on non-critical witnesses. The outline is the basis for any written work in almost all environments including casino complexes. By having an outline, the investigator can then use it to discuss the recommendation and process to his supervisor and not attempt to merely verbally request and miss potential facts or information. It also establishes to your supervisor that you are organized and actually have a plan to hopefully solve the matter at hand.

The case outline will also assist in preparing what order interviews or collection of evidence are to be conducted and will keep the investigator on track and focused during the course of the investigation. It will also be an integral part of the investigator's work file, which will be helpful when preparing updates and in the final written report. Additionally, in the event of litigation for inadequate investigation, it will demonstrate an organized and professional approach to conducting the investigation.

The outline is the roadmap of the processes the investigator will take from the initial discovery of the loss or incident through the chronological investigation. Very few investigators can have total recall of their progress or the sometimes large volumes of information or pieces of the investigation and the outline will keep the investigator on track to the desired objectives.

These outlines are included with any notes in the master file, which the investigator indexes at the conclusion of the investigation with a table of contents and evidence. In today's electronic world the entire file is then scanned and it goes on a portable hard drive, from which the investigator can access any file they have ever worked on. The ability for text and character recognition allows for quick searches of large documents for similarities or common names that may just solve that difficult case.

Key Takeaways

- A common mistake made by investigators is to jump in and try to solve the case early on without considering all of the factors that should be established.
- Start with what you already know and develop the case from there.

Best Practices

- Start with a case outline.
- Confirm that a loss has actually occurred and is not a supervisory or management issue.

Chapter 7

Written Reports

> Your written work product will be important and will be the basis of action by others in the future.
>
> Alan W. Zajic

Report writing is an art unto itself. The investigator refines his/her art as the fundamentals of report writing are followed and experience is gained. As each component of the document is developed and placed into its proper location and format the report becomes the representation of what the evidence tells us occurred. The written investigation report is the results of all of the work that has been completed and chronologically identifies the process taken.

These reports should not contain any supposition, opinions or conjecture; they should contain only factual information. If a theory results in interviews or document review, it is acceptable to identify that theory and that it was either confirmed or discounted. It is important to produce written work that flows, is grammatically correct and in which all spelling is triple checked including proper names.

Investigations require a comprehensive written record by the person conducting it and are typically not prepared using report-writing software, at least in gaming environments. These reports are typically written using standard business software with features to allow for references, footnotes, insertion of photographs or other items into the body of the report and other features. Typical security and surveillance report software is not conducive to most written investigation reports.

Consistency in general format will be helpful for long-term record keeping and use by the people who will review and supervise content, and prosecute the perpetrator if desired. Inconsistent format between reports also creates the opportunity for errors or unintentional omissions in the written record.

Your written work product will be important and will be the basis of action by others in the future. The basic concept of report writing in the gaming environment is much the same in the criminal or legal environment. The style and formatting of the report is often dictated by the investigator's supervisor and is not always modern and contemporary and may be based on the practical experience of your boss.

It is incumbent on the investigator to produce an accurate and comprehensive written report that not only memorializes the investigation from start to finish; it also is the document that will provide sufficient cause for some form of action.

The style of the written report should be prepared in the first person. The archaic third person written reports are not utilized as much today as they were decades ago. Speaking in plain language on a written report will make it easier to convey what occurred and what was done during the investigation. It is also easier for the trier of facts or others to understand.

Report Summary Section

The more common method of reporting in gaming environments also includes a summary section at the beginning of the written report. This summary section will basically establish the basic facts to include who, what, where, how and hopefully why the incident occurred in abbreviated form. The summary is designed to provide the reader with the basics of what is in the report. The targeted reader should be able to understand how the loss or incident occurred, who committed any offenses or the primary suspect, what the loss or impacts were and what action was taken by the investigator in a few short paragraphs.

The summary is designed to provide the targeted reader with sufficient information of what the investigation is about and the results without having to read the entire report and exhibits. It is designed to allow the reader to stop reading if they are satisfied and they understand what is contained, or continue reading details if needed, desired or required.

List of Players

The list of players or anyone involved in the investigation or interviewees is also a critical part of an investigation report and is typically listed in the front end of the report. This listing should include full name, department or relationship and a brief summary of their involvement. This will be valuable for reference purposes later when in the middle of a prosecution or employee action.

All persons involved in an incident should be listed. The principal participants, initial responding personnel, management and supervisor involvement, percipient witnesses and the all-important independent witness should all be contained in the list of players at the front end of the written report. Every witness interviewed, regardless of involvement, should be contained in this list.

Evidence Listing

All evidence including paperwork should be listed in the report to clearly demonstrate what was reviewed and what is included in the written report. This is the table of contents section of the report, which will list out all attached documents in an organized format for use later. This table of contents will include any written statements, receipts, accounting materials, laws or regulations, policies and procedures involved and any other form of evidence.

Video evidence may be listed but is typically maintained by the regulator or the surveillance department. Regardless all video evidence should be meticulously listed by segment, camera, location and what the segment shows as it relates to the investigation even if it does not show anything pertinent. This will be helpful if a future allegation of spoliation or failure to save a particular video segment is alleged.

Offenses or Infractions

The next heading in the report that should be in the front of the document and before the narrative is a listing of what specific criminal offenses, violation of rules, procedural violations or rule of misconduct are evidenced throughout the report. The preferable method is to restate the infraction in this section. This allows the summary of all offenses to be easily extracted from the report for action against the person. A separate page allows for that to be utilized from a human resources application without distributing the entire report.

Narrative

Most investigators complete the detailed narrative report based on the progress of the investigation in chronological order. The process is not as important as the content and being able to prove that some form of violation occurred. Again, the supervisor will typically dictate formatting in the report. The final section of the report should verify and establish who the suspect is, what evidence has been collected and who the results of the investigation were turned over to for action.

After the formal investigation is completed there will always be addendums that will be added to the written report. The addendums may include supplemental evidence collection, additional interviews, debriefing meetings, court-related updates including convictions or lack of them, follow-up on final actions and finally any restitution that may be collected. The written report should be comprehensive all the way through the process.

The narrative is the body of the report that will describe the investigation typically in that chronological manner. Using spell check and carefully examining the spelling and grammar is highly recommended to make sure nothing can be misinterpreted. Some operations prefer the base narrative to be completed and then dated supplements be added in a chronological manner. Regardless of the style, it is the roadmap to the final result and should be given utmost priority.

Visuals and Link Charting

Regardless of the methods and processes that are developed to solve cases, many investigators will utilize some form of visual charting that will assist them in understanding relationships to the players or connecting all the dots in determining a loss. The *link chart* is a very common method, which can be highly visual with a whiteboard or flipchart or can be a simple charting program on a computer terminal. This is used on television programs extensively to assist the viewer of the program to follow the plot or story.

Casinos will have many different employees who will cross some path during an investigation. Identifying interpersonal relationships between employees and managers is important before conducting comprehensive interviews. There are many different sources that supply this information, which include personnel files, results of other investigations, surveillance reports, anonymous tips and other intelligence gathered for other reasons.

Almost every employee has some form of interpersonal relationship with another employee. This can be as simple as a work acquaintance that spends break times with another employee to a romantic relationship between employees past or present. Roommate relationships are very common in employee populations and should also be identified, past and present, during the interview process, review of personnel files or other information collected during an investigation. Witnesses should be questioned regarding these interpersonal relationships during interviews as it will prove valuable for the process.

Addresses, beneficiaries, telephone numbers and even vehicle information will provide associations that will lead the investigator to clues in solving the matter at hand. It is remarkable how many of these common pieces of information merge in a gaming environment. The employee population is one of the greatest sources of information if used appropriately. The link charting will assist as a roadmap of the players and assist in understanding the relationships and sometimes motives.

Link charting will help put a visual in front of the investigator that may assist in zeroing in on a potential suspect or at least develop background information important to the investigation as a whole. As an example, in a case involving an armed robbery of a cashier's cage at a casino, a past roommate of the cashier had committed the crime. That past roommate worked in the beverage department and had been the roommate of the cashier for several years.

Once the information was developed by the property investigator through link charting it was turned over to local police who interviewed and obtained a confession from the perpetrator. It was determined during the course of the investigation that the cashier provided information that led to the robbery and the roommate had convinced the cashier over time it could be done and split the take. The roommate was not living with the cashier at the time of the robbery event.

If a whiteboard with markers is used for the basic linking, it should be located where other employees cannot see it or in a locked office that is not used for interviews. Taking digital photographs of the charted information before changes are made will also benefit the process.

Key Takeaways

- Investigations require comprehensive written records by the person conducting them and are typically not prepared using report-writing software, at least in gaming environments.
- The more common method of reporting in gaming environments also includes a summary section at the beginning of the written report.
- The list of players or anyone involved in the investigation or interviewees is also a critical part of an investigation report and is typically listed in the front end of the report.
- All evidence including paperwork should be listed in the report to clearly demonstrate what was reviewed and what is included in the written report.
- The next heading in the report that should be in the front of the document and before the narrative is a listing of what specific criminal offenses, violation of rules, procedural violations or rule of misconduct are evidenced throughout the report.

Best Practices

- Regardless of the methods and processes that are developed to solve cases, many investigators will utilize some form of visual charting that will assist them in understanding relationships to the players or connecting all the dots in determining a loss. The link chart is a very common method, which can be highly visual with a whiteboard or flipchart or can be a simple charting program on a computer terminal.

Chapter 8

Interviews

Never take away a person's self-respect.

Alan W. Zajic

Conducting interviews will occur in all investigations and will be critical for a successful outcome to resolve a loss or determine a cause for a breach or loss. The process that an investigator uses during interviews will serve as a foundation for the investigation and will be referred to many times as the investigation evolves. An investigator needs to be well prepared before they start the first interview, which will save time and effort in the long run.

The objective is to reduce the number of interviews of a particular witness if possible and not to keep going back with routine questions that should have been asked in the initial interview. This will not only project to an interviewee that you are professional and knowledgeable; it will also save valuable time and effort to solve the case or resolve the issue. The investigator should not rush to conduct an interview if there is plenty of time for them to take a deep breath and think through their process before asking the first question.

There are times when the investigation will require follow-up questions of a person that has already been interviewed regardless of the preparation. In many cases this will be used as impeachment of that witness to the original answers to the investigators questions after it has been determined that there were incorrect answers or that a person has lied to the investigator. It is also important not to rush for an answer and make sure the conditions are right and support information is collected and analyzed prior to confronting them with the discovery.

Foundational witnesses are those that assist the investigator in understanding what has occurred and in what manner the incident giving rise to the inquiry manifested. Foundational witnesses could be auditors, surveillance agents, security personnel, supervisors or managers, and the reporting person. These witnesses should be interviewed first to establish what has occurred, what losses are known at the time, what time frames are involved and what employees may have access or involvement.

Foundational witnesses will provide sources of information to establish the basis for the investigation and the written and unwritten protocols for the environment. Work and break schedules, logs, camera coverage and access control data are all examples of documents and information that are obtained during interviews of the foundational witnesses.

Wherever local law permits, an interview room with audio recording should always be utilized to accomplish a record of the interview, to allow for careful playback and to demonstrate the seriousness of the incident to the person being interviewed. In some environments this is required by regulation to include specified retention periods of video with audio. In other environments it is specifically prohibited by statutory provision or by common law.

It is very important to research your jurisdictions laws and regulations before conducting recorded interviews and the legal requirements including those found in applicable national wiretap or eavesdropping laws. Posting of appropriate signs warning of recording of video and audio are typically required. Be sure to check and confirm that the equipment is functioning properly when possible before starting these recorded interviews. In many environments this is completed on a 24/7 basis by the surveillance department independently of the investigator who also has the ability to monitor it live.

When possible a quiet interview room with lawful recording devices should be available that can be used without interruption. Using a busy security office to conduct recorded interviews that will have constant employees in and out, radio chatter and other distractions is not conducive to a productive interview.

Another self-improvement tool for the investigator is to observe themselves videotaped while conducting interviews with witnesses and suspects, watch and listen to the reactions to answers and make notes of what worked and what did not. It is also helpful if a peer also watches and can give feedback and constructive criticism on technique and result. This will not only improve the investigator's skills, it will also help to ensure enunciation of questions, identify bad habits and observe *kinesics* or body language of the person being interviewed and yourself as an investigator.

An example of an investigator displaying bad habits during a recorded interview is one investigator who would tap his pen on the desk during the interviews he conducted by first tapping one end of the pen then reversing it and tapping the other end. Careful observation would allow the interviewee to observe the body language being telegraphed in the wrong direction. Not only did the tapping come through the audio recording in an exaggerated way, the action was also telegraphing to the person being interviewed when the investigator was frustrated. In one case the person being interviewed was using the investigator's body language to understand whether his lies were being accepted.

As an example, some investigators will telegraph their feelings and perceptions during important interviews, which may help or hinder the outcome of an investigation and sometimes prolong the final result unnecessarily. On the flip side I have experienced situations where telegraphing through your body language that you are skeptical of an answer may move the investigation rapidly to a conclusion. Only the skilled investigator will know how and when to use these types of tactics.

The mere action of you making a note after being told something has an effect on the interviewee. Some investigators over the years have purposely made notes large enough for a suspect of embezzlement to see and recognize and have had very positive results in solving a loss and following it through to prosecution. Care should be made not to exaggerate or amplify a note to an extreme that may backfire on the initial intent.

The investigator must prepare the room in which interviews are conducted, collect all of the possible documents, reports, statements and other evidence, and plan the interview carefully to obtain and retain the valuable evidence they will later need. In the casino and gaming environment the most critical piece of evidence is typically some form of video or electronic evidence that requires corroboration or verification.

There are always considerations when determining if a piece of video should be shown to a potential suspect. Many surveillance and security professionals avoid this practice until absolutely necessary and usually at a criminal or disciplinary hearing. The first concern is divulging what the cameras can and cannot see and letting the potential suspect see what evidence is available. The use of still shot captures can be useful and have a positive effect on the interviewee without showing the moving video.

Independent witnesses are probably the most important witnesses in most investigations. An independent witness is one who is not known to the principal participants and who is not an employee. In civil cases the independent witness will carry much weight especially if a jury believes both sides of the case and is having difficulty making a decision. The independent witness is one who has no vested interest in the outcome and is not associated with either side.

It is very difficult during a field investigation to get initial responders to canvass for independent witnesses. The focus is not on bystanders and is usually on principal participants. The ideal time to identify, interview and have written statements to include contact information is during the field investigation when those potential independent witnesses are available. The investigator should always request independent witnesses and assist in training those who respond in automatically canvassing for them.

It is possible to reconstruct witnesses through data that is constantly streaming in a casino. The obvious method is to observe video segments to determine who was in the immediate area at the time and prior to the event in question. Employees, known customers and others can be identified by having surveillance print screen captures of the persons in order to search for their identity.

Player tracking systems will prove valuable in these instances also in that the video may identify a particular machine and the player tracking system will identify the player that may have had a bird's eye view of the incident. Customer privacy issues and impacts of contacting certain customers should be evaluated.

Cameras over POS systems such as restaurant cashiers or servers will also prove valuable in identifying a person using a loyalty card or credit card for purchases. Many cases in casino environments are solved by identifying persons in this manner from hotel records through the casino IT systems.

Key Takeaways

- Conducting interviews will occur in all investigations and will be critical for a successful outcome to resolve a loss or determine a cause for a breach or loss.
- The process that an investigator uses during interviews will serve as a foundation for the investigation and will be referred to many times as the investigation evolves.
- Foundational witnesses are those that assist the investigator in understanding what has occurred and in what manner the incident giving rise to the inquiry manifested.

Best Practices

- Foundational witnesses should be interviewed first to establish what has occurred, what losses are known at the time, what time frames are involved and what employees may have access or involvement.
- Wherever local law permits, an interview room with audio recording should always be utilized to accomplish a record of the interview, allow for careful playback and to demonstrate the seriousness of the incident to the person being interviewed.
- The investigator must prepare the room in which interviews are conducted, collect all of the possible documents, reports, statements and other evidence and plan the interview carefully to obtain and retain the valuable evidence they will later need.

Chapter 9

Ethics in Gaming Investigations

> The investigator must keep an objective and unbiased frame of mind when conducting the gaming investigation.
>
> Alan W. Zajic

The integrity of an investigation relies heavily on the ethics of the investigator and how they approach the process. The ethical process involves honesty, fairness and the overall truthfulness of the investigator. The integrity of the investigator is a prime factor in how the investigation will be conducted, received and, just as important, perceived.

It seems as though every few months the media reports another case cleared by using new forensic technology in DNA analysis to establish that a person who has been incarcerated (sometimes for decades) did not commit the crimes they were convicted of. These injustices are typically linked back to the investigator and the ethics of that investigator in pursuing a criminal conviction and closing the case. Sometimes the desire to close the case will impair the impartiality of an investigation and will compromise the ethics of that investigator.

As investigative reporters and producers of television programs dig into the case files later it becomes evident that the criminal investigator either ignored evidence or forced the investigation with an obvious bias to convict the person they thought committed the crime rather than find the objective evidence proving they did not. The pressures from prosecutors and police administrators in decades past did not help the problem.

The investigator must keep an objective and unbiased frame of mind when conducting the gaming investigation. We have experienced investigators who worked for us that developed such tunnel vision that they let their personal suspicions drive the investigation instead of the facts and important input from witnesses. We can also recall specific investigators who did complete comprehensive witness canvassing and would always look for the alternative suspect or cause as part of their complete investigation. One such investigator went on to be a security and surveillance executive in the northwest United States.

Again let's take a cashier's cage loss of $1,000. There are four cashiers, a supervisor, a cleaning person escorted by a uniformed security officer and the cage manager who all had access from the time when the bank was in balance until a loss was discovered on the front line by a cashier closing out their bank at the end of a busy shift.

The inclination is to focus on the cashier where the loss occurred, and that should be done first to eliminate them as a suspect if possible. Realistically all persons who were in close proximity to the cash are suspects until absolutely cleared. The investigator has an ethical obligation to clear all employees during the course of the investigation, to take a look at all of them in the event a past or future loss may involve them and to clear them from any suspicion.

As a case example, the cage loss of $1,000 actually occurred and the investigator working continued to dig, interview and cover each and every employee seen on the surveillance video in the area of the cashier's cage. The cashier of the bank where the loss occurred had financial problems, a history of small overages and shortages, and had been an employee for six years. She did not interview well and displayed body language that was troubling to the investigator.

As the case moved on and the investigator continued to investigate each person, match their interview details to the surveillance video and be cleared, there was no objective evidence that the cashier took the $1,000. She was placed on suspension pending investigation, which made it more difficult to solve the case.

The investigator finally interviewed the department head and the uniformed security officer who escorted the cleaning staff into the cage. The video review of these people proved negative to anyone obviously taking cash. The security officer proved to be an interesting interview. The investigator did not suspect the security officer because he worked with him and thought, in his mind, that he would not steal, and the video did not reveal an obvious theft.

At first the security officer was matter of fact and straightforward in his official interview and then as the experienced investigator asked more questions the officer got more and more nervous. The security officer displayed classic signs of deception to the well-trained and experienced investigator. This changed the focus of the investigation.

The interview was concluded and the investigator went back to the video to observe the officer while he was in the cage. A closer, frame by frame video analysis resulted in the detection of a suspicious move where the officer leaned against the counter with his hands behind his back. The video showed a stack of cash on the counter before and then, after a long period of time and after the security officer moved away, the cash was no longer there with no one else near it. The video was not conclusive to lay blame. A second interview by the investigator resulted in a confession to the theft by the very person who was charged to watch others for theft.

When debriefing the case later, the investigator confided that he was not going to interview the security officer initially and was convinced the evidence, although circumstantial, was pointing towards the cashier on suspicion. The investigator also did not believe that the cashier was lying to him when directly confronted. The ethical process by which this investigator continued to pursue the theft and assurance that he would not go after an employee who was innocent of the theft was profound when the easy approach would simply have been to blame the cashier, terminate her employment and close the file. Ethics in investigations is a constant and needs to be stressed to all employees charged with seeking to solve internal theft and embezzlement-type cases. A clear honesty and acceptance of the true evidence is crucial and a mandatory quality in the professional investigator.

There are many philosophers that have proffered on the subject of ethics in general but few who do so in the investigator world and more specifically the gaming investigator environment. An investigator holds great power in the direction and end result of the future employment and criminal record of the employees he interviews or involves in a case or incident.

Ethics are not typically learned in a class or course of instruction. Basic ethics are ingrained in a person's personality and can be nurtured and improved upon by competent managers. We learn ethics at a young age from our parents or role models as we grow and mature into adults. This process also occurs as events take place during our lives that shape our personalities and mold us into adults.

A great philosopher by the name of Cicero in 200 BC proffered many sayings and writings on the subject of ethics. Many others have written on ethics and how a person should hold to them in conduct. The following are some of the more common ones that apply to investigators.

Always Tell the Truth

We have often heard from our elders that we should always tell the truth. As investigators this is crucial in obtaining the facts and evidence in a criminal or other type of investigation. Most people in my experience are basically honest yet most people will embellish, exaggerate or tell "white lies" in everyday life and in routine activities.

Dating is a good example of this in that most people will make some utterance that is not completely true about an ex-lover or person they dated in the past. This social phenomenon is quite common and accepted by most people because of the nature of social interactions. It becomes exaggerated based on social media and can be hurtful.

Most parents know as their children grow up and develop that it is easy to detect when a young child is lying. Their actions, eye contact and body language give them away. Then they will have a tendency to lie again to cover the first lie and eventually realize they have been caught.

Adults are more skilled at lying but the characteristics remain detectable. When an investigator does not tell the truth, it is difficult to catch them at lying absent a keen supervisor or manager that is analytical and detail oriented.

If you catch an investigator lying it is a serious ethical violation and should be dealt with immediately and with serious consequences. Even a simple untruth in a report can dramatically affect the process and outcome of a case. The investigator is charged with seeking the truth in order to solve the mystery they are entrusted to solve. Even the smallest embellishment in an investigator's report or work product can nullify the entire investigation.

Treat People as You Would Like to Be Treated

Many old-school investigators believe that accusing and badgering a suspect or witness will result in solving the case. These are typically the ones that are always in a rush to work on the more exciting cases or the person who is long past retiring and does not have that passion anymore.

There is nothing more damaging to the perception of security, surveillance or the regulator than to accuse a person of a crime they did not commit. An example in this regard is the abduction of Jaycee Lee Dugard in a rural area of Lake Tahoe on June 10, 1991. She was later rescued from her captors some eighteen years later.

We were working in Tahoe at the time and the security and all of the law enforcement community within 500 miles was somehow involved in the search for the vehicle, the suspects and the eleven-year-old victim. Every car that remotely resembled the suspect vehicle was reported, stopped, searched and also examined in our parking lot.

In this disturbing case the law enforcement community badgered, accused, threatened and publicly embarrassed the stepfather who was the sole witness to the abduction. The police mocked his description of the vehicle and suspects and indirectly kept him from obtaining long-term employment as a result. That same vehicle was discovered when Dugard was rescued, and it matched the original description by the stepfather perfectly. The perpetrator was prosecuted and sentenced to 431 years. The impacts of this investigation are still being felt by all of the victims, including the family.

How we treat people is crucial not only in soliciting cooperation, but also in the perceptions that the employee population has and therefore the morale of an organization. A calm and professional approach will generally yield positive results.

The investigator should always be polite, truthful, respectful and patient. People in general like to talk and explain things and again the most important skill for the investigator is to listen carefully. The creative investigator will still get the same information from a potential suspect without taking away their self-respect. Anyone who ever worked for us knows that taking away a person's self-respect was a termination offense including dealing with suspects. You do not know where a person has been in their life, what they have had to endure or what circumstances forced them to do that they did not want to do.

Always Do the Right Thing and Follow Your Heart

Our moral compass drives us in our day-to-day life and steers us to knowing right from wrong and, when the time comes, to doing the right thing. Regardless of the circumstances, the investigator has to rely on their years of professional and life experience and training, yet make the right decisions for the right reasons.

I once had to terminate a security officer for taking two dimes from a drop box sleeve and putting them into his shirt pocket during a box drop. The man was truly a family man, needed the job desperately and was working two jobs to support his family. I agonized over the decision, did not sleep, tried to rationalize that it was not theft and questioned my own ethics, decision-making and professionalism. I thought in my heart that I should forgive him and discipline him in another way but my firm and proven policy was to terminate for any theft regardless of the item.

I finally decided to fire him but I spent a long time talking to him when I did. Although he knew it was wrong, he admitted that when he changed out of his uniform, he found the two dimes and did not turn them in. The surveillance video was conclusive of him taking the money from the box area and putting it into his pocket.

It is not always the best course to do what you think in your heart should be done, but instead to send a strong message that you will not tolerate theft. The general rule should be that if you feel in your heart that you should do something and it is the right thing to do, you should follow your heart. If that is in conflict with department philosophy, you should seek guidance from your superior and get the monkey off your back and onto theirs.

Key Takeaways

- Do unto others as you would have them do unto you. Treat all people the same with respect, courtesy and professionalism in every investigation.
- Follow your heart. Strive to always do the right thing for the right reason and not for expediency or other reasons.
- Always tell the truth in your investigation, reporting and conversations with peers, law enforcement and superiors.

Best Practices

- The investigator must keep an objective and unbiased frame of mind when conducting the gaming investigation.
- The investigator should always be polite, truthful, respectful and patient.

Chapter 10

Prosecution

The investigator must be able to meet and document the elements of the crime.

Alan W. Zajic

Depending on the jurisdiction, it is incumbent upon a gaming facility to request and facilitate the prosecution of criminal offenders whenever possible. This is accomplished by presenting the evidence to law enforcement who typically then complete a written report and attach the investigator's, security personnel's or surveillance agent's work product and report. This does not conclude the work on the file and is the beginning of the next phase of the investigation, called prosecution. Prosecution is the process by which local authorities comply with law and prove that a crime was committed and present the person that committed the crime to pay their debt to the victims and society.

We have encountered many investigators who were upset because a local district attorney (DA) reduced or dropped a criminal charge to a lesser offense and even dismissed a case without the investigator's knowledge. The reality is the burden of case management and communication to the local prosecutor is the job of the property investigator or other security or surveillance officer who was directly involved in the criminal investigation or the arrest.

It is a smart practice to require that the investigator or shift supervisor in security or surveillance be required to follow the case they initiated or investigated all the way through the process of hearings, trial, restitution and hopefully conviction of the perpetrator. A requirement to complete a follow-up on the final result will not only ensure closure with a satisfactory conclusion, it will serve to document the success of the enterprise to prosecute for criminal behavior and give the opportunity to demand and collect restitution for costs associated.

Meeting the Elements of the Crime

In reality the circumstances in many instances during prosecution are a result of the fact that the evidence presented to them does not follow and meet the very basic elements of the crime being prosecuted. Most DA or city attorney offices screen all files when initially received to make a determination if the elements have been met and the evidence is clear and convincing before they even start to schedule hearings or a trial. It is at this juncture (typically authorized by law) that a case is thrown in the "do not prosecute" pile and no further action is even contemplated.

In each and every case being investigated and when the written report is being prepared, the investigator must rely on the specific criminal charges that the case involves and document each and every element of the criminal offense or infraction as it applies to the incident. Without this very basic inclusion, the case that took many hours and much effort to prepare will be dismissed or the prosecutor will not pursue the charges. Remember the elements are all of the factors described in the law to prove that the criminal offense was committed by the person being presented as the suspect.

A very simple method for an investigator to follow is to prepare a binder of all the possible crimes they will investigate and place a copy of the statute or ordinance in that binder as a constant reference when completing the written investigation report. If the crime is grand larceny for instance, the occurrence, the amount that makes it a felony, the method of the larceny, the time and date of the larceny and the details must all follow the theme of what the crime of grand larceny is in the jurisdiction. As the investigator conducts more and more investigations and includes the elements of the crimes they will become experienced at not only documenting the elements but also looking for each required element during the course of the investigation.

Another common reason a case is not prosecuted, or charges are reduced, is that witnesses do not show up for the criminal trial. The transient employee population in casinos and the lack of communication and coordination of employee witnesses typically creates the void of witnesses at a criminal trial and therefore the case cannot present that critical witness evidence in the form of live testimony. Payroll issues in some enterprises will also create issues when employees are requested to go to court on a company or tribal incident and do not receive appropriate pay for their time.

As previously covered in Chapter 7, the investigation file should include a cover sheet with all of the players listed along with their basic involvement, whether it is as a suspect, witness, victim, police officer or compliance officer. This cover sheet should also contain the basic charges and important dates for placement on the investigator's calendar for preliminary hearings, trials and sentencing. As a case draws near trial, the investigator should initiate contact with the prosecutor to express the desire to prosecute and request an opportunity to present a demand for restitution should the case be negotiated. They should also make contact with witnesses and help facilitate the appearance at the hearing or trial.

Key Takeaways

- Depending on the jurisdiction, it is incumbent upon a gaming facility to request and facilitate the prosecution of criminal offenders whenever possible.
- Making sure that the elements of the criminal offense are met and well documented will increase the likelihood of succesful prosecution.

Best Practices

- It is a smart practice to require that the investigator or shift supervisor in security or surveillance be required to follow the case they initiated or investigated all the way through the process of hearings, trial, restitution and hopefully conviction of the perpetrator.

Chapter 11

Jurisdictions, Regulations and Gaming Environments

> Every casino has a unique regulatory process and includes the personnel and reporting relationships within the management structure.
>
> Alan W. Zajic

The evolution of legal gambling in the United States is interesting and very diverse. From 1931 when gambling was first made legal in Nevada as a benefit to the thousands of workers building Hoover Dam, the road to gaming today has been a complicated and interesting journey. Illegal gaming was the order of the day until Nevada became the first state to legalize gaming, bringing regulation and control to an industry that had operated without any before.

The traditional gaming environment in Nevada was developed over time and included integrity of gaming and protecting the industry from the criminal elements or gangsters of the day. Nevada was the start of regulatory oversight in casinos and has continued to be the leader in all forms of legalized gambling. Almost every jurisdiction in the world involves the lawyers and regulators visiting Nevada to assist in setting up their regulatory oversight.

The MICS in other jurisdictions are outlined using Nevada's basic regulatory structures and, in many cases, the regulatory restrictions have evolved to become much more stringent than those found in Nevada. When New Jersey decided to enter into the gambling business in the mid-1970s the regulators came to Nevada to review the oversight system by the Gaming Control Board (GCB). The Atlantic City environment was quite different and the paranoia that organized crime would take over the casinos prompted the New Jersey regulators to impose harsh and costly regulations on casinos. Many of these still exist and arguably may have been the cause of declining business.

The proliferation of Native American casinos took the regulatory industry to a new level, involving a self-imposed regulatory structure that may or may not have included a state agency where the sovereign casino was located. Tax structures and regulations are still very much in flux in these environments, as well as challenges through court actions.

The Riverboat phenomenon came into play in the 19th century and continues today in a much different fashion. The first modern-day riverboat designed as a casino appeared in 1989 on the Mississippi. The rush by companies to create gambling on the river, because gambling on land was illegal in most states, was massive and unprecedented in gaming at the time. Many restrictions, including that the riverboat had to pick up its gamblers, move away from the dock and return back several hours later, soon became problematic and in today's gaming market the vessels park permanently or are located on barges with attachments to land-based facilities. The law still requires that the casino be floating on the river, although slow changes in state laws are occurring.

Every casino has a unique regulatory process and includes the personnel and reporting relationships within the management structure. The common thread is that the regulatory personnel will typically report independently to the corporate or enterprise level of the organization or as an oversight by a state or federal agency.

All regulations are not the same, regardless of the common perceptions. Each and every casino is located in its own unique environment and has distinct rules, regulations and laws that govern the operation. Familiarization and memorization of whichever of these apply to the facility is an imperative to surviving the investigation process.

The investigator's library will include the most current laws and regulations that are applicable to the facility and the environment. The investigator must understand law enforcement actions based on tribal affiliation versus customers that are not tribal, all the way through the team members' association or demographic.

Key Takeaways

- Every casino has a unique regulatory process and includes the personnel and reporting relationships within the management structure.
- Each and every casino is located in its own unique environment and has distinct rules, regulations and laws that govern the operation.

Best Practices

- The investigator's library will include the most current laws and regulations that are applicable to the facility and the environment. The investigator must understand law enforcement actions based on tribal affiliation versus customers that are not tribal, all the way through the team members' association or demographic.

Chapter 12

Investigations and Liability

Investigations are full of tripwires that could ultimately involve a lawsuit against the enterprise and even individually for the investigator.

Alan W. Zajic

Liability exposure is a constant in all business environments and gaming facilities are an attractive target for the litigious and the people who have a legitimate legal claim. Investigations are full of tripwires that could ultimately involve a lawsuit against the enterprise and even individually for the investigator. No investigator is fully immune to a lawsuit if it can be proven that there was negligence or an intentional act that caused a plaintiff damage. The concept of a litigation claim will be that the conduct of the investigator was not reasonable under the circumstances and caused some form of harm to the litigant.

Generally, when an investigator starts the process of an investigation it is based on the initial field investigation, which does not necessarily have the correct information. Again this is a great reason to confirm that initial information, especially potential suspect information collected by others.

Once the investigator starts the process they may become culpable in a negligence claim if the facts are not correct and there was no reasonable attempt to obtain the truth or to correct facts and as a result a plaintiff was injured in some way including reputation, loss of income and many other ways. The investigator should step back and ask the following questions in a liability check of their end product:

- Is the basis of the incident correct and is the correct person named as the suspect?
- Are the damages exaggerated to move the crime into a felony category?
- Were all persons with access interviewed and due diligence completed to rule them out as a suspect?
- Were all alibis thoroughly researched and documented?
- Is there anyone else who could be the suspect?

- Are you willing to stake your personal wealth including your home on the results of your investigation?
- Have you been ethical in your investigation including the written report?
- Is there any appearance that the investigation was initiated in retaliation to some form of claim or complaint?
- Have you complied with and respected the individual rights of the person named in the investigation?
- Could it be perceived that there was some form of discrimination in your work product?
- Are there statements in your report that could be considered defamation, slander or libel?

The investigation should be conducted in an impartial, fair and thorough manner and should not leave any question in the reader's mind that it was not. The investigation should also be conducted in a reasonable manner based on all of the circumstances. Remember if there is a lawsuit, the trier of fact (most likely a jury from the community in which the suspect lives) will determine if your actions were reasonable and professional.

The report and testimony of the investigator should always be completed in a manner that minimizes any liability or exposure to the enterprise or the investigator individually. Litigation is a common factor in all businesses and the investigator should always lean towards avoiding any potential litigation and be able to prove that they were in fact impartial, were thorough in the process and exhausted all other leads. If the evidence is marginal or does not meet the burdens of proof criminally or civilly the investigator will have exposed themselves and their employer to liability exposure.

Spoliation of Evidence

As video technology has improved over the last several decades, so has the ease in retention and saving video. However, the decision to save a particular piece of video evidence is still a human one. Although technology improves the amount of digital video data that is automatically saved, the sheer volume of data makes it impossible to save all video data in the current server storage technology (although this technology is rapidly changing). As a result, the personnel in a surveillance or security observation function make the decision to save video segments and the critical sub-decisions on how much time, the number of cameras and the number of views of an incident or area to save.

In almost all litigations in gaming environments the video is the focus of the lawsuit in one way or another. Since there are regulatory mandates that video be recorded in gaming environments the chances that at least some video was captured are fairly high. Plaintiff attorneys will attempt to convince the trier of fact that the casino is hiding something or that critical video evidence was purposely removed, erased or destroyed. As a result, the video is always the *smoking gun* of their case and a jury will rely heavily on what is depicted in video evidence and what is not.

There are two basic pitfalls in trial that need to be avoided. The actual charge of spoliation or an intentional not saving or deleting of important video is commonly known as spoliation of evidence. The other concern at trial is if the plaintiff can prove some form of negligence in that the video was not collected and the data was written over by the software and server through the normal operation of the video system.

In spoliation legal causes of action the penalties can be severe in that the judge has the ability to determine liability based upon the intentional acts by an employee or agent. This is very dangerous because then the only thing to be decided is the damages, or amount of money, including punitive damages, to be awarded. Punitive damages are the headline makers when a case reaches the millions of dollars level in a verdict.

Every surveillance and security manager has to balance the staff time to investigate and collect the video evidence against the severity of the incident being investigated. The investigator is typically charged with determining how much video should be reviewed and saved, although a manager is typically involved because of operational impacts.

In a civil trial there will be many allegations by plaintiffs that the casino did not save enough video, did not save a different angle, saved only the actual event and not the video that would explain the start of the event, or any other imaginable allegation. Anywhere the video evidence does not support plaintiff's allegations will be disputed and exploited against the casino at trial.

Surveillance agents and security officers rarely have the foresight to collect the necessary video on high-risk events absent a supervisor or manager's directives. The investigator should be very cognizant of the video capabilities and direct the review of video or at least the collection of video for future review. At least one large server should be dedicated with a backup for video pulled from the system. Ideally the investigator should have direct access to that server to perform further investigation. It is relatively easy to save many views of an entire area post-incident for later review. It is impossible to collect the data from the system once it is written over after the retention period.

We have included the International Association of Certified Surveillance Professionals' best practice for *Video Review, Investigation, and Retention in Gaming Environments* in the back of this publication as a resource for the investigator and for surveillance personnel (see Appendix 5). The document will help in the process of determining the severity of an incident and the commensurate video retention and investigation process.

The investigator will uncover details not known at the time of the initial review and can also ensure adequate *chain of custody* of the video evidence. The chain of custody is again important in that the possession of the video evidence should be proven to be secured, not accessed by anyone unauthorized and not tampered with while secured. Although security features such as watermarking make alteration of video near impossible for the typical employee or manager, it is very possible to remove or delete a video segment that will be part of a spoliation claim.

In a negligence issue the trier of fact may allow that a jury instruction is given that they may assume that the missing video would most likely depict images most favorable to the plaintiff, which could turn a defense case into a plaintiff verdict. These instances are more common in casino litigations in that the evidence and testimony might reveal that the surveillance agent or investigator failed to review and save all available video of an incident.

There are other pieces of evidence that may come into a spoliation or negligence claim at trial. The more common ones besides video would be witness statements, POS records, lock interrogation reports, electronic security patrol records, daily activity reports, logs or any written reports, or photographs taken at the time yet not available for a jury to look at. Witness statements are very commonly used by a plaintiff when not included in the original report as fodder for an attempt to demonstrate negligence or unprofessionalism, or to project a negative corporate attitude.

The investigator is the backup plan post-incident in ensuring the incident is thoroughly documented; evidence is collected, organized and maintained through and beyond the statute of limitations. The statute of limitations is the time period in which a person can file a civil action against a casino. The investigator should be the one to, for instance, interview every security officer involved in an arrest where the arrestee was seriously injured, collect a written statement from each, and collect all available video evidence, any logs associated and any other perishable electronic data.

Most gaming facilities are still in the hard copy mode for logs and documents. The age of electronic data and scanners allows for huge volumes of documents to be stored in a single server. During any major incident a smart practice would be for the investigator to collect all work schedules, break schedules, logs, summary reports, POS reports, player loyalty reports, hotel folios and registration documents, PABX call records and any other document that could possibly relate to the incident being investigated. The hard case file or binder should be maintained and a scanned electronic copy of all documents should be made with the case name and number on the file for future reference and backup. This also allows authorized users to access the information and produce consistent evidence during the case discovery period or fact-finding legal process.

Key Takeaways

- Liability is a constant in all business environments and gaming facilities are an attractive target for the litigious and the people who have a legitimate legal claim.

- Investigations are full of tripwires that could ultimately involve a lawsuit against the enterprise and even individually for the investigator.
- In almost all litigations in gaming environments the video is the focus of the lawsuit in one way or another. Since there are regulatory mandates that video be recording in gaming environments the chances that at least some video was captured are fairly high.

Best Practices

- The investigation should be conducted in an impartial, fair and thorough manner and should not leave any question in the reader's mind that it was not.
- The report and testimony of the investigator should always be completed in a manner that minimizes any liability or exposure to the enterprise or the investigator individually.
- Every surveillance and security manager has to balance the staff time to investigate and collect the video evidence against the severity of the incident being investigated.
- The investigator should be very cognizant of the video capabilities and direct the review of video or at least the collection of video for future review. At least one large server should be dedicated with a backup for video pulled from the system.
- We have included the International Association of Certified Surveillance Professionals' best practice for *Video Review, Investigation, and Retention in Gaming Environments* in the back of this publication as a resource for the investigator and for surveillance personnel (see Appendix 5). The document will help in the process of determining the severity of an incident and the commensurate video retention and investigation process.

Part 2

Non-Gaming Investigations

Chapter 13

Non-Gaming Investigations

> A hotel room has a high exposure for criminal events to occur based on the nature of the design and the privacy that can also be an attractor to criminals to include crimes such as sexual assaults, robberies, assault and battery, and even homicide.
>
> Alan W. Zajic

The hotel in a casino complex is an amenity that supports the gambling and revenues for the enterprise. The hotel is essentially the temporary domicile of the guest who has rented the room from the enterprise. There are statutory laws and ordinances in every jurisdiction that address the hotel operator and the traveling public. The investigator should collect these hotel laws, commonly known as *innkeeper laws*, which apply to the jurisdiction where the hotel is located. A check with the company or tribal attorney will establish which jurisdiction is applicable, if state laws or compacts mandate jurisdiction, or how it applies to innkeeper laws.

The highest exposure for internal theft in gaming operations is the removal of consumable goods or inventory. This happens in all departments and is especially prevalent in non-gaming areas of the property. Additionally, non-gaming areas are typically monitored to a lesser extent by CCTV than the casino areas, which are heavily regulated. The less comprehensive camera placements and monitoring create opportunity for losses or damage to company and guest property.

Hotel Areas Investigations

The primary area for a hotel is the hotel rooms themselves. A hotel room has a high exposure for criminal events to occur based on the nature of the design and the privacy that can also be an attractor to criminals to include crimes such as sexual assaults, robberies, assault and battery, and even homicide. Hotel rooms are also frequently used for prostitution and drug sales or use, and the ever-present potential for parties involving minors or other high-exposure events. Many premium players will obtain a room for a minor relative who has a party in the room, which eventually becomes a crime scene.

For every room type within a casino resort, an accurate to-scale diagram should be maintained by the investigator for use in a hotel room investigation to identify evidence locations and as an attachment to the report. A file with copies of these room diagrams including reverse layouts will be very helpful. The architectural drawings or *as built diagrams* can be obtained and copied from in page size, which can include housekeeping quarters, floor hallways, vending areas, maintenance accesses and other valuable locations.

The investigator should prepare, in advance, all of the security features that are located in and around a hotel room. This is best done with basic floor plans and a key to identify each and every item that is designed to keep a patron safe when they are inside their hotel room. The following are examples of these security features:

- Solid core or metal door
- Automatic door closer, hinges
- Chain or security bar on entry door
- Working peephole
- Mortise lock mechanism
- Strike and latch assemblies
- Dead bolts
- Changeable key access or electronic key
- Electronic key interrogation capability
- Smoke detectors, speakers, strobe lighting
- Window locks
- Window slider stops anti-lift devices
- Television safety videos
- Bathtub safety devices
- Guest book safety chapter
- Emergency phone number
- Hotel safe in place and operable
- Local Hotel Law Card is posted as mandated

These items should all be checked off on a copy of the room diagram when investigating crimes that have occurred or have allegedly occurred inside a hotel room including reported loss of personal property, cash or medications. By having a pre-prepared diagram this will ensure that all of the safety features in the room were in place and functioning and that the hotel took reasonable safety precautions to protect the hotel guest.

The hotel registration computer system should always be checked, and documents to include all registration cards, signatures, number of keys issued, folios and specific charges made to the room should be collected when initiating a hotel room investigation. They can also prove valuable in other investigations such as a claim of a theft from the casino floor where a folio demonstrates the guest was in their room eating room service when they allege a theft occurred elsewhere.

In most hotels the changeable key card access system is a valuable tool for the investigator and once again is a perishable piece of evidence that should be collected early during any investigation. It is easy to read the electronic lock and retain the printed report and it is impossible to collect it days or weeks later. These interrogation reports will determine who used any key, including masters, to access the room. Note that the systems do not identify if a key was taken or stolen by someone else, and are not identity specific. They also do not determine who opened a door and exited from the inside.

This is valuable to determine maid and maintenance access, guest access times and time intervals in between. Regardless of the type and severity of the investigation, the lock interrogation report should always be collected for future use and documentation. In the event of a future investigation into employee thefts of customer property, for example, these reports will assist in solving multiple thefts.

Many hotels also have uniformed security officers utilizing an electronic patrol system that documents security patrols by location and time. The newer versions of these systems utilize a pen or wand that is used to read a metal button or bar code that is located in strategic positions throughout a hotel property. Android phones or iPhones are also being utilized for ease by the patrolling security officer; the phone immediately records its location into the tracking program, which is integrated into the dispatching software. At the conclusion of a work shift the data is downloaded into a device that exports the data into a computer and will reflect where the security officer was at various times throughout a working shift.

In cases of third party crimes where a suspect who is not an employee commits a crime against another guest these logs will become valuable to demonstrate that a security officer patrolled the location a certain number of times at certain intervals. This is used to demonstrate that the security measures were reasonable and within what is known as the *Standard of Care* or common practices comparative to similar hotels.

Most hotel facilities built in the last decade include CCTV cameras that are monitored by security or surveillance. In the case of a serious crime inside a hotel room, that video will become critical and as much video as possible based on retention should be initially saved, hopefully from the time the victim first entered the room.

Theft Inside Hotel Rooms by Employees

The most common thefts inside hotel rooms are cash, chips, jewelry and, surprisingly, prescription drugs. The crafty thief will stay under the radar and only take a single ten-dollar bill from a stack of cash in a drawer, a ring from a jewelry case or a couple of Percocet from a full prescription bottle. The casual professional maid thief can operate for years without being detected in this fashion if they have the self-control not to get greedy. Although it does occur, larger items are typically not taken from hotel rooms.

Housekeepers will also remove an item and hide it in their maid's cart or in the linen closet on their work floor. This is done to determine if anyone will report the loss and the maid can then return or "find" the item and turn it in. An occasional check and inspection of maid's closets and carts will reveal these items and whether there is theft of guest property occurring. Care should be taken in the event that the items are merely left by the guest in a checked-out room and they were not turned in to the official lost and found.

If a particular housekeeper is suspected of theft through recurring losses in rooms that they have cleaned, law enforcement should be contacted to assist in a legal sting project. Care should be taken in making sure that the setup in the room is not overly tempting to the employee such that it could be considered entrapment, in that the employee was baited into committing the crime when they would not have under normal circumstances.

In field investigations the taking of pictures inside the room is important to document items in the guest room and their particular location. Many pictures should be taken of the guest room, locks and safety devices, and the condition of the room. These photographs will assist the investigator in solving the loss and potentially arresting a bad employee. The pictures will also assist in the credibility of the victim in the event they are making a false claim.

The employees in the hotel are well aware of the electronic key system capabilities when it comes to the lock interrogation. This will demonstrate any person who entered the room by using an electronic key. It will not assist if the employee used a purposely unlocked connector door or defeated the strike in the mortise lock with tissue or tape to allow them access without using a key. The field investigation should always include inspection and photography of the entry points into a hotel room, which will detect any attempt to defeat access control, including windows and patio doors.

Any and all employees in a hotel can gain access into an occupied room. Another guest can also access a room, especially if a room is double rented or a desk clerk mistakenly issues a key to another guest. Room service employees who deliver food and observe a thing of value may want to come back when the guest is away and possibly enter the room. Maintenance personnel, vendors such as honor bar resuppliers, and just about anyone has the ability, with some creativity, to enter a guest room without being detected by the lock interrogation.

Trick Rolls and Prostitution

Hotel room incidents and crimes are common in that the private hotel room environment involves people who bring with them their conceptions, habits, prejudices and problems that cannot be detected by the normal protective employee. The case of a *trick roll*, where a guest encounters a prostitute inside the casino, brings them to their hotel room, pays for sex, is drugged and all of their valuable possessions are stolen, is very hard to prevent at the hotel room location.

Trick rolls become problematic in that the victim will rarely want to call the police and have a police report that will memorialize the encounter, which they may have to explain to their spouse, partner or employer. Prostitution also involves a surprising number of homosexual encounters with men and women and should also be considered during the investigation as a potential motive or circumstance that may be important to the investigation. The following should be considered when investigating a potential serious trick roll:

- Preserve any drinking glass, can or bottle the perpetrator may have touched as it may contain prints or evidence of drugs.
- Request and document the request that the victim go to the hospital and have blood and other samples taken to determine the intoxicant used.
- Look for and collect any biological evidence from bedding, from the bathroom or from towels that may contain DNA.
- Request the police are involved. If refused, still perform a comprehensive investigation to prevent future trick rolls, and document the refusal.
- Prepare a *Be on the Lookout Bulletin* (BOLO) with the full description of the suspect, the time of the incident and basic details about the incident. Distribute internally and externally through law enforcement.
- Collect detailed descriptions of all items taken and what items were available and not taken by the suspect. Include claimed dollar value.
- Broadcast to all physical security personnel to look for items discarded in trash or other locations. If found, photograph and document.
- Request video coverage of the victim to determine the identity of the perpetrator. Track the coverage of the victim for a sufficient period to determine if they were followed by, approached by or left with a particular person.
- Check the hotel safe and determine if it was operable and used. Determine if the perpetrator looked over the victim's shoulder when and if they opened the safe.

Anywhere people have disposable cash and there is any amorous sexual desire, prostitution will occur, regardless of the location or local perceptions.

Another common theft method for prostitutes is the *grope and grab*, which occurs frequently in gaming environments and is a variation of the classic *distraction crime*. A distraction crime is one where a person or persons create a distraction to direct a victim's focus to something other than the valuable item they are stealing.

In the grope and grab the perpetrator will approach the victim, flirt with them and even pretend they are just looking for casual sex. During this process they will place their hands on the person's body, including genitals, in an attempt to arouse them and while the arousal process works, the perpetrator will take a wallet or even a watch right of the wrist of the *mark* or intended victim. This can happen in any location, including a hotel room, and, when the perpetrator leaves, the loss is discovered.

A distraction crime that can also occur inside a hotel room can be an instantaneous one. Instances where a guest invites someone to their room, discovers they want money for sex, declines and a distraction occurs, the perpetrator will typically attempt to leave the room immediately and make up an excuse that they need to go get something. The valuable item is then discovered missing.

Sexual Assaults

In any reported sexual assault case the local police should always be called, regardless of the wishes of the victim. Law enforcement has trained professionals available to them to deal with both adult and juvenile sexual assaults and it should not be primarily investigated by the proprietary security department or investigator. Support and assistance should be provided to obtain and provide the police investigator with as much evidence as is available.

The most common mistake made during a field investigation by initial responders is the perceived interrogation of the victim and allowing the victim to tamper with evidence such as potential biological evidence that is collected in a rape kit. Allowing a victim to go to the bathroom, shower, clean up or change clothes can be a huge mistake in collection of evidence and eventual identification and prosecution of a perpetrator of a sexual assault.

The investigator can certainly collect video records, canvass for possible witnesses, obtain lock interrogation and gather other important or potential evidence in cooperation with the police. Any hotel environments, including those attached to a casino, have a higher risk of sexual assaults than other businesses. Employees also commit a surprising number of sexual assaults in these environments and should always be considered. In a sexual assault investigation any employee working in the hotel including but not limited to room service, housekeeping, maintenance, security and outside vendors should be identified, interviewed and documented in the written report.

A sexual assault is very disturbing to a victim and it should be left to the trained professional to interview and collect the necessary evidence. An isolated sexual assault and the related circumstances are handled differently than cases where there is suspicion that a serial rapist may be preying on unsuspecting hotel guets and each incident must be handled appropriately. In cases where several guests have been raped at the same hotel over time, the liability exposure would most likely be greater.

Push-in Robberies

A phenomenon that was popular in Las Vegas during the 1990s was the *push-in robbery*. This was being perpetrated by several groups of suspects along the strip. These criminals would merely walk the hotel floors looking for a hotel door that was ajar, or would follow a person and as they entered their room they would hold and push the door open, force their way inside and commit a robbery, sometimes with fatal results. During that period of time cameras on hotel floors were uncommon and these incidents had negative impacts on the casino resorts including local press reports. Casinos worked together and put plain clothes teams in place along with police assistance and the perpetrators were eventually caught, or left for another city.

Also common in the 1990s was the placement of a security officer checking keys to ensure all persons entering the hotel towers were registered guests. In most hotels this was only marginally effective in that anyone who could find, steal or appropriate an electronic key could pass into the hotel undetected. A small percentage of hotels still maintain this feature. Many hotels use the access controls inside the elevators to record usage and allow access to hotel floors only by legitimate users.

Push-in robberies still occur in casino complexes and the evidence collection is a crucial element that takes patience and due care. These criminals are typically serial in nature in that they will continue to commit the push-in robberies and they believe the rewards outweigh the risks of being caught. In a push-in robbery the evidence that should be collected in a serious incident should include but not be limited to the following:

- Coordination with local police for crime scene processing. Do not disturb the scene, and protect the entry door and anything that the perpetrators touched. Interview victims to determine which items were touched. Include door jamb, door, locks, hardware, etc.
- Determine if any biological evidence may be present. Locate and identify any bodily fluids that may be present, to include glasses or bottles where saliva may be present, or determine if the perpetrators used the toilet, blew their nose, smoked a cigarette, or any other evidence available.
- Look for and collect any item that is foreign to the room and not the property of the victims. Perpetrators leave things behind frequently.

- Pull the trash cans on the hotel floor and any ashtrays and bag the contents for potential evidence.
- Interrogate the lock on the entry door.
- Check to see if any elevator or corridor camera captured video.
- Check the security logs and electronic patrol records to determine who was near the room and when. Interview them as soon as possible to determine room activity.
- Collect any room service tickets, night maid deliveries, maintenance work or any other logs that may identify employees in the immediate area during the time frame of the event.
- Collect player tracking information from the casino to determine when and where they may have been gambling.
- Request a video review of the victims in any area where cameras may have captured them or anyone following them to include elevators, lobbies, casino, restaurants, outside areas, etc.
- Check the hotel safe to determine if it was operable and used. Determine if the perpetrator looked over the victim's shoulder when and if they opened the safe.

The severity of the crime or loss will generally dictate the amount of law enforcement crime scene work that may be required. The local police should be told that the enterprise is very concerned to prevent future incidents from occurring, and that they should talk to a supervisor if they meet resistance in crime scene processing by the patrol officer. Most police officers do not want to complicate what they perceive as a routine crime. It is incumbent on the investigator to prevent future incidents. These processes will also train the physical security, surveillance and others in what is required for the appropriate field investigation.

A proven camera location that assists in investigating these robbery events, trick rolls and even more serious crimes such as homicides is ensuring there is ample video coverage of all elevator lobbies and elevator cars. All elevators manufactured in the last forty years have video wiring already in the traveling cables of the elevator and it is relatively easy to install a video camera.

An additional covert camera using a pinhole or other concealable method is also useful. The camera is concealed in a wall at eye level in the elevator lobbies, which will capture clear facial video pictures of all persons who enter elevators. The installation of cameras at eye level is becoming more popular to include door frame cameras for clarity in identifying suspects or confirming victim identity. Natural choke points where all people pass are ideal locations in elevator lobbies.

Illegal Drugs in Hotel Rooms

Because of the proliferation of what are classified illegal drugs by the federal government as well as the abuse of prescription drugs, hotel rooms can sometimes be used as a location for sales and distribution, or parties involving juveniles or consenting adults. Great intelligence can be gained from the hotel staff regarding indicators of drug sales or use in the confines of a hotel room. A housekeeper's observation of bulk pills or the smell of cannabis can initiate an investigation and point to the spider web of people involved in the illegal drugs.

Hotel rooms offer a temporary location for sales and distribution and can be vacated or relocated on short notice. These dealers typically have a social network of customers and communications are made via text or social media with simple code words to identify product. They will let customers know they have product, where they can come to and the price, and then the sale and some use occurs inside the hotel room.

Hotel employees can be involved and care should be taken when initiating an illegal drug operation to include local police early on and coordinate with them. Because of the nature of employee social interactions inside a casino resort, drug investigations will tend to go on forever with a new suspect being developed each time an interview or other information is added. The investigator, along with the police, should know when to cut off the investigation before it consumes the property.

Front Desk Investigations

The front desk is the central location where all guests interact, check in and out, conduct business, pay for services and make requests or lodge complaints. It is one of the highest locations for guest dissatisfaction and complaints. As a result, many investigations will involve the front desk in some form including records, larceny by employees, or providing upgrades or services with no charge for tips, and can become problematic if a bad employee wishes to take advantage of the facility or its guests.

Investigations in this area will generally start out with a simple complaint from a guest such as a charge on their bill that they did not make. Inquiry may reveal that there is something suspicious in the charge or that it had occurred previously with the same clerk. These cases will sometimes result from human error and sometimes involve a conversion by a clerk; conversion is when an employee converts some item such as a coupon into negotiable currency.

The common methods to steal at a front desk are to either shortchange a customer or manipulate a charge to allow for a claimed refund in the paperwork. These investigations are time-consuming and will typically leave an electronic trail that is fairly easy to follow and solve. The case of employee who is shortchanging a customer in cash or services is much harder to solve absent clear video or other evidence.

In many front desk operations, the employee will offer upgrades in room types, services or amenities in the hopes of receiving a generous tip from the lucky guest. It is usually prefaced by the employee stating "I could get in a lot of trouble for this, but I like you and would like to upgrade you at no charge". The chance of getting some form of tip is high at the expense of the hotel revenue stream. These instances are often suspected by a hotel manager or supervisor and communicated to the investigator.

Front desk employees who turn to larceny can also do many things to access a credit card, manipulate charges and refunds, and even make a duplicate key assigned to the guest and access their room during one of their work breaks. Another common practice is to convert a cash payment for an incidental and then transfer the charge to another guest folio especially a premium player who is not likely to notice it on their bill.

Bell Desk and Concierge Investigations

The reported loss of luggage or items missing from luggage are the most common incidents an investigator may get involved in depending on the circumstances and the value of the loss. In addition, bell staff and concierge personnel are the likely suspects if there is some prostitution going on in the hotel. Prostitutes and pimps will attempt to befriend a bellman or concierge and tip them for every person that they refer to "party" with a hotel guest. These instances may very well fall into the category of pandering depending on local laws and is a serious problem in that local regulators could fine the operation or suspend a gaming license. These instances should also be reported to police and their vice officers should be allowed to investigate with the confidential help of the investigator.

Luggage claims are problematic in that the guest is already suspicious and upset at the hotel for losing an item or allowing an item to be removed while in a bell desk's custody. Most hotels have several cameras installed for employee deterrence and assistance in investigating a claim of missing items while in the bell desk custody. It should be noted that these employees are well aware of the camera locations and any potential blind spots and a concealed camera may be in order if a pattern develops.

Bell tags and stickers are usually difficult to follow with an internal theft inside a bell storage room in that it is relatively easy for a dirty bellman to switch or replace tags making it appear to be a mistake or to deflect suspicion on another employee not well liked.

Concierge investigations typically involve kickbacks and occasionally prostitution. Unfortunately, whenever the offer of cash for a referral is made by a criminal or legitimate business it becomes problematic to the smooth operation of the hotel. These employees believe that their actions are not wrong and there is no victim involved. That employee at the concierge desk that gets ten dollars for every referral to a restaurant regardless of customer complaints will create operational issues and will create motivation to step over the line to more criminal events. Concierge employees who work with a cash drawer also have the same opportunities for larceny offenses as a front desk clerk.

Clearly defined policies and procedures that identify the dos and don'ts for a concierge will assist in these types of investigations. If tips are permitted, a clear and understandable procedure will deter and help control abuses and greed.

Intoxication and Alcohol Incidents

There are instances where an investigator may be involved in an investigation involving a guest becoming intoxicated and possibly injuring themselves or others up to and including death. Most states have *dram shop* liability laws that impose liability and therefore potential judgments if it is proven that employees served alcohol to an intoxicated person and they subsequently were allowed to leave intoxicated and caused death or serious injury. States without liquor liability or dram shop laws are Delaware, Kansas, Louisiana, Maryland, Nebraska, Nevada, South Dakota and Virginia.

Care should be taken when conducting interviews and collecting evidence in these cases to be objective and professional. The investigator needs to keep in mind that most likely a lawsuit will be filed and everything they do and document will come under great scrutiny. If the investigator is not objective and has any type of bias, the investigation will be compromised and they will basically be admitting to violations of law through inaccurate reporting and through opinions and conclusions. Ethics will also come into play and the investigator must take care to do the right thing during these intense emotionally driven incidents.

For example, compiling composite video of only negative observations can skew the evidence and create additional liability rather than objectively document the investigation. If the investigator or surveillance agent compiles what they think should be collected it may very well present only negative video clips. In these investigations composite video should be avoided and instead you should collect individual video segments from a period before a subject enters the view until after they exit the video view. If law enforcement wants to edit your video evidence they would have to explain why to the court.

These investigations should be thorough and complete, and video composites are for summary purposes. This only benefits the plaintiff in a civil case and can be misinterpreted based on an initial compiling of a composite. Playing only the negative video documentation and not the hours of pro-active activity to a jury can be very misleading. As a general rule composites should be avoided in investigations especially if there is a potential for civil litigation. Your attorneys can strategically put together a composite video later. Original evidence should be a series of video clips that are collected and not an edit and composite based on an original observation.

All activities involving intoxication investigations should be collected including cut off logs, POS charges, and interviews of all servers found in surveillance video, any security personnel, managers and supervisors who may have had contact with the subject including table games and slots, and any independent witnesses that could shed light on the perceived intoxication level. Safe ride transportation documentation on logs or other records will also be helpful in the investigation.

Key Takeaways

- A hotel room has a high exposure for criminal events to occur based on the nature of the design and the privacy that can also be an attractor to criminals to include crimes such as sexual assaults, robberies, assault and battery and even homicide.
- The most common theft inside of hotel rooms is cash, chips, jewelry and, surprisingly, prescription drugs.
- Because of the proliferation of what are classified illegal drugs by the federal government as well as the abuse of prescription drugs, hotel rooms can sometimes be used as a location for sales and distribution or parties involving juveniles or consenting adults.
- The front desk is the central location where all guests interact, check in and out, conduct business, pay for services and make requests or lodge complaints. It is one of the highest locations for guest dissatisfaction and complaints. As a result, many investigations will involve the front desk in some form including records, larceny by employees, or providing upgrades or services with no charge for tips, and can become problematic if a bad employee wishes to take advantage of the facility or its guests.

Best Practices

- The investigator should collect these hotel laws, commonly known as *innkeeper laws*, which apply to the jurisdiction where the hotel is located.
- For every room type within a casino resort, an accurate to-scale diagram should be maintained by the investigator for use in a hotel room investigation to identify evidence locations and as an attachment to the report. A file with copies of these room diagrams including reverse layouts will be very helpful.
- The hotel registration computer system should always be checked and documents to include all registration cards, signatures, number of keys issued, folios and specific charges made to the room should be collected when initiating a hotel room investigation.
- Many hotels also have uniformed security officers utilizing an electronic patrol system that documents security patrols by location and time.
- Most hotel facilities built in the last decade include CCTV cameras that are monitored by security or surveillance.

Chapter 14

Food and Beverage Investigations

> The highest level of fraud is found in food and beverage areas where there is value and lack of controls.
>
> Alan W. Zajic

All food and beverage investigations involve multiple parties with and without interpersonal relationships. Because of the fact that the regulatory scrutiny will typically stop at the border of the casino, these investigations can sometimes take on a life of their own and involve many people. In most instances losses will occur as a result of internal theft, abuse or misappropriation of consumable inventory or conversion to personal property in some fashion.

Generally, the inventories of consumables are not well maintained, and losses occur as a result of theft, spoilage of product or lack of accountability. The *shrink* or inventory losses in this area are subjective and will fluctuate based on the competence of management and the ability to manage employees and inventory to maximize the profit to the outlet.

In most cases an investigator will not get involved deeply into these areas because of the dynamic and lack of controls found in casino areas. There are some areas that consistently produce internal theft and are cyclical based on the employee and management population and turnover. The following are some of the types of losses an investigator may get involved in.

Liquor Sales and Storage

We believe that when training a new surveillance agent, the most productive department to let an agent catch a thief is the liquor service areas with bartenders or servers. The temptations are strong, gratuities are a common motivator and internal controls are not always well designed or audited by the food and beverage department. Additionally, the POS program is typically not utilized as designed and theft goes on unabated until an outside investigator gets involved.

In many cases a careful analysis with accounting of the POS system and comparative sales to other servers will indicate inventory discrepancy or sales volume decreases without explanation when compared to others in the same capacity. Again, the POS systems are designed to flag exceptions of all servers and compare them to each other to find anomalies that will identify a potential suspect.

The bartender is the easiest internal thief to catch for an investigator in that they will get greedy quickly especially if they believe no one is watching or checking them on their pour or collection of revenues. A major source of theft by a bartender is the complimentary authority given to them in those jurisdictions that allow comps. This dangerous practice allows any server to convert a cash payment for a drink to a comp in the system and allows them to pocket the cash they collected. These instances are not difficult to catch and periodic audits will also be beneficial in identifying the abusers.

Not all bartenders will steal from the company directly but have a tendency to at least over pour or give away drinks to their benefit. Regardless of the circumstance or the quantity, giving alcohol away without collecting payment is still theft. The use of various sized jiggers for premium liquor will not be detected by surveillance and over pour can occur merely by using the larger jigger and charging for the smaller content.

There are some bartenders who are very adept at shortchanging often marginally intoxicated patrons. They believe that because they are not stealing from the casino and the customer will never know, they can add to the gratuity jar every shift. Unfortunately, this will not always go undetected and surveillance audits again will typically catch this type of theft from the customer.

Liquor storage rooms contain an amazing amount of alcohol and value overall. Although some operations are very good at inventory control of liquor storage areas there are many thefts that can still occur. A simple act of a dishonest employee bothering his supervisor for liquor when they are tied up may result in that supervisor giving up the liquor room key and that employee then taking a case of expensive champagne or liquor and stashing it for later removal.

History shows that the placement of a covert camera inside a liquor room will yield much entertainment and document what occurs there for investigation purposes. Although permanent installation of covert cameras should be avoided, an occasional one in the liquor storeroom will yield everything from theft of bulk alcohol to abuse of inventory by vendors, drinking of alcohol by employees, drug use and even sexual misconduct.

Food Servers and Service Employees

Again, the massive amount of consumable inventory that goes through an operation is difficult to track and manage in the best of operations. Theft by food servers is typically as a result of not following a protocol or procedure and not charging the guest for what they have ordered. In the case of a restaurant server a single server who does not charge the customer for desserts or drinks can amount to hundreds of dollars of revenue short-fall in a week. Multiply this by several servers and the amount annually is staggering. Although this is not always intentional there are those servers that will "forget" to charge in the hopes of receiving an additional tip. They will sometimes even tell the customer that they did not charge them for the item.

The *friends and family discount* merely involves those dishonest employees who manipulate the operation or circumstances to allow them to serve their friends or family without collecting for the food consumed. This can be done in many ways to include coupon conversion, manipulation of comp tickets or simply telling their supervisor the table was a walkout. Again, these are not difficult to track and prove but become very time-consuming for the investigator. The internal auditor charged with review of restaurants can be very helpful in these investigations.

Another common area of theft is the abuse of the POS system. Merging of tickets, leaving checks open and manipulating them are typical methods for a server to commit theft. Other abuses include supervisors who merely give their access keys or cards to employees and allow them to void a check. A voided check should always be investigated.

Theft of Supplies

The question of whether the theft of food inventory is occurring at your facil-ity is not an "if" but a "how much". The opportunity for theft is highest in the food department and should not be underestimated. A cook on the front line can take a single steak to her locker on each break and have a great BBQ at home. She just tells her supervisor there were two steaks in the meat drawer that were spoiled and could not be served. The waitress that decides to steal a dessert to bring home for the family just removes it and places it in her purse located nearby.

These thefts are difficult to catch or investigate based on the circumstances and the lack of camera coverage in food service locations. The best method is to frequently conduct bag and backpack searches of employees both in their work areas and as they leave the facility. An unannounced ten-minute period where security is deployed in both plain clothes and uniforms con-ducting bag checks will serve as a great proactive and preventative measure and will occasionally yield a theft in progress. This demonstrates to those employees who are tempted to steal that at any time they could be caught with company property as they leave work.

Because of time and attendance issues with overtime and pay, most casinos have moved away from a single location through which all employees must enter and exit work. Time clocks are placed in numerous locations and employees are typically permitted to come and go without passing a backdoor security officer. This makes it difficult for the investigator attempting to track employees, although not impossible. Access control system records, times of actual employee punching in and out, and other data systems including work station computers will at least give basic locations of employees.

A very common location where supplies are stored temporarily is the garbage room or compactor. Based on the loosening of backdoor controls because of the time and attendance changes over the last few decades, the physical security around the garbage room has lessened overall. As a result, an employee simply places whatever they are taking into a plastic bag and places it somewhere they can pick up after they punch out or simply have an accomplice come and pick the items up. The investigator should check this location when investigating routinely missing items that include silver, meat, seafood and many other items.

Another common way that internal theft out of the food areas occurs is when the employee is permitted to leave the work area and they go to their vehicle and place an item in their car during a work break. This occurs more frequently than most security professionals believe and should not be overlooked.

Employees also go to their vehicles to commit violations of policy including the consumption of alcohol and illegal drugs and many other things. If an investigator suspects this is occurring a coordinated effort between the camera operators and the investigator will also yield positive results and signal to employees it is not a good idea to go to their vehicle mid-shift to steal or to use intoxicants.

Key Takeaways

- Inventories of consumables are not well maintained, and losses occur as a result of theft, spoilage of product or lack of accountability.
- The *friends and family discount* involves those dishonest employees who manipulate the operation or circumstances to allow them to serve their friends or family without collecting for the food consumed or product sold.

Best Practices

- We believe that when training a new surveillance agent, the most productive department to let an agent catch a thief is the liquor service areas with bartenders or servers.
- History shows that the placement of a covert camera inside a liquor room will yield much entertainment and document what occurs there for investigation purposes.
- Another common area of theft is the abuse of the POS system. Merging of tickets, leaving checks open and manipulating them are typical methods for a server to commit theft. Other abuses include supervisors

who merely give their access keys or cards to employees and allow them to void a check. A voided check should always be investigated.

- An unannounced ten-minute period where security is deployed in both plain clothes and uniforms conducting bag checks will serve as a great proactive and preventative measure and will occasionally yield a theft in progress.

Chapter 15

Background Checks and Vender Due Diligence

> The investigator must always be aware that a database in a background check is only as good as the thousands of people who enter the information and should not be relied on solely.
>
> Alan W. Zajic

Every jurisdiction completes vendor and employee background checks, which vary widely in scope, detail and time devoted to each person or entity. The process is typically highly regulated and there are also many different laws that must be complied with on a national, state and specific regulatory jurisdiction. As a result, there is no one single process that is followed consistently throughout the gaming industry. The concept is to ensure that every person who works at or does business with the facility is not a known criminal and does not have any other undesirable trait or history of negative or undesirable behaviors. Regardless of the process, it is important for any investigator assigned to this tedious task that there should be no shortcuts taken in the process.

There are many companies that provide very basic background services that include checking the sex offender registry, no-fly lists and other public and nonpublic databases for a reasonable fee per check. The investigator must always be aware that a database in a background check is only as good as the thousands of people who enter the information and should not be relied on solely. There are also statutory laws in some jurisdictions such as California where criminal history cannot be obtained after a certain number of years. Regardless, the local laws need to be consulted regarding background checks along with federal regulations.

Criminal background checks are difficult to get details of, especially if a file has been sealed or a felony was committed when a person was a minor. Traditionally the concept is to perform a due diligence check of the person or entity to determine if there is anything present that may create liability or if a person may have the propensity to harm persons or take from their employer.

Some environments have very comprehensive background checks completed and the sheer volume of people in current pending status creates a huge operational problem in that pressure builds to complete the check rapidly and either clear the person with a pass or fail them to allow the operational management to hire and submit the next applicant for background. Evolution will typically balance this dilemma and processes that are not critical are streamlined or additional investigation staff are hired to clear the backup and process checks.

The investigator must meticulously follow the guidelines provided by the regulators because a violation could result in a fine or suspension of a gaming license and could sometimes result in thousands of employees being out of work for some period of time. Although very mundane and not always exciting, the process of a background check must pass the legal test in covering the following areas: did the enterprise conduct a reasonable background check and if they had, would they have found evidence of a crime or event that would give them notice that the person either was dangerous or had a propensity to commit other crimes?

An example might be if a hotel houseman is hired to stock linen rooms during the evening shift when there is little or no direct supervision. That houseman also obtains a master key to hotel rooms and is charged with delivering housekeeping requests from guests, or an emergency room cleaning on occasion. This employee then decides to commit a sexual assault of a teenage girl in the hotel, who he stalked and watched for several days.

If the facility failed to complete a reasonable background check on the employee and the police investigation results in the discovery of the history of the employee doing the same at other hotels and even being arrested for the same, there now is a high risk of liability exposure. If there was media coverage of the prior arrests or convictions the plaintiff attorney will have a great opening statement at a civil trial when he makes a statement to the jury "They did not even do a Google check on this employee where there was obvious evidence of this employee committing sexual assaults against young girls prior to him being hired".

Documentation of the background check is also very important and will always become the subject of arguments between attorneys and a judge to allow or not allow that into evidence during a criminal or civil trial. Anytime a background check is completed there should be detailed notes of contacts, information obtained and copies of any database results. These notes could very well be the detail that proves either that the due diligence occurred or that it did not.

Compliance Investigations

Much of the work that is done by an investigator involves compliance in some manner. As stated in numerous portions of this book the major cause for most internal theft or incidents is the failure to comply with those self-imposed and regulatory standards well established in the structure of the facility. The reports and work in a compliance investigation are very straight forward and probably the easiest as a result.

In these types of investigations there is truly a black and white process that should be followed. Once it is determined that there appears to be some form of compliance violation, the investigator starts with the regulation in question and develops the investigation based on what is required to be complied with and then matches the documents and any associated video to determine if the subject employee violated the regulations.

Compliance investigations have continued to increase in all gaming environments and are predicted to continue those increases due to the U.S. Treasury Financial Crimes Enforcement Network (FINCEN) regulations and involvement in gaming operations. As a result, proof of compliance to critical financial controls including Title 31 will fall under the investigator's umbrella in conjunction with internal auditors. The accuracy and importance of compliance investigations, regardless of perceived importance, will become critical to sustained operational solvency and survival.

Compliance investigations are not exciting or interesting in nature and tend to receive little attention unless forced by management. They are also extremely unpopular to operational departments based on the fundamental purpose to find, rectify and cause employee discipline because of a failure to follow regulations designed to prevent internal theft.

Claims/Workman's Compensation

This is the most undesirable type of investigation most staff investigators will work. Most investigators complain of the mundane work and little rewards from working on these types of claims. Only the rare case where an employee is caught working a second job lifting heavy materials during an investigation fulfils most investigators' desires for catching the bad guy. That being said, it is the costliest type of investigation collectively involving casinos overall.

Between the costs of basic medical care, disability benefits, rehabilitation, retraining and extended impacts workers' compensation claims chew up profits faster than internal theft does. Accounting executives know this fact well and understand how investment into claims investigation and worker safety can impact the bottom line both immediately and long term.

Because of the nature of employee investigations and the fact that off-property work is typically involved, staff investigators should utilize licensed private investigators to perform the majority of claim work. Any property-related investigation will fall upon staff to determine the ability to refute a claim or prove that it is exaggerated by the employee. Certain states and jurisdictions require a specific time before and after an employee's shift to be covered by worker's compensation coverage and will need outside investigation also.

Some instances are merely looking for video coverage and a determination whether the incident was caught on a camera view. In serious incidents of injuries a review of the entire video retention period (usually seven days) may be required and that video should at least be collected as soon as possible to preserve it for future close review.

In some other instances a video review may prove that the accident did not occur altogether, was exaggerated by the employee, or was a result of horseplay or violation of established safety rules, which may very well impact claim payments and benefits depending on the circumstances. Surveillance personnel are not always aware of all of the factors and a comprehensive review of that video may require a trained investigator to do the review and document the findings.

In serious employee accidents, OSHA (Occupational Safety and Health Administration) will become involved and especially in the case of a workplace death there will more likely than not be an OSHA investigation and subsequent fines. These types of investigations require in-depth processes and working with the OSHA investigator to enable the internal investigator to communicate potential action against the employer to management as the federal investigators do their work. This allows for potential mitigation of any pending fines before the final reports are submitted.

These investigations are very time-consuming and labor intensive in most cases. If there is a suspicion that an employee has exaggerated or falsified a claim of injury the witnesses and fellow workers will need to be interviewed by an experienced investigator and not necessarily a department supervisor.

Key Takeaways

- Every jurisdiction completes vendor and employee background checks, which vary widely in scope, detail and time devoted to each person or entity. The process is typically highly regulated and there are also many different laws that must be complied with on a national, state and specific regulatory jurisdiction.
- Some environments have very comprehensive background checks completed and the sheer volume of people in current pending status creates a huge operational problem in that pressure builds to complete the check rapidly and either clear the person with a pass or fail them to allow the operational management to hire and submit the next applicant for background.
- Compliance investigations have continued to increase in all gaming environments and are predicted to continue those increases due to the U.S. Treasury Financial Crimes Enforcement Network (FINCEN) regulations and involvement in gaming operations.
- Between the costs of basic medical care, disability benefits, rehabilitation, retraining and extended impacts worker's compensation claims chew up

profits faster than internal theft does. Accounting executives know this fact well and understand how investment into claims investigation and worker safety can impact the bottom line both immediately and long term.

Best Practices

- The investigator must meticulously follow the guidelines provided by the regulators because a violation could result in a fine or suspension of a gaming license and could sometimes result in thousands of employees being out of work for some period of time.
- Documentation of the background check is also very important and will always become the subject of arguments between attorneys and a judge to allow or not allow that into evidence during a criminal or civil trial. Anytime a background check is completed there should be detailed notes of contacts, information obtained and copies of any database results. These notes could very well be the detail that proves either that the due diligence occurred or that it did not.

Chapter 16

Vehicle Accidents and Auto Theft

Parking areas are a fertile environment for larceny crimes.

Alan W. Zajic

Most vehicle-related accidents will be dealt with by first responders who can collect and document the fender benders and minor incidents. The investigator may become involved in more serious or high-value vehicle investigations. Just due to the mere fact that sometimes thousands of vehicles will move into, out of and within a property on a daily basis, the risk exposure for some form of accident is high. Depending on the parties operating the vehicles or the ownership of the vehicles, there may be incidents that will require more than the uniformed officer's initial report.

Understanding your local law will assist in understanding the risk exposure to vehicle accidents from an employee driving a patron's car to an on-duty employee colliding with another vehicle on site. Worker's compensation laws may apply to include a period of time before and after the employee's work shift and responsibility or statutory liability for vehicles damaged while in the care and custody of the property such as valet.

In valet instances where a casino offers parking services to patrons either free or for a fee, there is typically liability should something occur to that customer's car or truck. If a customer entrusts the casino with their vehicle, that vehicle is accepted and a claim ticket is given, there is an expectation that you will reasonably care for that vehicle.

Understanding that valet is a gratuity-driven enterprise, expensive vehicles will typically receive preferential treatment to include parking in a special place or in a prominent location to showcase them. Unfortunately, the security of the vehicles is not always effective. Valet attendants will want to utilize shortcuts and therefore will self-modify the controls or departmental rules and regulations for their own benefit and not always the company's.

The investigator will also get involved when that valet employee decides to take that Ferrari on a spin around the block for fun and runs into a light pole or rolls it on a curve. This will create a six-figure financial problem for the enterprise that must be thoroughly investigated. Liability may not be a factor depending on the local laws and the investigator must first determine what exposure the enterprise has. The incident will still need to be investigated thoroughly to determine what exactly occurred. The loss may be to a high-value customer or dignitary that may warrant an exception.

As previously stated in Chapter 13, the collection of architectural diagrams will be helpful in demonstrating the accident on a map of the parking lot, or a section involved, shrunk down to report page size. These diagrams are typically found in facilities and are used for permitting, occupancy load and parking management and will include light poles, walkways, parking spaces, intersections and drive lanes. These will be helpful when interviewing witnesses and identifying specific locations in parking areas. These should also be utilized when investigating serious criminal events such as robberies, assaults, rapes, homicides and any other crimes against persons where there is a risk exposure.

In serious incidents it may be valuable to video record the route and locations to demonstrate at a later time what the exterior conditions were. This may prove beneficial if there is a pothole that contributed to the accident or some other physical characteristic is present.

Key Takeaways

- Most vehicle-related accidents will be dealt with by first responders who can collect and document the fender benders and minor incidents. The investigator may become involved in more serious or high-value vehicle investigations.
- In valet instances where a casino offers parking services to patrons either free or for a fee, there is typically liability should something occur to that customer's car or truck.

Best Practices

- As previously stated, the collection of architectural diagrams will be helpful in demonstrating the accident on a map of the parking lot, or a section involved, shrunk down to report page size.
- In serious incidents it may be valuable to video record the route and locations to demonstrate at a later time what the exterior conditions were.

Chapter 17

Post-Investigation Best Practices

The last step in any investigation is to attempt to recover losses and prevent future ones.

Alan W. Zajic

In this chapter we discuss the best practices to use after the investigation is complete. These practices are used to wrap up the case in the best ways possible. The following key questions should be addressed: Will the loss that occurred be recuperated? Who needs to know about what happened? And maybe the most important point of all: How do we prevent such an incident from reoccurring?

Restitution

Restitution is a much-misunderstood function that has great redeeming value to the investigation process and a method to capture losses and generate a simple form of income. Many gaming operations do not take advantage of this process and should always be prepared to present a demand letter for restitution on all criminal cases being prosecuted. There are many judges who will grant restitution especially if the demand is clear, with proof, reasonable and presented to the court in a timely fashion. Restitution is much more than the actual provable amount or value of items taken. The following are some examples of restitution that can be demanded:

- Security personnel time. Take the average wage and add the payroll expenses and benefits and calculate the number of hours and minutes it took to investigate the incident.
- Surveillance personnel time. Again, take the average surveillance agent's wage and benefits and calculate the time it took for review, report writing and all work or expense related to the incident.
- Investigation time and expense. The time and expense of the investigator to include all the witness interviews, evidence collection, report writing

and management meetings as a result of the incident. Direct costs of office supplies, travel expense, etc.
- Actual payroll costs of all employee witnesses that had to be interviewed at regular or overtime costs as applicable. Include overtime costs to cover for employees directly as a result of the incident.
- The actual loss in dollars.
- The replacement costs of the item(s) if applicable.
- The cost of rental or temporary replacement of items if applicable.
- The loss of any revenue associated to the loss.

It is important that the restitution demand is reasonable, is accurate and reflects any and all costs associated to the perpetrator's behavior in the commission of the particular offense. The demand letter should be professional, include a respectful request of the court and identify the losses being requested.

In most circumstances, a judge will gladly add the restitution to his findings and judgement of conviction if it is presented professionally and with proof. It can at times be the deciding factor on whether a suspect will spend time in jail or pay back the damages they caused, which is preferable. The investigator should understand that as long as a conviction is recorded, it matters not how much time a person serves or how long they must be on probation. The court will then issue a check back to the casino when paid by the perpetrator, which is then entered into the restitution log and account located at the cashier's cage.

Your accounting department will assist in setting up a ledger account that is specifically for restitution and damage to property. This account is also used when a customer damages property, such as punching a belly glass on a slot machine, and agrees to pay for it. This account should be used for restitution for criminal charges as well and is a mechanism to receipt and track how much the process of restitution will generate overall to the enterprise. It will also serve as the starting point to reimburse the various department budgets for items damaged or lost.

There is a certain satisfaction in showing your boss a restitution check for a major crime that created much work and was collected as a result of good solid investigation and the foresight in seeking lawful restitution.

We recommend that with each and every criminal case a letter be sent to the prosecutor with the request or demand for restitution in the event that a binding legal deal is reached between legal parties that restitution is part of the judgement of conviction or a condition for the reduction of charges. It can even be used to require restitution on casino incidents where criminal disorderly conduct or trespass occurred; in this case restitution would charge an amount for the security personnel tied up in a detention and for report writing, along with any hard costs if the perpetrator caused damage.

Executive-Level Debriefing

The overall objective should be to mitigate the need for future investigations through educating executive-level decision makers of the breaches in policies and procedures and the impacts on the enterprise. If a routine part of any investigation is to debrief the stakeholders with the highest level of management included, the investigation will prove productive in that goal.

The debriefing should be brief, concise and impactful and should not drone on and on and become a dreaded exercise to the busy executives. A simple memo with important bullets and explanations is desirable to get the message across quickly and with the most impact. Included should be the following:

- Key players
- Security breaches
- Direct costs
- Indirect costs
- Prosecution results
- Restitution demand and satisfaction
- Remedial training of staff involved
- Follow-up disciplines and/or positive feedback to staff
- Policy and procedure violations and future recommendations

Regardless, there should be some form of communication in a manner that demonstrates concern and oversight by the executive level of the management staff. This will help move the departments to a more professional and secure operation.

Procedural Changes

Ironically there are usually policies, procedures, rules and regulations that are designed to protect the people and assets of an enterprise from most internal thefts or losses. A violation, breach or *workaround* of an established protocol has typically been mismanaged or ignored on the supervisory level of an organization. This failure by supervisory and mid-level managers creates the need for an investigator when those imposed standards are violated.

Post-investigation review should include a review of the specific protocols that were breached and any recommendation to ensure future compliance. Based on the complexity of most regulatory environments, changing MICS or other regulations is a slow and painfully arduous task that requires many people in the approval process.

If there is a documented pattern of abuses or noncompliance to those established protocols, it becomes easier to push through the needed changes for future compliance, and the need for investigation. Included in the executive-level post review should be a short comment on whether the incident being discussed and the causation for it has a history with either the affected department or particular employees. The investigator should become a stakeholder in the development and changes to any regulation, rule or procedure that involves anything of monetary value in order to reduce losses overall.

Future Audits for Compliance

Internal audit compliance and surveillance should also schedule post-event audits at least every quarter for the first year and annually thereafter. These audits are merely a simple check to ensure that the original procedural cause for the loss is not being slowly eroded again due to the environment or changes in personnel. It does not need to be complex or involve massive amounts of time.

Simplistically, ten- to fifteen-minute surveillance audits of the employees on an infrequent basis will typically reveal whether the procedure is being followed and the risk of future violations has been reduced. It is important that the surveillance agent be familiar with the specifics of the past breaches in order to look for indicators that it is resurfacing.

Key Takeaways

- Conduct a post investigation review to summarize findings to include operational failures, identifying policy and procedure loopholes or work-arounds and any lack of management oversights.
- Quantify the monetary loss to the company in realistic amounts to include estimated overall losses.
- Determine if any losses can be recovered through restitution demands during criminal proceedings.
- Establish employee audits to help prevent future similar internal theft.

Best Practices

- Develop a process to recover costs for conducting an investigation and demand restitution for any associated expenses to the prosecutor to include staff time involved and direct losses. Include attempts and succesful restitution collection in the executive final report and briefing.
- Develop a tracking system for criminal hearings involved in the investigation and participate in them as allowed to recover costs.
- Develop and recommend strategies to prevent or minimize future similar events or losses to include reinforcement of existing policies and procedures and development of new ones.

- Make general recommendations to operational management regarding staff oversight and supervision improvements related to the loss and recommend future audits of affected areas.
- Prepare and conduct a final briefing to the highest executive-level stakeholders to include video segments, duration of negative or criminal activity and final conviction/restitution results.

Part 3

Gaming Investigations

Chapter 18

Investigative Concepts

The bad guys train every day to beat you; you then must do the same to beat them.

Derk J. Boss

This chapter discusses important investigative concepts, beginning with the need for proper training, use of proper investigative tools and fundamental techniques when investigating. Casino security and surveillance personnel don't normally receive investigative training. Some personnel may have had such training or experience from prior careers in law enforcement or the military but most of our protective personnel do not. Investigative best practices can assist the new investigator with investigating appropriately and effectively. Tools such as video investigation and surveillance tradecraft are used heavily in the casino hotel environment and can provide a wealth of information and leads and can be the investigator's best friend.

One thing I noticed right away when I started in surveillance was the lack of training, especially in the field of investigation. For a position that is supposed to catch sophisticated bad guys, advantage players and inside jobs (not to mention the stupid criminals), that didn't seem very smart. But it was the reality.

I began my surveillance career in a two-man room (two men total, not two per shift) in Laughlin, NV. I had received a one-week training course at the Mint in downtown, Las Vegas. The agents were all very nice and seemed very knowledgeable to me. They taught me about card counting, and that was about it. In those days (1987) counters were believed to be the biggest threat out there. I was taught that it was us against them and to find them at all costs!

We didn't spend much time on anything else. We looked at slots minimally and not at all at the bars, keno, poker or the employee areas.

At that time in the gaming world nothing else besides the pit was important. Consequently, we focused our time and energy in those areas and really left everything else alone.

The problem with that was crime kept popping up in these other areas. I would be protecting the pit and we'd get slugged in slots. I would be involved in evaluating a twenty-one player and I would get a phone call reporting a potential internal theft problem in keno. As this continued it became obvious to me that I had to come up with a better method to protect the property and hopefully a method that would help me identify potential problems or at least small problems before they became large problems.

One thing I was beginning to realize was that waiting for something to happen was getting me there too late (I wouldn't have the answer to this until I was taught the IOU patrol). As everyone I knew in surveillance operated much the same, I was pretty much stuck on what to do at the time.

When I moved over to the Ramada Express and was made the surveillance manager my need for a proactive system became critical. Now I was responsible for a property and had to answer to a GM as well as corporate. I sure didn't want to get beat by cheaters or card counters and have to explain to my bosses that I didn't have a clue as to what happened!

Luckily, when we first opened our GM brought in a surveillance consultant who taught me the IOU patrol. IOU is an acronym for a systematic method of camera patrol that has three components: Identification of subject, Observation of subject, and Understanding of activity. That changed everything for me and my staff. We went from being notified of a problem or loss to, in most cases, detecting the issue on our own. This was a major sea change for us. The IOU patrol made us proactive.

We will discuss the IOU patrol later on but the reason I mention it is that it is part of the surveillance training process. It is a fundamental technique that, in one form or another, should be included in a surveillance program.

The IOU patrol started it all for me. Within weeks my team was beginning to detect crime and advantage players on a more consistent basis. The patrol put us on the map! People sat up and took notice that something good was happening at the Ramada (not the bad guys, of course). The IOU became the stepping stone I used to train and develop my personnel from then on.

Over the course of a number of years (the process continues to this day) I developed, along with members of my various staff members from my surveillance teams, a training program that provides the fundamental concepts of surveillance operation and investigations.

I also recognized the value of a well-conducted investigation. During my career I was involved in hundreds of investigations, from petty theft to executive fraud. Most of the cases were successful: meaning that we identi-fied the suspect and stopped the crime. However, we often didn't finish the investigation completely. Frequently we were unable to have the suspect arrested or obtain restitution, or put someone out of the business that deserved to be kicked out. This was due mainly to my inexperience in how to investi-gate and put together a case. We hope, through this book, to provide you the information you need to perform a thorough and legal investigation, avoid the common pitfalls involved with investigations, and to assist you with case preparation so your bad guys don't get away. When you can do all that you've performed a successful investigation.

In this chapter we will discuss security and surveillance concepts and operations especially as they apply to conducting investigations.

Fundamental Investigative Concepts

In my mind, the following concepts, as they pertain to investigations, should be a part of every surveillance training program and operations, including security surveillance. These are the building blocks that a training program should be built around to address investigations. Utilizing these concepts allows a surveillance operation to work proactively, and will generate consistent detections and leads to follow up for investigation.

These concepts are as follows:

- IOU patrol
- Tri-shot coverage
- Audits and close watches
- Risk analysis/threat assessment
- Appropriate gaming statutes and regulations
- Appropriate criminal laws and statutes
- Property and departmental controls, policies and procedures
- Tells of cheating, advantage play, theft and fraud
- Loss prevention theory and techniques
- Case management
- Evidence handling

As we continue through the chapters I hope to show you how to use these fundamental techniques to detect and investigate criminal activity.

IOU Patrol

As discussed in our previous book (*Casino Security and Gaming Surveillance*, D.J. Boss and A.W Zajic, Auberbach, 2010) an IOU patrol or other systematic method of patrol observation (I've heard it also called Recognize, Respond, Resolve) should be used to generate and develop leads. Patrolling and operating randomly is not an option. This is true in any environment. The crime is out there, and it will be hidden from you, so you must search for it in a manner that will provide you consistent results. Further, you must be proactive in order to have consistent success in the detection of criminal activity in the workplace. Using a proven patrol system is one of the basic building blocks used to obtain consistent and continuing success. See Appendix 1 for a more thorough discussion on the IOU patrol.

Tri-Shot Coverage

Another fundamental building block to effective surveillance operation is tri-shot coverage. This is a term that just means getting enough cameras on the scene to see what is going on, who is doing it and who else may be involved. In other words, gathering evidence. It is a required minimal camera setup consisting of three cameras: one placed to cover the table or area, another placed to provide an overview of those on the game and in the immediate area, and the third placed to observe the specific suspicion, concern or activity. You may add more cameras that provide additional angles, if necessary, but you should always place at least three.

Establishing proper and complete coverage is essential to the detection and investigation of crime. Most people think that internal theft and fraud is detected by luck or being in the right place at the right time. I believe that you create your own luck and you place yourself in the right place at the right time by using the right system.

The system begins with the IOU patrol. The next step is placing proper camera coverage immediately the moment you suspect anything whatsoever. The reason for this is twofold: 1) bad guys usually try to hide their crime from you; you will probably notice something else first that just doesn't look right or is outside procedure. That should be your trigger to be suspicious, and 2) if you wait to set up your coverage you may miss valuable elements of the incident you will need later such as suspect identification and/or activities, witnesses, others involved, etc.

A lot of surveillance people wait too long to place proper coverage of a developing issue or crime and miss critical elements that will be needed later. See Appendix 1 for further information.

Audits and Close Watches

Audits

Since crime happens in every area/department in a business, especially in a casino resort, we must look at that area or department in depth and on a regular basis in order to detect developing or existing crime. We use the audit to do that.

Audits are, in my mind, the single most powerful weapon in the surveillance arsenal. I define it as: "An assigned observation of employees working in key areas or performing critical transactions, for a specified period of time, for the purpose of detecting illicit activity or inefficiency of operation."

Typical audits conducted in key areas are: player ratings, player's club, bars, gift shops, receiving and kitchen areas, etc. Examples of critical transactions that should be audited are: slot jackpots, marker and buy-back transactions, issue and redemption of free play, and issue and redemption of comps, to name just a few.

Audits, invariably, detect activity that occurs under the radar. They can and should be triggered by an IOU patrol or due to information received or developed. An audit then turns into an investigation of the activity that was observed.

Close Watches

Close watches vary from audits in two ways: 1) they are implemented because of information received or developed (an audit can trigger a close watch), and 2) close watches are performed on an individual or group of individuals and/or an area for specific reasons.

Close watches are normally used when you are pretty sure of your information and want to get the crime on video for prosecution, and/or are trying to verify information or an investigative theory. Close watches require a significant use of your resources (staff and time, as well as cameras being locked down) so you should be pretty comfortable with your information or theory before assigning.

A word of advice: assign your best people to audits and close watches. A lot of surveillance personnel are unable to audit or investigate properly and will just use the time to stare at the screen. The investigator must have the ability to identify or deduce critical information or activities that indicate what is pertinent to the case. If you don't have anyone capable of proper investigation, ensure you monitor the progress of the audit or close watch daily in order to keep it focused and to obtain what you're looking for.

See Appendix 1 for further information on audits and close watches.

Risk Analysis

In order to operate proactively you must identify where and what your risks and threats are. It is better to prepare for incidents to happen than to wait for them to occur. Ideally, we'd like to prevent incidents from occurring at all or to detect such incidents in their earliest stages.

To do so requires that we identify what the risks are, where and when they may occur, how often, their cost and impact should they occur, and how we will mitigate the cost/impact of the incident if it does occur.

Proactive operation and audits evolve out of identifying the risks and threats that occur on your property. When you complete identifying those risks and threat (start with most costly, impactful, and likely to occur), then begin your audits of those areas to locate indicators that they may be occurring.

Risk and threat analysis should be conducted at least once a year and anytime a significant change is made to company operations. See ASIS International's

General Risk Assessment at: www.asisonline.org/Standards-Guidelines/Pages/default.aspx

Law, Statutes, and Regulations

Knowing the law, statutes and gaming regulations is paramount to every surveillance agent, manager and director. You must know the law to recognize when someone is violating it and/or when someone is not. It is not enough to know how the law, statute or regulation reads; you must understand how each of its elements may apply to your case in order to ensure you have a solid case.

As an investigator, you must prepare your case with the specific law you believe has been violated and ensure that you've proven the necessary elements of the law to prevail. When you prepare your case in such a manner you will find that law enforcement and prosecutors will accept your case much more readily because they have what they need to take it to the next level.

Additionally, nowadays security and surveillance personnel must be able to "control" responses made by executives and department managers. In today's litigious society we can't just have someone arrested on flimsy evidence, parade them through the casino in handcuffs, and just hope the charges will stick! We will be on the local news and not in a good way! We must control the response: if we don't have the evidence necessary to satisfy the elements of the law in a particular incident, we should not have someone arrested. We must live to fight another day. Don't let anyone talk you into doing something you are not prepared to do. Trust me, when things go bad you will be standing alone and the others who were involved won't help you. In fact, they will watch as you're thrown to the dogs! It is your duty and responsibility to control the response. No one on the property will know as much about the law as you.

If you are forced to do something you know may cause the property harm down the road, document everything you can and keep it for a rainy day. Enough said!

The good news is that in those situations when you feel it prudent to allow someone you feel committed criminal activity to leave your property remember that, more than likely, they will be back. Criminals return to where they had success. You will see them again and get another shot at them, and this time you will be ready!

Also consider that while you may not be able to have someone arrested in a particular case at a point in time, remember that you may be able to respond at a lower level such as eighty-sixing the person or stopping/limiting their play, or in the case of an employee, perhaps termination is the answer.

Remember: control the response to protect yourself, your department and the property.

Property and Departmental Controls, Policies and Procedures

For your protection program, your property and departmental controls, policies and procedures are just as important as laws and regulations. Most of your investigations will be triggered by an observation of a violation of a control, policy or procedure. Most of your internal investigations will use these types of violations as evidence to support discipline issued by a department or human resources. And as mentioned previously, observed violations are used in operations to assign audits and/or close watches.

Surveillance personnel must have a strong working knowledge of the controls, policies and procedures for every department on the property. This means that each agent should read and understand each department manual and be able to locate any information needed.

Tells of Cheating, Advantage Play, Theft and Fraud

In almost all cases of cheating, advantage play, theft and fraud the perpetrator(s) goes to great lengths to hide what he or she is doing from employees in the area, security personnel and of course us in surveillance. In fact, if those responsible for the game or area don't know what they're looking for, the bad guys may continue their scam for a long time.

The point is that we will never know all the cheating moves or scams that are out there but you can detect them through tells or behaviors that are normally present in even the most sophisticated scams or moves.

Recognizing the tell or behavior leads to what the scam is and allows you to respond accordingly, properly and effectively to the incident.

Again, when we operate proactively our investigations will move closer to the actual incident as opposed to days later, and of course this is where we need to be in order to stop the crime and recover our losses.

We must know the tells for as many known scams, fraudulent activities, cheating and advantage plays as we can. Knowing the tells allows us to protect the gaming areas and the retail areas, as well as the back of the house, under our guardianship. See Appendix 3 for a list of common tells.

In the next chapters we will discuss applying these practices to the investigation of gaming crimes.

Key Takeaways

- Consistent training must be provided to investigative personnel (this is especially true for surveillance personnel).
- Use a patrol system such as the IOU that looks at each area regularly and thoroughly.
- Immediately establish a tri-shot (at a minimum) upon detecting suspicious activity.

- Utilize audits and close watches to develop or verify information.
- Take the time to know what and where your threats and risks are using risk analysis.
- Ensure your staff and yourself are thoroughly familiar with the statutes, regulations and laws of the jurisdiction you're in.
- Know your property's controls, policies and procedures as well.
- Bad guys have tells and behaviors that will allow you to detect them; know them!

Best Practices

- Develop, implement, and maintain an ongoing surveillance training program.
- Require surveillance agents to patrol systematically (use a patrol technique such as the IOU).
- Place camera coverage effectively to gather evidence properly (such as tri-shot coverage).
- Conduct audits of critical areas and key transactions on a regular basis.
- Perform a risk assessment survey annually.
- Know your tells!

Please note that we've included in the Appendices several investigative tools and tells for your use.

Chapter 19

Covert Surveillance Investigations

> In the casino, people get used to working under the eye of a camera; they are completely unprepared for a hidden camera.
>
> Derk J. Boss

There are occasions and situations when covert surveillance investigations are necessary. Such investigations are almost exclusively handled by the surveillance department. This is due to obvious reasons: surveillance has the personnel and equipment to dedicate to and conduct covert investigations; in fact, it is part of their job description.

What are covert investigations and how do they differ from what surveillance normally does? How are they used? We will answer these questions and others in this chapter.

Covert Investigations

Covert investigations are those that are performed secretly, hidden or under-cover. Surveillance usually operates with cameras behind smoked domes so that no one really knows what they're looking at; how is a covert investigation different?

Covert investigations usually are based on information such as that received from a close watch and/or information received from an informant. Covert investigations may also be based on routine audits or a routine practice such as an integrity check used to see if housekeepers are stealing lost and found items.

Covert investigations are usually performed with hidden cameras or by individuals such as employees working undercover or outside shoppers.

Hidden cameras placed in store rooms, hotel rooms and other areas where an individual does not have a reasonable expectation of privacy can be very effective when battling internal theft. Such cameras are placed, for example, when we are battling the theft of lost and found items, and we believe the housekeepers may be responsible (or at least some of the housekeepers).

Most surveillance departments have cameras in hotel hallways but, of course, don't have anything in the hotel rooms. Housekeepers know this and can take advantage of it.

An effective method to combat such theft is for the investigator to place items into the room to see if the housekeeper will take them. These items such as jewelry, electronics, cash or any other item that can be taken and hidden easily should be marked and/or photographed (with identifiers in the shot), and left in the room to see what the housekeeper will do. A covert camera isn't necessary but it is a best practice. As a covert camera nowadays is a self-contained unit that can be placed into almost any item such as a radio, clock, briefcase, or even a hat or doll, it can be easily deployed. Modern technology allows video to be recorded for extended periods using batteries, wireless or hard wire.

Covert investigations differ from normal surveillance investigation in their focus and/or in the cameras or personnel used. For example, surveillance when performing an audit normally uses cameras already in place to observe and follow an employee such as a bartender as he/she performs their duties.

A covert investigation is almost always a close watch with a specific objective or person in mind. Existing cameras and/or newly placed or positioned cameras or any combination of any of the three may be used.

Usually a covert setup is used because there is no other way to perform the investigation. The housekeeper issue described earlier can only be investigated covertly: we have to be able to get into the room and/or place marked items within the room to catch the thief.

Use of Undercover Personnel/Shoppers

At times using cameras only will not provide the information required and undercover personnel must be used. An example is an investigation that must be performed within a restaurant. Let's say we received information that one or more of the wait staff is comping off cash paying customers. In such a case we may have to use surveillance personnel or shoppers to enter the restaurant and order a meal. In this fashion we can pose as customers and cause a ticket to be generated for the type of payment we made.

As most surveillance operations do not have many, if any, cameras in restaurants one of the few ways to address issues in the restaurant is to use undercover personnel. You can also cover your operatives with whatever existing camera coverage you do have.

In such cases there are additional issues and concerns we must consider.

First, is the issue at hand important or significant enough that undercover personnel are necessary? The use of undercover personnel can be costly and requires a lot of resources. You will usually require at least one operative and possibly a team of operatives depending on the type of investigation and its scope. Ideally, when your undercover operatives are working you are monitoring their activities with surveillance cameras. This ties up at least one surveillance agent whenever the operation is in progress.

Please note that it is a best practice to provide camera coverage of undercover operators and shoppers as they operate as much and whenever possible for verification of their reports and activities, and for evidentiary purposes.

Second, it is imperative that a method of communication between the operative and the surveillance team is in place. The operative should be able to signal to the camera that something has occurred or is about to occur that surveillance must take note of. The signal can be simple: removal of the operative's hat, running a hand through the hair or pulling on one's mustache. Whatever is used it should appear to be innocent and not capture the attention of those around them. When receiving such a signal surveillance should log the time and details of what they observe for later review.

Additionally, the ability to directly communicate with the operative is critical. Invariably the mission will change, or due to information developed the operative must be moved to observe another person or area, or possibly the investigation has been compromised and we need to remove the operative from the scene. Set up a way to communicate with the operative prior to initiating the investigation. Today, because cell phones and texting are everywhere, the use of either doesn't alarm anyone and can usually be used without raising anyone's suspicions.

Finally, you must have a case handler or manager to manage the undercover operation. This often is where we go wrong. Just because surveillance has an undercover operation going on doesn't mean the casino stops. Surveillance agents are still handling their normal business and may not pay strict attention to what the operatives are doing on the floor, and may miss entirely a critical moment or fail to move a camera when the operative moves, losing necessary coverage. A case manager should be in place to make sure this doesn't happen.

The case manager is also responsible for ensuring the operation is progressing and attaining its objectives and/or changing the objectives as information is developed. Such operations have a natural tendency to move in different directions; there are so many moving pieces that come to light that may require attention, that a constant hands-on approach is needed. The manager must make decisions as to the direction of the operation, and ensure agents are assigned and on task, video and other evidence is obtained and stored, and the undercover operatives submit their observation notes and final reports.

Please note that sometimes an undercover operation must be terminated due to it being exposed, management instruction, or the likelihood of physical harm to those involved, or just because the operation is deemed ineffective. In any case, when the decision is made to pull the plug, a case manager will be necessary to make it happen.

It will be helpful at this point to discuss an actual case.

Case History

Surveillance was performing an audit of the coffee shop on the property. The coffee shop was a branded operation that was leased, but managed by the property. The operation had been on the property for a number of years and was considered successful.

The audit focused on food and liquor sales and consisted of observing what was sold and comparing what was entered into the register. The liquor sales were easy and appeared to be handled properly. However, surveillance couldn't always see what food was ordered and served so could not verify what was being entered into the register.

One thing was noted: a number of waiters and waitresses were using a certain key called the service recovery key on the register to comp off the meal. This key was supposed to be used to resolve customer service issues and complaints. As the key seemed to be used frequently it appeared that the restaurant had problems with customer service.

As the investigators continued to review the receipts it soon became apparent that the key was used almost exclusively for cash customers.

Investigators determined that there weren't enough cameras in the area to provide the information needed. They needed to determine that the meals comped off due to service issues were for legitimate reasons.

Undercover surveillance personnel and shoppers were sent in to pose as customers and order a meal in the restaurant. They were told to pay in cash and keep their receipt to allow their payment to be tracked through the system. They made no complaint about the food or service.

Investigators watched as the waiters entered the transactions for the undercover agents. Each time the meal was comped off for "customer service issues". The cash paid for the meal disappeared (it was later found that it became part of the waiting staff's tips).

Now the investigators knew it was internal theft, and not a customer service issue. They also knew how the theft was being perpetrated. It was time to identify all employees involved and determine how much money had been stolen.

More shoppers were sent in and soon ten suspects were identified. Their transactions were traced through the system and the investigators were actually able to pinpoint when each suspect began stealing: it was when their cash sales dropped dramatically and their tips increased. This was a trend noted with each of the suspected waiters.

Because of the downswing noted in cash sales and the ability to calculate sales comped off by the service recovery key they were able determine that the fraud began about four years prior and that one individual, an assistant manager, had performed the majority of the thefts over those years.

The investigators also estimated that over $100,000 was probably stolen by the assistant manager and the other suspects. During the investigation it was found that to use the service recovery key a manager's card or the number on that card had to be input into the register. All of the suspects, of course, had the number (in fact, most of the restaurant staff had the number to use for "efficiency"). It was believed by the investigators that the prime suspect had taught others how to do it.

I think it is important to note the assistant manager was a woman in her mid-fifties, lived with her mother, had worked at the property since day one, and was loved by everyone. She had even been an employee of the month and was widely considered to be one of the best managers on the property.

I note this because we run across this a lot: one of our best employees is so trusted that he/she can commit fraud for years and no one ever suspects a thing. Also, a lot of security personnel think that it is the younger generation that is the face of fraud. Not so: remember what we learned in the ACFE Report to the Nation (see www.acfe.com); the perpetrators we should worry about are those who are in trusted positions. These are usually individuals who have worked at a business for a number of years and have attained a level of access and authority allowing then to commit the fraud. Trust no one.

Also of interest in the case history: again we see the importance of reviewing transactional and other departmental reports. Investigators used receipts, register transaction reports and register check out reports to detect, investigate and prosecute the crime.

Two huge tells that were missed by the department manager and auditing were: 1) cash sales turned in by the involved suspects were ridiculously low as compared to the rest of the staff; and 2) the overall service recovery expense was incredibly high. At the very least someone should have noted that the restaurant had very poor service!

Everyone was interviewed and later terminated. The assistant manager readily admitted that she'd been stealing. She had a lot of bills due to taking care of her mom and she needed the money.

The manager was terminated also. Although she wasn't involved in the theft she failed to prevent it or detect it, or even what I call "mind the store": she failed to review her daily paperwork. Had she done so she could have stopped the theft the first day or at least in the first week.

The theft wasn't reported to the police due for reputational considerations. The property was located in a small town and would have reflected badly on the casino.

This case could not have been investigated or even detected without the use of a surveillance audit (covert by its very nature) and the use of covert shoppers.

Covert investigations are an additional tool that can be used by a loss prevention team to either further an investigation or to initiate an investigation in areas not traditionally covered by surveillance cameras.

Covert Investigations Concerns

There are a number of concerns that should be addressed prior to initiating a covert investigation. Without careful forethought you may unintentionally invade someone's privacy. Everyone has reasonable expectation of privacy, even in the workplace, that we must take into consideration when planning our investigation.

There are areas in which we know we must not install a covert camera. Bathrooms, locker rooms, occupied hotel rooms, private offices and any room where employees change clothes (even in unauthorized locations) are such areas.

In general, it is okay to install a covert camera in the workplace in any area where an individual has no expectation of privacy. This includes areas such as an unoccupied hotel room, an office that is used by several individuals such as an open office with individual cubicles, a store room, etc. I usually go by if the door can be opened at any time by another person then an individual does not have a reasonable expectation of privacy.

I also will shut down an investigation if it becomes a situation where the individual obviously expects privacy and is not involved in a crime. An example would be two individuals having sex in a store room. This is something you should put a stop to through other means but is not necessary to continue to observe and gather evidence on. Continued observation will be hard to explain.

Another potential concern when you're planning to use a covert camera to observe a specific individual is that you should have a good reason for doing so. We don't want to install a covert camera to determine whether someone is at their desk or not. There should be a substantial reason such as theft or other illegal activities to justify a hidden camera, and there should be no other means to investigate the case.

You should also consider the cost of using a covert camera. Not only is there a cost for the equipment and its installation, you will also have the cost of assigning one or more investigators to monitor the camera and pursue the investigation.

A word of caution and advice: you should always obtain legal counsel prior to initiating a covert investigation program or investigation. Laws pertaining to the use of covert cameras vary from state to state. Additionally, you may be required to adhere to laws or regulations within the workplace such as union requirements or other contracts. Always check before initiating a covert investigation.

Key Takeaways

- Covert investigations can be an effective tool to investigate those areas or activities not covered by surveillance cameras or those requiring undercover operatives.

- Covert investigations are usually initiated due to information received from an informant or developed through criminal activity, exception reports or statistical information.
- Always obtain legal advice before initiating a covert investigation.

Best Practices

- Monitor the activity and operations of undercover personnel and shoppers with camera coverage whenever possible to provide verification of reports and incidents, and for evidentiary purposes.
- Use covert cameras for significant issues only and when there is no other method to investigate the issue.
- Respect privacy. Ensure you are following the law. Do not install a hidden camera in an area where privacy can be expected. The cost to defend your company against a violation of privacy will far outweigh any information gained.
- Assign a case manager to manage any undercover operation.
- Seek legal counsel for advice prior to installing a covert camera or operating a covert operation.

Chapter 20

Employee Theft Investigations

Cheats and advantage players attack you a few times a year; corrupt employees attack you every day.

Derk J. Boss

This critically important section discusses employee theft. The casino hotel investigator will spend, by far, more time investigating employee theft and fraud and discipline issues than in other areas of crime. Businesses suffer their largest theft and fraud losses to the employee. As such, the investigator must understand why employees steal from their employer, what is vulnerable to theft and the common methods used to commit the theft or fraud. Understanding basic concepts about employee theft will allow the investigator to successfully investigate an employee and even, in some cases, predict where theft may occur. Performing at this level allows the investigator to protect their property proactively!

It is a predominate theme that resonates throughout our industry: the biggest and costliest threat to the casino is the cheat. I disagree totally. It's been my experience that it is the dishonest employee who is the threat that will cost us the most money, as well as the most time and resources. While you may see a cheat a few times a year, your employee is there every day, and already knows how to beat you with the tools we provide.

The cost of occupational fraud to businesses nationwide as reported in the 2018 Report to the Nations compiled by the Association of Certified Fraud Examiners (ACFE) is about five percent of a company's gross revenue (www .acfe.com/report-to-the-nations/2018/). Another way I like to put it is that it costs $9 per day per employee. This is one of the first methods to estimate fraud used by the ACFE and I still use it because it really brings the cost home for us in the gaming industry. That means that a gaming property with 1,000 employees can expect to lose over $3 million annually to occupational theft. That is a tremendous amount of money!

When I first calculated that number I didn't believe it. But after years of investigating internal theft cases there is no doubt in mind that it's true.

Keep in mind that occupational fraud also includes time fraud such as fraudulent overtime, petty theft such as office supplies, comp, expense fraud and many other types of theft and you begin to understand why employee theft is such a big problem.

I can also tell you that most executives and maybe you yourself won't believe those numbers. So let's say that it's only half of that, $1.5 million. Still a large amount. Or let's say it is twenty-five percent: that's an amount of $750,000. Still don't believe it? How about ten percent of that initial $3 million? That would be $300,000 annually! Any amount you want to consider is a larger number that most companies don't want to lose from their bottom line.

By the way, I really do believe it's closer to the $3 million more or less depending on how many employees you have.

Employees steal from their employer because they can commit the crime and hide it more easily than if they tried it outside the workplace. Why would an employee rob a bank when they don't know anything about robbing a bank and they are more than likely to get caught? An employee will stick to what they know.

For example, think of an employee at any POS. That employee works with that register, hour after hour, day after day. After all that time the employee knows that register inside and out and can make it dance and sing, if he or she desires. That employee also knows what their supervisor checks and looks for as far as controls, policies and procedures are concerned, if at all. Keep in mind that the POS, the cash register, is really just a computer, meaning that it can be manipulated if you have the right access levels.

Let's see what we have now: an employee who knows their register better than anyone, a supervisor who doesn't check exception or register reports (highly likely), and a computer that if accessed by a person with the right access (again, highly likely, a lot of supervisors leave their card, codes or logins at the register) leaves the company open and vulnerable to theft and fraud.

That employee can now (using the manager's access or, in some cases, their own) sell an item, void the transaction and pocket the cash. The supervisor won't catch it because they don't check voids. The item sold won't be missed because the inventory is rarely balanced.

The crime is done and probably won't be caught for a long time, maybe not at all. It can, and usually does, go on and on. You say that you can't take much from a gift shop, nightclub, theater, or pool admittance. I say I've seen such cases in the tens of thousands of dollars. Keep in mind that we're just talking about one POS here. How many POS systems and computers do you have on your property?

There are many opportunities for a dishonest employee to commit theft. In fact, it would be wise for those responsible for preventing theft to keep in mind that employee theft can and probably does exist in every department of the casino hotel resort.

Employee theft will happen on your watch. It is important that you understand four key concepts that will aid in your investigation (and detection) of employee crime:

1. In almost all cases employees must commit their crime clandestinely.
2. In almost all cases employees must violate or bypass a control, policy or procedure.
3. In almost all cases there is a paper (or electronic) trail.
4. Employee theft occurs every day, on every shift, in almost every department.

The first concept we should understand is that the employee commits their crime clandestinely meaning that the employee makes every attempt to hide and cover up their crime. That's an obvious statement but one that few really understand. It means that not only do we have to break through the camouflage to detect the crime in the first place, we also have to decipher and unravel the false information (usually the paper trail) the employee used to cover their crime.

This is very important for the investigator to remember. At first glance the crime may remain unseen, unprovable or even minimal. It is only through effective investigation that the true nature and depth of the crime will be exposed. Employee theft is like an iceberg; most of it is hidden below the surface and must be brought to light.

The second concept to remember is that in almost all cases the employee must violate or bypass a control, policy or procedure that exposes him to detection. Usually the cases where he does not violate or bypass a control are because he is working in collusion with another.

This is usually where an employee can be detected by their supervisor or surveillance. Most controls are designed to protect the company from theft. We all forget this over time and think that a control that is violated is a training issue or indicates the employee is lazy. That may well be but our first concern should be that the employee may be stealing.

For example, a bartender who fails to issue a receipt to a customer has broken a procedure. While this may be because the bartender was never trained properly or that he is an employee who doesn't follow the rules, it is also indicative of a number of methods used to commit internal theft.

The observant supervisor or surveillance personnel should determine what type of issue it is and take appropriate action. The investigator should use this as a starting point in the investigation.

The third concept is that there is almost always a paper trail, especially nowadays and certainly in the casino hotel. We forget this, I believe, because when we say paper trail we really mean an electronic trail. Most everything we do at POS systems, player ratings and player's clubs, and in table games and slots, is tracked and/or maintained by a computer. In fact, POS systems are computers!

To the investigator this means that a lot of the evidence will be found on the computer.

Our final concept is that employee theft occurs every day, on every shift, in almost every department. This is a premise that the investigator must believe. If you believe you'll find it out there, you will. If you don't believe there is any crime out there in the casino (and a lot of properties feel this way) you won't bother to look for it.

Let's use a case history to illustrate what we've learned and put it into action.

Case History

The surveillance department reports observing a clerk at one of the property attractions (roller coaster and other thrill rides) selling tickets and placing some of the cash received under his cash drawer. The transaction was entered into the register and a receipt usually issued to the purchaser. The clerk did not have anything other than small variances when checking out. He did, however, remove the cash from under the drawer and placed it into his pocket.

The individual assigned to investigate decided that he must determine first why the clerk hid the money under the drawer (our first concept of hiding their activity) and if the cash placed under the drawer (second concept: policy violation, no funds should be removed and separated from the company bank-roll) and later removed by the clerk were tips or company funds (tips should be clearly indicated as such and not commingled with what appears to be company funds).

As review and live observation of the clerk's activities does not show, in this case, a view of the register transaction, a review of the register transaction tape from that time period, compared to the video, should be performed (third concept).

Our investigator, John, starts his investigation there. Please note that the register tapes are now usually obtained electronically. However you may find the old-fashioned hard copy. If the surveillance system is up to date you may have the transaction information overlaid on your video. It will be available in one form or another and can usually be located through the accounting department or the controller.

Once John begins comparing the transaction tape to the video, he quickly finds unusual activity. Most of the transactions he observes are normal and no suspicious activity is noted. As he digs deeper he first observes a - five percent locals discount to two people. He notes that no identification was asked for or presented. Cash is received for payment and placed into the register, and a receipt is generated. However, after the customers leave, the clerk removes cash from the drawer and sets it underneath.

He next observes that an all-day ride ticket (signified by a wristband worn by the customer) is given to a customer but is entered as a regular ticket.

The correct amount is collected from the customer and proper change given. Again after the customer leaves, the clerk removes cash and hides it under the register. In this instance, the investigator knew the clerk took ten dollars because that is the difference between a regular ticket entered and the all-day ticket sold.

Continued review of the transaction report with the video indicated that every time the clerk gave a discount (local, senior and employee) it was incorrectly applied and that nearly every time he sold an all-day wristband he entered the sale as a regular one-time ride ticket.

John estimated that just during the eight hour period he reviewed the clerk stole over $175 of company funds!

John decided that he should determine if at all possible how much the clerk had taken and check to see if there were other employees involved. To do this he would have to check with surveillance how far back video was available and if there was video of other ticket stations.

Upon checking, surveillance reported that they had about ten days of video and that they would review the activity of the other clerks for the same type of activity.

John reviewed the video available and determined that the clerk used the same techniques to steal approximately the same amount each day over that time period. John calculated the clerk stole over $1,600! The investigator knew that the clerk, now identified as Kevin, had been hired three months prior and wondered when he began stealing from the company, and how he'd learned to do so.

Surveillance reported that they were unable to locate any other clerks that exhibited the same type of behavior.

John believed that he had evidence that Kevin had committed the crime of embezzlement over a period of eleven days resulting in the loss of over $1,600. He reviewed the Nevada Revised Statutes, which can be seen in the boxed text.

NRS 205.300 Definition; Punishment

1. Any bailee of any money, goods or property, who converts it to his or her own use, with the intent to steal it or to defraud the owner or owners thereof and any agent, manager or clerk of any person, corporation, association or partnership, or any person with whom any money, property or effects have been deposited or entrusted, who uses or appropriates the money, property or effects or any part thereof in any manner or for any other purpose than that for which they were deposited or entrusted, is guilty of embezzlement, and shall be punished in the manner prescribed by

law for the stealing or larceny of property of the kind and name of the money, goods, property or effects so taken, converted, stolen, used or appropriated.

2. The value of all the money, goods, property or effects misappropriated in separate acts of embezzlement must be combined for the purpose of imposing punishment for the offense charged if:

    (a) The separate acts were committed against the same person within 6 months before the offense;

    (b) None of the individual acts is punishable as a felony; and

    (c) The cumulative value of all the money, goods, property and effects misappropriated is sufficient to make the offense punishable as a felony.

3. Any use of the money, goods or property by any bailee thereof, other than that for which it was borrowed, hired, deposited, carried, received or collected, is prima facie evidence of conversion and of intent to steal the same and defraud the owner or owners thereof.

4. The term "bailee", as used in this section, means all persons with whom any money, goods or property has been deposited, all persons to whom any goods or property has been loaned or hired, all persons to whom any goods or property has been delivered, and all persons who are, either as agent, collector or servant, empowered, authorized or entrusted to carry, collect or receive any money, goods or property of another.

[1911 C&P § 388; RL § 6653; NCL § 10340] – (NRS A 1985, 978) (www.leg. state.nv.us/Statutes/63rd/Stats198504.html#Stats198504page978)

NRS 205.305 Prima Facie Evidence of Embezzlement

If any clerk, apprentice, servant, or any other person whatsoever, whether bound or hired, to whom any money or goods, or chattels, or other property, shall be entrusted, for any purpose whatsoever, by his or her master, employer, or any other person or persons, corporation or corporations, by whom he or she may be entrusted, shall withdraw himself or herself and shall go away with the money, goods, chattels or property, or any part thereof, with the intent to steal the same, and defraud the master, employer or any other person or persons, corporation or corporations, of the same, or being in the service of his or her master, or employer, corporation or corporations, or any other person or firm, shall embezzle the money, goods, chattels or property, or any part thereof, or shall otherwise convert the same to his or her own use, it shall be prima facie evidence of the intent to steal the same, and every such person or persons so offending shall be punished in the manner prescribed by law for feloniously stealing property of the value of the articles so taken, embezzled, stolen or converted.

[1911 C&P § 389; RL § 6654; NCL § 10341] *(www.leg.state.nv.us/Statutes/63rd/Stats198504.html#Stats198504page978)*

John believed that he had identified evidence demonstrating that Kevin had committed the crime of embezzlement and could prove that he had stolen over $1,600. He decided to contact both the Nevada Gaming Control Board (NGCB) and law enforcement to see if they would be interested in taking the case at this point.

When he contacted NGCB he was informed that as it wasn't a gaming crime and wasn't related to gaming he should contact Metro Police.

He spoke with the Financial Crimes Unit of the Metro Police Department who recommended he try to obtain a signed admission from Kevin as this would assist them in submitting the case to the DA and aid the DA in prosecuting the case.

John contacted the director for the ticketing department and brought him up to date on the case. As usual, the director said that he thought something was wrong with Kevin's work because he had noticed that his gross sales, especially in cash sales, had gone down. He had also noted that Kevin's sales were lower than the other clerks working the same shift. However, he hadn't followed up to see why.

It was now time to talk to Kevin. John called security dispatch and instructed the officer on duty to send officers to pick Kevin up and bring him to his office.

As soon as Kevin walked into the office John could tell he was nervous and knew he was busted. Kevin looked like an intelligent young man who was about twenty-two or twenty-three years old. Working as a clerk was probably his first job out of school. John wondered how he had figured out how to get around the system so fast.

Kevin, after just a few questions, opened up and told everything. He was told how to use the discounts and all-day passes by another clerk, Jeremy, a five year employee who worked on swing shift. Jeremy knew that the supervisors never bothered to check the paperwork or review sales, and had been stealing for years.

Kevin stated that he stole anywhere from $150 to $200 a day. His thefts were only limited by the amount of time he had. Kevin said that Jeremy was correct that the supervisors never asked any questions about his sales or the low amount of cash he turned in. They just closed him out at the end of the day and moved on.

Kevin stole because, unusual for someone so young, he had already developed a gambling problem and got behind with his car payment. Once he started he couldn't stop. Kevin also said that Jeremy was stealing much more than he was.

John had Kevin write out an admission statement and sign it. He placed Kevin on suspension pending investigation. He would then turn over the case to Metro for prosecution. Kevin would ultimately be fired and face criminal charges.

John pulled Jeremy's paperwork and immediately saw the same pattern of discounts and unusual number of regular ticket sales and all-day passes, albeit on a much larger scale. He would determine that Jeremy was stealing almost $400 a day! John figured that Jeremy may have stolen well over $100,000 during the two years he worked as a ticket clerk. Jeremy, during his interview, refused to admit anything. He was suspended and would be terminated. His case was also submitted to the police for prosecution.

Although John knew that Kevin and Jeremy had stolen much more than he could prove, he did have enough for each of them to be charged with a felony. That would have to do.

John's work wasn't done yet. He had identified the thieves, documented how the crime was committed and established how much was stolen by each perpetrator during a specific time frame, and, in one case, obtained an admission of guilt. Now he had to determine why they were able to get away with it for so long.

John discussed the case with the ticketing manager, the controller and surveillance. It became apparent that there were several breakdowns.

- There wasn't a system in place to verify discounts issued. In fact, employee didn't have to even record why a discount was given or to whom.
- Tickets sold were not checked against the inventory of tickets maintained. In this case while all-day tickets were registered, it was regular tickets that were actually issued, meaning the physical counts of both types of tickets would be incorrect.
- Cash sales by both Kevin and Jeremy were significantly lower than any other cashier, and discounts issued by them were higher.

Please note this part of the investigation must be handled in a spirit of cooperation and team work. The investigator will be dealing with department heads, and others who are responsible for ensuring that employee theft doesn't occur. Because a theft has occurred these very same people may feel the need to have to defend themselves from the investigator who, in their eyes, may be trying to make them look bad. The investigator must be sensitive to this and get the message across that he is not there to point fingers, but to assist in determining what can be done to ensure this type of theft does not occur again.

It is critical that this last step be taken. Too many properties seem to just accept that employees will steal and that there isn't much you can do about it. This is absolutely the wrong way to look at it. We can do a number of things to deter, detect and reduce employee theft.

In the case discussed both Kevin and Jeremy were arrested and charged with felony embezzlement. Although they didn't serve any time they were required to perform community service and pay restitution in the amount of what the investigator was able to prove they stole. This is usually the amount that you can demonstrate was stolen through video and/or the paper trail: a good argument for going back as far as you can to document the crime.

Audit Departments

It is important to note that this fraud (and the others discussed in this book) were *not* detected by anyone in the financial or compliance departments such as casino audit or accounting, revenue audit or internal audit. These departments (whichever one was assigned to monitor the involved department) missed a number of red flags that probably occurred daily or weekly, or even monthly; the point is that the red flags were there. We are not blaming these departments for missing the red flags, however we are asking the reader to be aware that they were, in fact, missed by the very people and departments we expect to detect the red flags and other indicators.

It is critical for the investigator to bear in mind that auditors and accountants in most gaming and retail operations are *not* trained to detect theft and fraud, or suspicious activity. They are normally trained to ensure the numbers make sense and that everything balances, not to identify and determine the reasons that a bartender has too many voids or that the venue cash drop has dropped dramatically. Their perspective is to ensure the cash and credit receipts balance with the sales receipts.

This perspective results in existing red flags of theft or fraud often being missed by auditors and other financial personnel and not being reported to the surveillance department or other loss prevention personnel. Thinking back over our own careers we rarely received any leads from audit or accounting that led us to open an investigation. They, at least in most cases, are not trained to recognize those indicators.

On the other hand, once audit personnel are aware something is amiss in the number they are extremely adept and diligent in tracking down where the problem is and how it occurred. They are a wealth of information and can be counted upon to work closely with the investigator. We encourage the investigator to seek out assistance from the financial staff whenever necessary.

We would also recommend that whenever possible the financial staff be trained by the loss prevention staff to know what the indicators of theft and fraud are, where to find them and when it should be reported to the loss prevention team.

Deterrence of Employee Theft

The ACFE's 2018 Report to the Nations is a wealth of information for anyone involved in loss prevention and fraud detection. Please note this report is issued every two years and can be found at www.acfe.com. There are a number of key points in the report that I believe are critical to building and operating a successful loss prevention program.

- Employee theft incidents are often ongoing for an average of sixteen months before the crime is reported or detected.
- Most employees who commit theft are first-time offenders.
- Most employee crime is detected through a tip from another employee or outside source.
- Asset misappropriation is the most common type of occupational fraud.
- Those with higher levels of authority tend to cause much higher losses. This is because they usually have much more access to and control of assets.
- The longer a perpetrator has worked for an organization the higher the losses tend to be.
- The presence of anti-fraud controls assists greatly in the prevention and detection of occupational fraud.
- One of the biggest tells to look for in occupational fraud is an employee living beyond his or her means. In the gaming industry that can often be excessive gambling, alcohol or drug use by the employee.

It is important for an investigator to know these points. While the investigator will usually not be involved in the actual deterrence of crime, knowing these key points and behaviors will assist in identifying the perpetrator of the crime, and taking away the opportunities for others to commit the crime the same way in the future.

One of the most important points in the report, and it really should just be a reminder to us all, is that anti-fraud controls such as internal controls, policies and procedures really do work when put in place and enforced. This is how almost all internal theft occurs. In fact, I would say that of cases I've been involved in or researched ninety-five percent of them involved a violation or bypass of a control, policy or procedure. The remaining five percent involved collusion with an outside agent.

The investigator should always remember this point when conducting the investigation. The violation of a control, policy or procedure often indicates where the theft is occurring and/or hidden.

Proactive investigators such as surveillance personnel, auditors or fraud examiners attempting to deter theft and/or locate active internal theft should review any observed instance of a violation or bypass of a control, policy or procedure.

Note that departments that have solid controls in place and ensure their employees adhere to them will not suffer nearly the amount of internal theft as a department that fails to use standard controls or enforce them.

Another suggestion for your consideration is installing a confidential employee hotline that employees or vendors can use to report suspicious activity (see Chapter 4). The ACFE Report to the Nations 2016 states:

> Providing individuals a means to report suspicious activity is a critical part of an anti-fraud program. Fraud reporting mechanisms, such as hotlines, should be set up to receive tips from both internal and external sources and should allow anonymity and confidentiality.
>
> (www.acfe.com/rttn-archive.aspx)

I have had tremendous success obtaining tips to fraudulent activity. Of course, some employees use the hotline to air grievances or frivolous complaints. But you should also receive two to three calls a year reporting criminal activity, usually ones that you had no idea were occurring. Such calls, in my experience, are always truthful and right on the money.

Detecting Internal Theft and Fraud

Most investigators understand that you can't investigate a crime until it's been detected or reported. As mentioned earlier, investigators usually come in to do their job after the crime's been discovered. This is changing. Investigators now are being used proactively to detect the indicators of a developing or active crime.

A number of business organizations use proactive staff functions or individuals to actively hunt and review for employee theft and fraud. This is especially so in the gaming industry. Surveillance personnel especially are being trained to locate such theft before it grows into a large loss. The creation and use of fraud investigation units is becoming increasingly common. Such units are normally comprised of surveillance staff specifically trained and assigned to observe for and identify internal theft.

These teams are also using specialized equipment such as eConnect to provide live and retrievable POS transactions that are linked to video. These systems track just about any type of transactions you wish, such as voids, no sales, discounts, refunds etc., and are invaluable in the detection of POS theft and fraud. An investment in a program like eConnect can save your company considerable money in potential and actual loss.

Another system you can use that is not as sophisticated as an eConnect platform is a video interface system.

Please note that you can proactively hunt for internal theft and be tremendously effective without specialized units and equipment, it just takes longer. We use audits to perform this task. We will discuss audits shortly.

Whoever is assigned to detect internal theft must base their techniques on the four key concepts previously discussed. This is the fundamental approach to detecting such crime. Once detected, the investigator can and should use whatever reasonable approach and techniques necessary to solve the case.

The fourth concept, I believe, is one of the most important. We have to realize that, in our business more so than any other, we will get ripped off by our own employees. There is just too much opportunity. The investigator will do well to remember that employee crime is probably occurring on every shift and in every department. Of course, some departments will be more at risk than others, and will cost the company more. The proactive investigator will plan accordingly.

Risk Assessment

One of the better ways to plan proactive investigations is to perform a risk/threat assessment. Once completed the assessment should clearly indicate when and where an area should be reviewed.

The risk assessment guide I use is the General Security Risk Assessment Guideline developed by ASIS International. Please see www.asisonline.org. This guideline is well written and focuses on the key areas and concepts necessary for a thorough assessment that helps you identify your security threats. The guideline will take you through a seven step process to aid you in isolating such threats. There is a cost (under $100 for non-ASIS members) but it is well worth the investment towards protecting your property.

Once performed, the assessment will identify those areas and/or activities that are at the most risk due to frequency of occurrence, cost to the business in assets or reputation, and criticality to your business operation. This allows you to plan your audit schedule to be the most effective, i.e. to focus on the areas that can cause your company the most damage.

Risk assessments should be performed at least once annually.

Audits

There are two types of audits typically used in the gaming industry: those performed (normally by financial or internal audit) using reports and paperwork such as receipts and cashier reports submitted by the department, and video audits using surveillance video. Video audits usually compare the transactional paperwork and/or proper use of policy and procedure to the actual video of the transaction and are almost always more effective in the detection of theft. Video audits are usually performed by security or surveillance personnel to detect and/ or investigate theft.

We use the risk assessment or information such as tips, statistical reports or other indicators of loss to assign our audits.

A sample audit schedule is listed in Table 20.1. This is just an example of an audit program schedule. It can and should be adapted for each property.

Non-Video Audits

There are times when a video audit can't be performed. This is usually due to the fact that there are no cameras in the area, or it may just be the fact that a paperwork audit would be more effective. For example, we may know that the blackjack hold is too low but we don't know where we have a problem. A video audit can't be used at this time because we don't know where to look yet. However, if we start reviewing the win/loss and table analysis reports we should be able to narrow down where the loss is occurring and/or the reason for the loss. With this information we can now initiate an audit.

Audits are one of the most powerful weapons a proactive investigative team can use. It is much more effective to investigate to deter crime or to catch it in its earliest stages. It will also drastically reduce a company's losses to look for crime rather than being told about it when it is already fully engaged and you've lost thousands of dollars.

Table 20.1 Sample Audit Schedule

Location	Frequency
Bars and restaurants	Quarterly
Player's club	Quarterly
Cage	Annually
Count room	Quarterly
Player ratings	Quarterly
Table game procedures	Monthly
Warehouse/receiving	Biannually
Nightclubs/pools	Monthly
Gift shops	Quarterly
Hotel front desk	Biannually

Practical Steps for the Investigation of Employee Theft or Fraud

1. Determine that there is an actual loss.
2. Determine the extent of the loss.
3. Identify potential suspects.
4. Identify a contact person to obtain information, necessary reports and paperwork.
5. Establish timeline of when the theft/fraud occurred.
6. Gather evidence to identify individual(s) involved.
7. Brief the GM and/or executive team.
8. Determine if an outside agency should be contacted or if the case will be handled internally.
9. Contact human resources to obtain necessary evidence, statements and documentation.
10. Determine if interviews of suspects and witnesses will be conducted and by whom.
11. Conduct interviews and obtain written statements.
12. Review to determine what charge or level of discipline the evidence obtained can support. Discuss with human resources (and legal counsel, if available), the GM or the executive committee, and outside law enforcement agencies to ensure proper (and desired) action is taken.
13. Suspend employee pending further investigation, or terminate. File charges with the local DA or have them arrested by local police. This is dependent upon your evidence and what you, legal counsel, human resources and/or the GM/executive committee have decided to do.

Key Takeaways

- Employee theft and fraud is the single largest and costliest threat to any business. Gaming properties are particularly vulnerable.
- Most gaming properties spend too much time looking for outside thieves and cheats and not enough time looking at the inside threat.
- Employees already know how to steal from us. It is either their own personal integrity or strong internal controls that prevent them from stealing.
- Because gaming properties (and most businesses) usually have internal controls and transaction reporting, a paper (or electronic) trail exists to proactively search for and/or investigate internal theft and fraud.
- To commit internal theft or fraud, almost in every case, an employee must violate or bypass a control, policy or procedure.
- The video audit is probably our strongest weapon for the prevention, detection and investigation of internal theft and fraud.
- One of the biggest tells of an employee committing theft or fraud is living beyond their means.

- Computers and other technology that are used by a growing number of employees, while providing greater efficiency to the workplace, also allow the fraudster to steal more, faster.

Best Practices

- Observe or review for violations of controls, policies or procedures. Doing so will often lead to the existence of a theft or fraud in progress or assist in its investigation.
- Review data, statistics and exception reports on a regular basis.
- Perform regular audits of all departments, especially critical departments, for indicators of theft and fraud.
- Implement and maintain a strong internal control program to minimize occurrences of theft and fraud.
- Train the financial staff to recognize and report indicators of theft and fraud.
- Utilize exception monitoring systems whenever possible to detect exceptions in critical areas.
- Install a confidential reporting system to allow employees and vendors to report suspicious activities.
- Perform annual risk assessments of your property.

Chapter 21

Outside Agents and Collusion

Every day, every shift, every department, someone is ripping you off.

Derk J. Boss

This chapter discusses the ever-present potential for a dishonest employee to collude with another to perpetrate their crime. It can be another employee the first has convinced to join in the conspiracy, or it can be, and often is, an outside agent the employee brings in to serve as agent to complete the theft or appear as the innocent guest collecting their prize. This type of fraud is extremely difficult to detect because it appears legitimate: required signatures are present, attestations of verifications are made and wins are pronounced legitimate, but underneath it is all false. It takes the astute and persistent investigator to peel back the layers of deception and get to the reality of what occurred.

We've previously discussed that almost all internal theft and fraud can be detected by looking for a procedure break, and/or the violation of a control or policy. This is usually not the case when an employee is working in collusion with others.

It is a characteristic of collusion that the activity will look normal. That is, the presence of another employee or supervisor, or an outsider, provides the verification or legitimacy needed.

For example, most slot jackpots require two signatures of slot employees verifying that the jackpot actually was won. In fact, two signatures are required to prevent theft by one person. Traditionally in gaming it was thought that it is more difficult to get two people to steal than it is one. And that is usually true. Of course, such a requirement is fast disappearing; slot machine systems serve as one component of the verification, thus allowing one employee to sign for smaller jackpots. The point is there are two verifications.

When reviewed by the audit department, the jackpot form is checked for two verification signatures. In a false jackpot scheme the two signatures (or more) may be present because two or more of the employees are involved in the scheme. As a side note, one individual can commit the same scheme by fraudulently signing in the required locations.

Another example is a marker issue. A dealer and a floor person must each sign verifying that the amount being issued is, in fact, the actual amount listed on the marker itself. If the dealer and floor person are working in collusion the entire marker and/or any portions thereof may be stolen. The player doesn't even have to be a part of the scam. However, if the player is involved it makes the theft easier because now the dealer or floor person doesn't have to take the checks off the game; they can be carried away by the player.

The example above is representative of fraud committed by individuals working together to defraud their employer. Collusion can be defined as "a secret agreement, especially for fraudulent or treacherous purposes; conspiracy: Some of his employees were acting in collusion to rob him" (www .dictionary.com/browse/collusion).

What is important for the investigator to remember is that fraud involving collusion is much more difficult to find and investigate. In such cases, everything that needed to be done was done; it just wasn't accurate or legitimate. As we discussed in the marker issue example, the floor person and dealer both can "sign to verify" that the amount being issued is correct, when in actuality it may be that there are an additional $1,000 in checks on the layout.

What we need to detect and investigate in most collusion cases is verification. We will discuss verifying key processes and transactions later. For now, let's go over what we can do to detect and/or investigate collusion.

Key Concept/Technique

Whether we are looking at a slot jackpot or a marker issue, or any of the other myriad transactions occurring on the casino floor that we must trust our employees to perform, the key to detection/investigation is that the investigator must verify that the process or transaction was authorized, legitimate, accurate and actually occurred.

For the investigator this means that we need to determine whether we are in the detection or investigation mode. Each is described below.

Collusion Detection

As described in earlier chapters, operating proactively requires that we monitor key transactions and processes to locate any indicators of theft or fraud. As part of the audit observation process the investigator must also observe for collusion. This requires verifying that the transaction is authorized and accurate.

We can verify such a transaction live during the audit process by ensuring that the transaction is accurate; for example, that the amount listed on the issuing document matches what is being issued.

We also verify that the individual being issued the amount or property is authorized to receive it. While a transaction "looks" like it is legitimate, that doesn't mean that it is legitimate. An audit observation requires that we look more deeply to verify the transaction.

Again using a marker issue as an example let's walk through what can be done to verify the transaction.

Surveillance is notified electronically or by phone that a marker is being issued. The surveillance investigator places a camera on the game and observes that either lammers or a marker request form indicating the amount to be issued are displayed on the table. The agent observes that the checks placed on the layout are the same amount as indicated by the lammer or the request form, and that is the same amount given to the player.

Surveillance would also verify to the best of their ability that the player signing the marker is the person authorized to sign for the checks.

This is also the time to verify that the floor person and dealer are following established procedures and are also verifying their portion of the transaction.

By following the above process the investigator knows that the marker issue is correct and accurate. Or the investigator will know that the issue is not correct and should take appropriate action.

Please note again that to verify such a transaction we must take the step of actually monitoring it in process. In most cases this will be performed by the surveillance team using video observation.

Investigation of Collusion Type Crimes

Hopefully, we will catch criminal activity prior to it occurring. Realistically, we know that we can't catch everything. When internal theft or fraud occurs and it is suspected that collusion is involved we must determine where the opportunity for collusion exists and verify the integrity of the transaction at that point.

For example, let's say the slot audit team informs you that the reports from one slot machine show an unusual number of paid outs as compared to coin in. At this point all you have is the report information that tells you on what day and times the paid outs took place, and their amounts (all under $200).

You can do two things at this point: 1) request ongoing surveillance of the subject machine and 2) review as many of the paid outs (in the form of TITOs) that are still available on video as possible.

When you review the video of the day and time of the paid outs you find that no one is at the machine when the ticket was issued. Now we know through our video verification of the process that something is incredibly wrong!

The next part of the transaction we can attempt to verify is the redemption process. We know the tickets are being redeemed: that is what initiated our investigation. We obtain a list of the redemption days and times and again begin the review process.

This time we locate individuals redeeming the tickets. We quickly determine that the redemptions are performed by one of the same three individuals each time. Now we know that somehow these individuals are receiving redemption tickets without any play or even being on the machine in question. It appears now that the company is the victim of some type of fraud involving collusion.

In this case (an actual case that resulted in the loss of over $1 million) the investigator has enough information to detain any one or all of the three individuals in an attempt to find out from them where or from whom they obtained the tickets.

Or we can continue our investigation to its source, which is probably the best way to ensure we know what happened, secure all of the evidence and put in controls to prevent it from reoccurring. In this particular investigation we would ultimately trace the tickets back to three slot technicians who had found a way to print tickets from a machine in their shop using the test mode. They gave the tickets to friends and family to redeem.

The above case went on for far too long (which is why it was so costly). It wasn't caught until an alert auditor noticed that the coin in didn't match the coin out.

Case History

A routine audit of player ratings located a female player who was listed as playing on a blackjack game but couldn't be located on video playing the game at the time listed on the rating card. The investigator knew that the rating could just be a mistake but she also knew that the inaccurate information was indicative of a fraudulent rating.

The player's account revealed that she was a frequent player, wagered an average bet of $500 and generally played about two to four hours. She was a good player for the casino.

The first step was to pull all ratings associated with the player and review available video. As the investigator looked at one tape after another she was unable to locate the player on any of the dates, times or tables listed on the card. It was now apparent that the player may be being rated fraudulently.

Examination of the rating card determined that the same floor person rated the player on each occasion. It was verified by different pit supervisors.

The investigator now wondered if the floor person and the female player had any association. She began with comparing the player's address with the floor person's address on file. It matched.

Reviewing the player's comp history, she had used her points to obtain cash back and for gourmet meals. She had redeemed over $10,000 in comps. At this point the investigator had never located her playing on any game and highly suspected she never would.

It was time to interview potential witnesses or people who may be able to shed some light on what was going on, those responsible for verifying the rating, and of course, the floor person, now a suspect in a fraud.

The investigator spoke to several other floor persons and was unable to locate anyone who knew or remembered the female player playing. No one besides the suspected floor person had rated her.

She next spoke to the pit supervisors who had verified the player's rating. Each had admitted to "rubber stamping" the rating meaning they just signed it without performing the required verification of play.

She then interviewed the suspect who, when confronted with the evidence gathered by the investigator, admitted to creating an account for his girlfriend and rating her fraudulently. They were big gamblers and used the cash back to gamble at other casinos. The floor person stated it was easy to do because no one ever checked the ratings.

The floor person was immediately terminated.

As a follow-up and just to be sure no one else was creating false accounts, the investigator ran the addresses of all the floor persons against player addresses. An additional seven floor persons were found to have created false accounts for "friends and family". They were also fired.

All of the floor persons who set up the fraudulent accounts used the points to obtain cash back. Most gambled regularly but a few took the cash just because they could. Each of these employees worked in collusion with outside agents (i.e. friends and family) to commit their fraud.

In this case, the GCB wasn't called. It occurred during the early days of rating and the crime wasn't really understood. It was looked at by the company as more of a control problem. Nevertheless, the company did lose thousands of dollars and this type of fraud was placed on the radar to be prevented. The surveillance department would continue to check ratings as often as possible (as did surveillance rooms on other properties). This practice continues at most properties today.

The Role of Exception Reporting in Fraud and Collusion Detection

Most investigators, auditors and managers don't understand how valuable exception reports are in our efforts to deter, detect and investigate theft and fraud. This is especially true nowadays with the ubiquitous use of computer systems, programs and databases. As we've noted before, fraudsters using such systems to commit theft and fraud will look to an observer like they are performing their normal duties. Nowadays, we will very rarely see the employee placing cash directly into their pocket, especially with collusion with inside or outside agents. We must look deeper to find the scam.

Almost all critical and key transactions that occur in a casino generate reports that contain detailed information such as opening amounts or balances, the number, types and amounts of transactions, who performed the transactions, when, closing amounts, etc. The list can go on and on, and can be designed to provide whatever type of information the company desires.

Systems also provide exception reports. Exception reports list those transactions that were performed outside normal operating parameters. While exceptions may be an accepted and even a routine transaction they can, when abused, allow the perpetration of theft and fraud. For example, a "no sale" transaction is an exception to normal operation but is an accepted practice in most casinos because it is used to open the register to provide change for a customer.

Exceptions such as "no sales" become an issue when they are used to commit and camouflage theft and fraud. It is important that the investigator understand that the deception the thief uses to cover his theft is often the indicator that highlights his activity.

As mentioned previously, exceptions are transactions that fall outside the norm. Exceptions are tracked by the system and are usually detailed on a report that is generated automatically or upon request. Most systems, if not all, provide exception reports. Over the years common reports were developed for use by the end user because fraudsters use common methods to beat the system. These reports will allow the department manager to keep track of the department to identify arising issues, and the proactive investigator to identify and detect crime.

Unfortunately, we do not use exception reports as they should be used. In fact, we usually don't use them at all. We often forget that they are available and/or don't check them regularly for the indicators of theft.

Audit departments may actually check exception reports but may not understand what they mean. Auditors often are not trained in recognizing red flags that may indicate the presence of fraud. Auditors are usually looking to ensure that amounts balance and the proper forms are submitted.

Any auditor, investigator or surveillance personnel can and will improve their fraud detection rate by reviewing key exception reports as often as possible.

I recommend that key exception reports are reviewed daily. In fact, I recommend that one person be assigned to review each department's exception reports. This allows that one person to become thoroughly familiar with one department's operation, personnel and key reports. Assigning one person to monitor also increases efficiency. It should take less than an hour each day for the assigned person to check the previous day's paperwork for red flags. Of course, once you locate an anomaly you should begin investigating why the exception occurred. As an investigator you are exactly where you need to be: identifying and responding to a suspicious activity.

Key Takeaways

- It is a characteristic of theft and fraud committed by outside agents colluding with employees that the activity appears normal until you begin checking the details.
- Monitoring critical and key transactions for accuracy and authorization on a regular basis aids in the detection of theft and fraud.
- Detecting and investigating such activity requires that the investigator verifies that a transaction is accurate, authorized and occurred.
- Reviewing exception reports on a regular basis will provide indicators and red flags of theft and fraud, and allows the investigator to work proactively.

Best Practices

- When collusion is suspected, the investigator should verify that a process or transaction was authorized, legitimate, accurate and actually occurred.
- Performing regular audits of key areas and transactions will assist in the detection of theft and fraud involving collusion.
- Review exception reports daily to check for unusual and suspicious activities or transactions. Verify what occurred with video when possible.
- Assign specific personnel to review specific departments to obtain the best results.

Chapter 22

Gaming Investigations

> It is in our gaming operations where we are most exposed, but also where we are the most prepared.
>
> Derk J. Boss

Gaming crime, while based in traditional motivations such as greed and attempting to get something for nothing, differs from normal criminal activity in the methods used to commit the theft. Gaming has its own methods of operation, its own vocabulary, unique systems and types of gambling, as well as marketing programs. The casino resort is vulnerable to theft and fraud using the property's systems and games against itself. The gaming investigator should understand the differences and similarities between gaming crime and traditional crime. Applying fundamental investigation techniques within the gaming environment requires a thorough understanding of gaming operations, regulations and controls, marketing programs and the games themselves.

The more experience I've gained in loss prevention the more I've learned about traditional crime investigation. It amazes me to think back to when I began as a surveillance agent and how little I knew about conducting an investigation. I can't believe I caught anything at all and I often wonder how many of my cases would have had a better result if I knew more about proper investigative techniques.

One of the most important lessons I've learned is that while the crimes and incidents that occur vary in each department, the way we investigate follows a fundamental process. In other words, we should apply standard investigative techniques to any crime or incident we come across.

Regardless of the department or type of crime or incident there are certain things we can expect to be present to aid us and other things we must do to conduct a proper investigation. For example, a cage investigation or a table games investigation both require standard identification of suspect(s), review of video, if available, evidence gathering, interview of potential witnesses and suspect(s), etc. We can also expect that we will have the use of aids to our investigation such as: transaction and exception reports, video, witnesses etc.

You will find this to be true in all investigations of gaming departments. While the type of transaction, activity and paperwork will be different, the steps you take to investigate are similar.

Differences in Gaming Investigations

Gaming investigations differ from non-gaming investigations in several ways. First, gaming investigations involve departments directly involved with gaming or as a result of gaming. Slots, table games, sports book and poker are examples of departments directly involved in gaming. The cage and player's club are examples of departments that are a result of gaming and/or that support gaming. Normally, these are the departments that the GCB would want to get involved with should an investigation become necessary.

Retail operations such as the hotel, food and beverage, gift shops, ticketing etc., are normally not considered to be gaming related. I say normally because there are some cases where the GCB may be interested. Such instances are usually related to comps, redeemable points and free play earned from an individual's gaming activities.

The GCB is also interested in nightclubs, day pools and spas. These are retail operations that due to their very nature can operate in such a manner that they may negatively affect a casino's gaming license. Activities such as allowing minors, over-intoxication, drugs, fights, lewdness, prostitution etc. are all illegal activities that will be investigated by other agencies, and the GCB in most jurisdictions will monitor the results of those investigations and will (and has) impose fines to get the attention of the gaming property and the industry as a whole.

Nevada Gaming Commission Regulation 5 (www.gaming.nv.gov) states:

5.010 Methods of Operation

1. It is the policy of the commission and the board to require that all establishments wherein gaming is conducted in this state be operated in a manner suitable to protect the public health, safety, morals, good order and general welfare of the inhabitants of the State of Nevada.
2. Responsibility for the employment and maintenance of suitable methods of operation rests with the licensee, and willful or persistent use or toleration of methods of operation deemed unsuitable will constitute grounds for license revocation or other disciplinary action.

The above regulation allows the GCB to investigate non-gaming areas to ensure that the casino is maintaining a suitable operation.

It is recommended that the investigator consider which agency or agencies should be contacted during an investigation. While a particular agency may decide not to assist they can often provide valuable information and support. It is also always good to build a rapport by freely communicating with all agencies within your area.

Gaming investigations are normally highly regulated (as described above) and controlled. That usually means that there should be a number of controls that are required to be in place by the regulator. This is true for all gaming departments in a gaming property. The investigator can expect to find certain controls and/or reports for the department being investigated. While these controls can make the investigator's job somewhat easier, they don't mean that all crimes will be prevented.

Non-gaming areas such as retail operations are usually not regulated by gaming regulators. The operators of the property or the venue are responsible for installing the necessary controls. Of course, this is where things start breaking down because operators don't always ensure controls are implemented and maintained. This results in more thefts from these areas and more difficulty detecting and investigating them.

This certainly doesn't mean that gaming investigations are easy or infrequent. In fact, quite the opposite is true.

Let's look at some issues that arise almost immediately in a gaming investigation. Let's take, for example, a table games investigation. An anonymous report is made that floor personnel are inflating player ratings. Hopefully we know what that means. If not we have to take the time to learn what that means and that's the point; in most gaming investigations the investigator must develop a strong understanding of the game and/or operation of the game or activity in order to properly investigate.

The investigation of a ratings scam would require, as a bare minimum, knowledge of what ratings are, what they are used for and how they are computed.

This is a cardinal rule of gaming investigations (actually probably any type of investigation): you must understand as well as you can what you are investigating. An investigator who does not understand how the department, game or transaction works is doomed to failure. They will fail to ask the right questions, investigate the right areas or collect the right evidence.

Investigators must take the time to learn the subject matter as much as possible. Sometimes that is not possible. Either there is not enough time or the subject is too complicated. In that case, teaming up with someone who does know what you need to know is invaluable. Department heads or managers, consultants, friends in the business etc. can really assist you with the case.

Please do this with caution. You should be careful who you trust with knowledge of the investigation. Many times I've had department heads or managers talk about confidential investigations to others not involved. Obviously, this is not a good thing. When people are talking it's only a matter of time before word gets out to the very people or person you're investigating.

A good rule to follow is to discuss the case with only those with a "need to know". If they don't need to know, don't tell them. You should tell your GM and perhaps your legal counsel if you have one on property. This is for you to decide in the best interest of the property. If you do decide to ask someone for assistance, you must stress with them that the investigation is confidential and ask them to keep it that way.

Another issue that arises immediately in a gaming investigation is the securing of evidence, particularly video evidence. Surveillance video is normally kept for seven days, sometimes a little longer. The devices used to store video are expensive, limiting surveillance rooms in how long they can store video.

Saving the right video and/or all the video involved in the case is the next issue. The investigator at the beginning of the case usually doesn't have any idea of what video will need to be saved. Knowing what to save usually comes after working the case and gathering a lot of information. This is a common problem with gaming investigations. While the investigator is determining what occurred and who is involved, video that may be pertinent is disappearing each day.

I recommend that the moment you initiate an investigation you should save all video you believe is or may be pertinent. Of course at times you will save way too much and at other times not enough. But think it through and do what you feel is best. You won't get in trouble saving too much video.

An idea to consider is to purchase additional storage for the securing of evidence. Storage drives are becoming increasingly more cost effective and can allow the storage of virtually all video that may be involved in a crime. Purchasing such storage would alleviate the pressure of the clock and the potential loss of valuable evidence.

Additional evidence to secure includes, but is not limited to, any paperwork, reports, inventory, check out sheets or receipts used in that area, activity or station. Such information may also exist electronically. While paper and electronic reports and other information usually remain in existence longer, it's best to secure them as soon as possible. They will, at the very least, be moved to some type of storage, making them more difficult to retrieve, or in some cases they may be destroyed entirely. Getting the evidence into your hands as fast as possible is a good idea.

Another thing to consider in gaming investigations is obtaining statements from witnesses as quickly as possible. This is often overlooked during the initial stages of an investigation primarily, I think, because 1) we don't want to alert people we are investigating and 2) we believe that as we're dealing primarily with employees that we can always obtain a statement later.

What happens is that we usually don't obtain any statements, a few of which always become important later. I think that unless there is a reason for not doing so the investigator should obtain a statement from anyone they talk to in the course of the investigation. Even if they say they don't know anything, their statement may prove valuable as leverage later should it become apparent that they actually did know something that they "forgot" to tell you.

It is also amazing to me what happens if you don't take a statement at the time of the interview. It is a virtual certainty that the interviewee will disappear or otherwise become unavailable when you need to talk to him or her again. Vacation, hospitalization or termination all can happen when you need to circle back and pin down that person. Always, always get your statement as soon as possible.

Of course there are other things that arise in a gaming investigation, especially in the various departments with their operations, regulations and controls.

Let's take a look at an actual case and see how it works.

Case History

Surveillance received an anonymous caller who stated there were some weird things happening at the sports book between the director of race and sports book and a group of what the caller claimed were wise guys. Specifically, the caller claimed that the wise guys were getting better point spreads than anyone else. The caller suggested that surveillance take a look.

Surveillance immediately initiated a close watch of the director (Joe). It became quickly apparent that the surveillance investigators would need help in determining what was going on. Surveillance could see that on Monday mornings some bettors lined up at one of the betting windows to place wagers on upcoming NFL games. They were personally taken care of by Joe. The problem was that surveillance wasn't really familiar with the sports book beyond a basic understanding of its operations. Surveillance didn't understand why the bettors were there so early.

The surveillance director, recognizing he needed assistance, contacted a person in accounting who he had worked with before and who he knew had been a previous sports book director. After asking the accountant to keep what they discussed confidential he told him about the anonymous call and showed him the video of the betting line.

The accountant immediately said "he's letting them buy the early line". He explained further that the opening line was posted on Monday and as it hadn't been bet on yet it was a point spread that could and would move as money was wagered on the games. The former sports book director also said that this was a practice used by some books to attract business, however most books discontinued it as it attracted the wrong crowd. The wrong crowd consisted of wise guys and messenger bettors (runners working for gambling syndicates or big gamblers) who possessed inside information, bet large sums of money and were extremely hard to beat. Giving such a good line to such bettors was not a smart thing to do and put the book in a losing situation.

The surveillance director knew from many budget meetings that the book was losing consistently and that it wasn't the intention of the property to attract advantage players. He decided to focus on Joe to see why he was bringing so many wise guys in.

The accountant also provided the information that the sports book would have computer records and reports that would detail lines and line movements. He also showed the surveillance director where to obtain the "official line"; this was the line put out by a line service that set the spread. This line was used by all the books as a baseline and was normally followed exactly.

Comparing the official line to the line issued by Joe determined that the line he provided to the wise guys was always in their favor and not to the casino's advantage. In fact, as the surveillance director and his investigators researched further they determined that it was the games that the wise guys bet on that caused the most losses to the sports book and kept it from being profitable.

Knowing what they now knew, they began looking through the reports for unusual line movements. The day and times of such movements, as well as who made them, were listed and provided to surveillance. It was noted that all of the line movements considered unusual or suspicious were made by Joe.

Unfortunately, due to the time it took to determine and ask the right questions and read the right reports, not all the video was available. The investigation would have to be performed "live" meaning surveillance would have to monitor the book and develop new evidence. While the evidence they had already would help to prove the case, it wouldn't be useful in prosecution without video to support it.

Moving forward the surveillance team would focus on monitoring the individuals waiting in line Monday morning, try to identify them and determine what type of line they were getting.

Investigators quickly ascertained that the majority of bettors standing in line on Monday were not only obtaining the best numbers available, they were consistent winners. These players combined accounted for a large percentage of the loss incurred at the book. They were not tourists or casual bettors. They were almost all locals and known professional gamblers or associated with known gamblers. They were, in fact, wise guys.

The question now became why Joe provided such good lines to the wise guys. It was time to begin interviewing the people involved. Investigators were instructed to interview all employees in the book, including supervisors, as soon as possible. In the meantime, the surveillance director would look into Joe's background.

Investigators interviewed the sports book writers and the supervisors. They were able to interview everyone except for the swing shift supervisor who would be in later that night and a writer who was off. They decided to have the supervisor contacted by human resources the next day and requested to come in for an interview. While they were able to ultimately interview the writer when he returned from days off, human resources reported that the supervisor had begun a three week vacation and was unavailable.

Results of the interviews determined that a good portion of the supervisors and writers felt something was weird with the way the director handled the advantage players. The graveyard supervisor stated that the director wouldn't let anyone but himself change the lines or adjust other game parameters, which he had never seen in his career. The director also served as the day shift supervisor.

Joe's background was sketchy. Why he was hired at all was anyone's guess. He had been in the business for over thirty years and had worked at a number of large properties. However he had usually resigned or been terminated for reasons unknown.

There was one period of time when Joe had operated an offshore betting operation, which was illegal in the US but legal offshore. He must have been backed by someone, or a group of someones, but they were undisclosed. That operation suddenly failed and was abandoned quickly. That was the director's last job before he came to the book on the property. The surveillance director was concerned that, at the very least, Joe was involved with some shady characters, and maybe those shady characters were making bets on his property. He decided to take a closer look at their play.

The surveillance director and accountant pulled the computer records and reviewed the bets that were being made by those specific players. That was where they struck pay dirt!

Bets being made by this select group always got the best lines available on the events they wagered on. Further, they found a number of occasions where Joe actually changed the line for a bettor while he was making his wager! The computer report detailed the line movement immediately before the wager was made and then back to the original after it was made.

The investigation had determined that Joe was providing the best possible lines for certain individuals for reasons unknown. This practice had resulted in the loss of hundreds of thousands of dollars in winning wagers. At worst Joe was working in collusion with outside agents to defraud the casino. At best, Joe was guilty of poor decision-making (sports book directors were expected to make line decisions to increase play and the probability of winning for the casino).

It was time to interview Joe. He was interviewed by the surveillance director who was given some questions to ask by the accountant. Joe had been around and refused to admit he did anything wrong. His answer to everything was that he'd been hired to make decisions and set lines to attract business.

His answer to why he changed the line only for certain players who were beating the hell out of the casino was that "it happens, it's gambling". Joe was of no assistance to the investigation and only made the investigators more confident that he was guilty.

The surveillance director ran the case by the GCB and was disappointed to find that Joe hadn't really violated any laws or gaming regulations. Sports book directors, as part of the very nature of their job, were allowed to make adjustments. The GCB didn't like what Joe was doing and agreed he was up to something illegal but needed substantially more evidence to take the case.

The surveillance director presented his case to the GM. They agreed that while they may not have enough evidence to prosecute Joe, they certainly had enough to fire him for failure to operate the book properly. Joe was fired the next morning.

On a side note, after firing Joe the book soon returned to profitability.

Key Takeaways

- Gaming investigations should be treated as a criminal investigation.
- Gaming and non-gaming investigations are usually reported to and handled by different agencies.
- You should understand what you're investigating as well as you can.
- Review departmental operational and exception reports for red flags and evidence.
- Obtain assistance from a knowledgeable person(s) if necessary to allow proper investigation.
- Discuss the case with only those with a "need to know".
- Interview and obtain statements from witnesses and other involved individuals as soon as possible to prevent delay or loss of their information.

Best Practices

- Perform any investigation as you would a criminal investigation.
- Increase your video storage capability.
- Ensure you are thoroughly familiar with the area or operation being investigated. If you are not, you should do whatever you can to become so, or identify someone with the necessary information and knowledge that you can trust implicitly to assist you.
- Operate on a "need to know" basis.
- Develop a plan to identify evidence that must be obtained and secured.
- Obtain witness statements at the time of interview whenever possible.

In the following chapters we will discuss gaming investigations as they pertain specifically to key departments.

Chapter 23

Cage Investigations

The cage and count rooms are our most highly secure areas yet remain vulnerable to internal theft, fraud and collusion.

Derk J. Boss

The casino cage is where the gaming day begins and ends. It is the fortress that stores and issues our cash and checks and controls their return. Within the cage are our count rooms where the day's drop is counted and profit or loss is determined. The cage and its environs are our most sensitive and secure areas and yet, as we've learned, there is always a way, often many, to bypass the barriers and attack what's within.

The cage is balanced every shift of every day along with each department it works with. There is a great deal of paperwork generated and time spent to ensure that the cage remains balanced during the tens of thousands of transactions it performs daily. There are relatively few variances that occur in the cage that aren't resolved, often in twenty-four hours. When the cage does get ripped off it is usually minor theft from a cashier's drawer or major theft from the count rooms or the main bank.

Cage Operation

The cage operates very simply. It starts with a base or imprest (specified amount) level of cash and checks. Whatever it sends out or receives is replaced and documented with cash, checks, monetary transfers or receipts. It is balanced at the end of every day and then immediately opens for the next day's transactions.

The cage department is usually comprised of the main mank, front line or cashier windows, fill window and an employee bank. These are the primary areas for the cage. It may include an area for guest safety deposit boxes, a credit office and the count room.

While the count room may be located within the cage, count room staff normally report to someone other than the cage manager, such as the director of finance. This is to maintain segregation of duties and prevent one person from being in charge of the money coming in and going out.

The main bank is the heart of the cage. It supplies checks and cash to the cashier windows, provides fills to the pit and distributes cash for employee banks. One of the main bank's most important jobs is to receive the previous day's total cash drop from all sources and get it deposited into the bank. When a shift day is complete checks, cash, credits and employee banks return to the main bank to be counted and the cage balanced. The main bank also maintains and stores the property's chip inventory.

The front of the cage is dedicated to customer service with any number of windows for guests to cash checks, redeem checks and TITO tickets. The cash drawers at each window are stocked by the main bank.

A number of cages use employee windows to issue, store and maintain employee banks. Employees such as bartenders, waitresses, front desk clerks and others are issued a bank at the beginning of their shift. At the end of their shift they return their bank along with the cash, comp, sales and credit receipts from their sales for the shift. These funds are normally turned in to the count room to be counted and verified.

In some cases these funds are turned in to an employee bank, if used by the property.

The fill bank issues chip fills to table games and receives credits from the pit and other departments such as slots. It may or may not be located in the main bank. Surveillance cameras are placed to see either the fill or credit in the window and the accompanying documentation.

It is important to keep in mind that the cage must balance at the end of their day. Whatever is issued or received must be accounted for and attributed to a department or individual. In order to do so the cage maintains an excellent paper trail that the investigator can use to conduct investigations.

Types of Cage Theft

Thefts from the cage are usually relatively small (one hundred to a few thousand dollars) or larger (a few thousand to tens of thousands of dollars).

The smaller thefts almost always occur at the front line (cashier windows) or at the employee bank. They may also occur by theft of checks stored in the main bank.

The larger thefts usually occur in the main bank and usually from cash or checks that are stored in inventory.

Let's discuss the different types of cage theft and methods of investigation.

Theft from Front Line (Cage Windows)

Thefts occurring at the cage window are usually perpetrated by an individual cashier removing cash from their drawer. Such thefts are usually small: $1 to

$500. Most of these thefts are in the $100 to $200 range in order to stay below or at the cage variance policy (larger variances require investigation; smaller variances subject the cashier to discipline).

Variances, whether over or short, require response. Smaller variances under $100 usually are tracked and handled by cage management and aren't investigated by outside investigators. Almost all cage variances are of that variety and are handled internally by the cage.

It is a recommended best practice that cage variances of $100 or more are investigated by someone in loss prevention such as a security investigator or surveillance. In most cases it is best for surveillance to do so as most of the investigation will be done through the review of video.

We must first determine if the variance occurred due to a mistake made by the cashier. This may occur for a number of reasons but usually related to overpaying or shorting a guest or employee, or entering an amount incorrectly on the cashier checkout sheet.

Investigating a mistake or a theft starts the same: review of paperwork and video. The process begins with a review of paperwork by a cage supervisor or manager. If the variance is not found it is turned over to surveillance or a security investigator for a video review.

Video review begins at the start of the cashier's shift. Each transaction should be checked for accuracy, proper procedure and indication of theft. The investigator should begin by verifying the opening of the window. An oncoming cashier will either open a closed window or buy the window from another cashier.

Our first step is to determine that the cashier opened the window as per procedure and counted the bank properly. Cashiers should count each bill in a strap (other than $1 straps) to ensure the strap isn't short. A number of thefts occur due to one cashier selling a strap of cash (usually a $100 strap) that is short one or two $100 bills.

It is important to note that a variance, whether it is a shortage or an overage, requires attention. A shortage means something is missing. An overage means the cashier either shorted a customer or employee or is stealing and is unable to keep track of how much he/she has stolen, and was unable to remove the amount from the bank prior to the end of the shift.

It would be impractical to investigate every variance. Most properties begin investigating at $100 or $200. These amounts eliminate variance caused by small mistakes.

Cashiers use a buy/sell sheet to open or sell the window. The investigator should review the buy/sell sheet and attempt to verify the accuracy of the count as best as possible. This means obtaining a copy of the buy/sell sheet and verifying each of the totals listed on the sheet and comparing the activity to the video. Totals will consist of total cash, coin and checks in the bank, usually by denomination. Other totals may include TITO tickets, coupons, checks and receipts for any transfers made by the cashier during the shift.

Verification of the buy/sell sheet will usually locate an arithmetic mistake made during the opening process, which often occurs. If the variance isn't located at the opening of the window we know that it must have occurred during the shift and we can move on to reviewing each transaction.

When the investigator begins reviewing transactions they should keep in mind that there may be a number of transactions that can be moved quickly through. For instance, if the variance is a $100 shortage then transactions totaling less than that probably are not responsible for the shortage.

However, the investigator is reminded that each transaction must be reviewed to include the cashier's activities during the transaction. The cashier could use such a transaction to cover the theft of cash from the drawer.

In most cases the variance will be located during the review of transactions. Often the variance is the result of an incorrect payment to a customer during cash-out of a player's checks, cash in of a TITO ticket, or transfer of funds to or from the main bank. There are a number of other transactions where the variance can occur, requiring the investigator to check each transaction thoroughly.

Of course, the variance may not be located in any of the transactions reviewed. In such a case it becomes more likely that the variance was the result of a theft by the cashier or another individual who had access to the bank or its funds. A thorough review of the cashier's activity is warranted at this point with special attention being paid to the cashier's handling of cash and checks. The investigator should also review the activity of cashiers or other individuals, such as guests or employees who received a payout or funds from the cashier. There are frequent occasions when a guest or employee receives an overpayment and just pockets the difference. Their behavior after receiving payment may provide an indicator as to what happened to the money.

I think it is really important that we keep in mind that the money had to go or come from somewhere. Too many investigators give up the search and just say the variance can't be found. I disagree. Again, the variance is real, something happened. The money went somewhere.

One point to keep in mind is that because the cage operates on a twenty-four-hour basis in order to issue and receive funds to and from all departments, it can take twenty-four hours to allow all banks and other activities to clear. It is usually good practice to allow the twenty-four hours to pass before beginning your investigation to ensure that the variance isn't cleared due to a simple mistake. Of course, if the investigator believes the variance is an actual theft he should begin immediately.

Keep in mind that it is okay to work with the cage manager or a supervisor to aid in your investigation by allowing them to also review the video. As it is their department they should have a thorough understanding of their operations and how things should be done. They can often spot something that the investigator may miss. Obviously you shouldn't involve a manager or supervisor, or anyone else, if you feel they may be involved in the variance.

Main Bank Theft

Larger thefts in the cage usually occur in the main bank. The main bank is the central repository for the entire property and houses cash and chip reserves. As such, due to the sheer volume of cash and chips, thefts from the main bank are usually larger than those that occur at a cashier window.

The main bank also suffers different types of theft than do the cashier windows. Theft in the main bank is usually theft of cash or chips that are stored in vaults or in other locations that are not specifically counted.

Most of us have seen the vault and are familiar with the fact that often millions of dollars of cash and checks are stored within. The vault is a part of the cage and it is usually located in the main bank area. The main banker is the employee assigned to operate the main bank, and it is bought or sold to another main banker at the end of his/her shift. The main banker sends and receives cash and chips throughout the shift and is constantly counting and balancing the bank.

Because the main bank is central to the casino's operations it is almost always in balance. Should it become over or short it attracts a lot of attention and the variance is located as quickly as possible. When theft occurs in the main bank it usually happens where cash and chips are stored.

As mentioned previously the main bank stores cash and chips as a reserve for big wins, and to ensure enough is on hand as required by regulation. Many thefts have taken place from the cash and chips that are stored. This is usually due to main bank cashiers, or cage personnel in general, not completing a thorough count and inventory of the straps of cash or racks of chips stored for later use.

Theft can be committed by removing a partial or full strap of cash or high denomination chips from the storage area. This is usually accomplished by taking cash or checks that are not counted by cage personnel because of the inconvenience of counting each strap or moving each chip tray to verify that nothing is missing. Once a potential thief observes that not everything is checked it is relatively easy to remove cash or checks and place the shorted strap(s) or chip tray(s) where it won't be counted for a long time. Another technique used by thieves is to remove a high denomination check and replace it with a dollar check (or other small denomination check).

This is a common scam that it is actually very effective due to the fact that it won't be caught for a long time, usually well after the video is no longer available, making the determination of the thief virtually impossible. The investigator must resort to interviewing suspects and hoping for an admission.

The best way to prevent this type of theft is for cage personnel to rotate the cash and chips on a regular basis. Rotating the stock allows a good look at what is actually in the chip racks and allows staff to count each strap to verify nothing is missing. Potential thieves seeing that the stock is rotated regularly are less likely to steal from storage and, if they do, the missing cash or chips will be noticed much faster.

Fill Window Theft and Fraud

Theft and fraud from fill windows can occur when employees collude to steal from fills sent to table games or credits sent to the cage. When a fill is requested by the pit from the cage it is put together by the cashier at the fill bank. Once completed a security officer is summoned to verify the checks and deliver them to the table. It is verified at the game by the dealer and a floor person. High-denomination checks are broken down by the dealer to allow for easy verification by surveillance. Once verified the checks are placed into the tray.

There have been cases where the fill was issued correctly from the cage and when delivered to the game all or some of the checks were given directly to an agent on the game. Of course this requires security, the floor person and the dealer to collude, and for the fill to be under the amount surveillance would verify.

Fills can also be ripped off when they are sent out incorrectly with an amount over what is stated on the fill slip. A security officer or dealer can take advantage of such an error by taking the overage.

Both of the above cases are solved easily by review of video from the fill window and the game. It would require ignorance or laziness on the part of the casino management and accounting teams to allow such theft to occur for a long period. Unfortunately, such theft does happen.

Theft and Fraud from Outside

Theft and fraud committed by outside agents usually involves armed robbery, counterfeit cash, chips or personal and business checks, credit cards, money transfers and front money. Investigation of such activity normally will involve outside agencies because the method used to commit the crime often violates state and/or federal law.

The role of the investigator in this type of crime is to support the outside agencies by assisting in the gathering of evidence. Because the cage is so well covered by cameras and all transactions are well documented, including the requirement that you must present identification (regardless of whether it is fraudulent identification or legitimate), there are always potential leads and evidence.

Because the need to identify those who attempt to perpetrate crimes at the cage is so great it is a best practice that there are enough cameras there and that they are positioned properly to ensure a good facial shot of the suspect and of the transaction that is occurring.

It is also a best practice to retain video from cage cameras and ATM/credit machines for longer periods of time: thirty to forty-five days if possible. Most banking and credit institutions don't report suspect fraudulent transactions in the seven-day retention period used by surveillance rooms, meaning video won't be available for investigators if retention time isn't extended.

The investigator should gather and provide to law enforcement video, photos and documents involved in the paper trail. Documents may include player information such as buy-ins, win/loss, dates and times of play, etc. Please keep in mind that some properties allow such information to be released immediately to police, and others require a subpoena. You should check with your legal counsel.

Case History

Surveillance was notified that $50,000 was missing from a cashier booth. This booth was located in the slot high-limit area and was operated by the cage for the purpose of handling high-end slot players. The cash was stored in a locked drawer to be used as a cash reserve in the event of large cash-outs.

Operating procedures required that the $50,000 cash reserve be counted at the opening/closing of each shift. In practice, this was rarely done. Each cashier normally would simply accept that the cash was in the drawer and never checked.

One day a cashier from the main bank had to fill in at the slot booth due to a call in. She wouldn't accept that the cash was in the drawer without seeing it. The drawer was opened and the cash was gone!

Surveillance was faced with the fact that since the cash was never checked as required they had to go back as far as they could on their video (in this case eight days) and review every moment of the entire eight days to see if anyone had entered the drawer.

The review located one cashier (a white male who'd been there for several years) who opened and entered the locked drawer where the cash was stored. This occurred about three days prior to the cash being found missing.

It was observed that the packet of cash was placed onto a counter where the camera view was washed out by too bright lighting. The cash was lost from view in that lighting. The cashier was observed doing a lot of cash handling in that area but the surveillance couldn't see what exactly was being done or where it all went. Surveillance could determine that the packet of cash was not returned to the drawer but wouldn't be able to prove specifically where the money went.

However, the cash was missing and the cashier was the last one to handle it. Surveillance could also definitively prove that the money was not paid out to anyone through the window nor were there any errors found that could account for the missing funds. In other words, the cashier had to have taken the money!

Regulators were notified and reviewed the video and decided not to take the case! This was due to the camera angle that was washed out, preventing the regulators from proving that someone else didn't take the money.

The cashier was interviewed by the regulators. He refused to admit anything and couldn't or wouldn't say what happened to the $50,000. The regulators said there was nothing else they could do and closed their investigation.

The surveillance investigator assigned to the case knew the cashier took the money and decided to interview him one more time hoping to trip him up and get an admission of guilt. The investigator decided to pull him first thing in the morning for the interview.

The cashier never showed for work and, in fact, never returned to the property. He was ultimately terminated but, of course, the $50,000 was never recovered.

On a side note: the surveillance department didn't give up. They were able to trace the cashier using an outside investigator to Montana where he was living with his brother. This information was forwarded to the regulators in the hopes the case could be reopened based on the cashier's behavior of leaving the state after the theft. The regulators declined to do so.

In the end, the failure to ensure cashiers counted all the cash, chips and all reserve inventories allowed a cashier to steal thousands of dollars and get away with it. The cashier was never apprehended.

Count Rooms

The count room(s) are usually located within the cage. The count room department usually reports to the casino controller or director of finance and not to the cage director. This is to maintain segregation of duties to require more than one person to authorize or be responsible for all transactions in the cage and count rooms.

The count room is responsible for opening and counting the drop boxes from table games, and the bill validator units (BVU) from the slot machines. Each is picked up during the drop by the count team members. The drop is usually performed during the early morning hours. The table games drop is usually picked up once per day, and slots can range from once a day to two to six days a week. During the drop the "live" or "hot" boxes are removed from the games and slot machines, and empty boxes put in their place.

Slot drops used to be performed daily and the table games drop was done on each shift. I mention this because although it is cost effective to reduce the number of drops done per day and per week, our ability to identify where and when losses occur is also reduced.

During peak business hours individual boxes for slot machines or table games may become too full and must be exchanged for an empty box. Such exchanges are called emergency drops and are subject to the same strict controls required in the normal drop.

After the drop has been completed, the drop cart containing the live boxes is escorted by the count team and security into the count room.

Please note that in some jurisdictions the surveillance department is required to monitor the drop and count process, in others it is not. It is a surveillance best practice to monitor the drop and count at all times. If a lack of personnel prevents surveillance from doing so, frequent and thorough audits of both the drop and the count should be conducted.

Usually there are two teams with the count team operation: the drop team that picks up the boxes, and the count team that counts the funds. Some smaller properties may combine the teams. Of course, this depends on what is required by the gaming regulations and controls within the jurisdiction.

The count room is normally required to possess extensive camera coverage, and should provide camera coverage of the entire room. Audio coverage is also required. Other security measures are used, such as: controlled access; individual count team members must wear coveralls or smocks that prevent them from placing cash into their pockets; the counting table must be clear so that nothing may be hidden underneath; and all cups and/or glasses must be clear to prevent cash being hidden in them.

During the count process, the surveillance department must pay strict attention to what is occurring within the room, and that the count team members are following established policy and procedure. This usually requires at least one agent to observe the activity, and listen to the count team members as they call out the numbers of each box as it is opened.

The count room is the most secure area in the casino. Unfortunately, theft can occur in this area, and frequently does. In fact, I've never worked on a property where it did not occur. Hopefully, the theft is caught before the company loses a tremendous amount of money. I am familiar with cases that cost the property over a $1 million.

How does that happen in an area that is secured so well? It is usually due to inattention and negligence on the part of the surveillance team. Surveillance has the primary, if not sole, responsibility to monitor the actions of the count team during the count process. When the surveillance agents fail to closely observe what the individual count team members are doing, theft can and has occurred. A great majority of the thefts that happen in the count room are perpetrated in front of the cameras and in an obvious manner. In other words, surveillance can and should detect such theft activity. Unfortunately, we often don't detect theft activity within the count room, and that is directly due to inattention.

Observing the count process is extremely boring. It is important, and it is a critical process, but it is boring. Agents assigned to monitor the count process, especially for hours at a time and on a daily basis, eventually get tired of looking and don't really see what's going on in front of their cameras. They are observing but not seeing or understanding.

Agents also get tired of listening to the count team members as they work. While working the crew members usually fall into casual conversation that after hours and days of listening to becomes monotonous and frequently irritating; the audio from the count room is almost always turned down by surveillance personnel for that reason.

Effectively observing the count requires agents to be fresh in order to concentrate on what the count team members are doing. This requires that agents, if at all possible, take turns observing. I recommend that agents spend no more than two hours at a time observing the count room. After two hours another agent should take over the duty. The agents can rotate the duty back and forth but they do need that break.

Another best practice I would recommend is that surveillance perform frequent audits of the count process. An audit (see Appendix 1) requires that the count room be monitored intensely and continuously by surveillance for a specified period of time. During an audit the full weight of the surveillance department and its resources are applied to observing the count team and process. Each movement, drop box, transaction, activity and motion are closely observed for adherence to procedure and controls. Any exception or suspicious activity is investigated.

Audits are much more effective at detecting unusual or suspicious activity than daily monitoring (although daily monitoring must be done). A best practice is to conduct a thorough audit of the count room for at least two days to ensure the team is following established policies, procedures and controls, and that there isn't any indication of suspicious activity. Remember to audit the drop team and the drop on a regular basis also. Again, once per month is recommended.

Theft from the Drop and Count Room

The thefts that I've seen occur or been aware of during the drop and in the count room are described below. This is not an inclusive list. I'm sure there are scams and schemes I'm not aware of or that will be developed. The key to deterring and detecting existing and developing theft is to monitor the activities of the room often and thoroughly, and to know what you are winning/holding in table games, slots and other games. In other words, you should have a good idea what should be in those boxes through your following of the numbers.

The thefts I'm aware of that occurred in the count room are extremely simple in nature. In fact, the theft usually entails grabbing some cash and either hiding it in the smock, coverall or personal clothing, or hiding the cash in paperwork, or in a box, cup or other item.

One theft I investigated involved a count room employee who had cut a hole in her coveralls and sewn a pocket underneath. She would take cash and place it into that pocket. That's one reason why you shouldn't let count room employees take their smocks or coveralls home, and why you should inspect these items on a regular basis.

Another theft I'm aware of is a female count employee who, while counting cash, wrapped some of the bills in a piece of paper, then dropping the packet into the waste basket. As we all know, that waste basket is usually picked up by an attendant with security, or just security. In this case, it was a security officer who just happened to be the boyfriend of the count room employee. He retrieved the cash from the basket before dumping it. Again, please note that we usually check or should check any item coming out of the count room, and prohibit anything but clear cups, boxes, etc. For such thefts to occur as I've described, there had to be a breakdown in observation and the inspection of items leaving the count room.

Case History

A surveillance director who had just started at a property noted that the hold percentage for blackjack overall was down about three points from where it should be. What's more, the hold had been down for at least two years as compared to industry standards.

The director reviewed the numbers thoroughly and identified two blackjack games that continually were losing games and accounted for most, if not all, of the losses. However, the losses could not be explained by play, meaning there was no winning play to account for the loss.

The director set a close watch on the games and didn't locate any theft or fraud by the dealers or floor personnel. Fills and credits were correct, markers and buy backs handled correctly, wins and losses listed accurately, and cash placed into the drop as it should be. After eliminating each of these transactions it was apparent that whatever the reason for the loss, it wasn't occurring on the games.

The director then instructed his agents to record every bill that was placed into the drop boxes of both games, and to keep a running count. The total count obtained by surveillance was then compared to what the count team reported as a total for both boxes. The total reported by the count team was lower by a couple of thousand dollars. This meant that the money was disappearing from the drop boxes prior to the verification of the count.

The director then ordered his team to closely monitor the handling of the two drop boxes as they were opened. Immediately it was noted that as those two boxes were opened two members of the count team grabbed handfuls of cash and stuffed them directly into their clothing underneath their smock!

Continued observation determined that three members of the count team were stealing cash each day from the two boxes. It was ultimately revealed that the theft had gone on for over two years and that the company had lost over $2 million. All three were arrested by the GCB.

It is important to note that this theft should have been caught the first day it was attempted. The thieves made no attempt to hide what they were doing, yet it continued far too long. As we discussed, the reason the theft occurred and continued is because the departments responsible for detecting the activity were not paying attention to the count room. I'm sure the cameras were displayed on the monitors but obviously surveillance wasn't looking at them. The graveyard surveillance team was fired.

The director of table games and the casino controller also failed in their duties. They failed to note the continued low win percentage in blackjack, specifically on those two games. They, too, were fired.

Key Takeaways

- The cage and the areas located within it are highly sensitive areas and are usually well protected. However, it can be attacked from within and from outside.
- The cage should balance each day. Variances should be investigated by an outside department such as surveillance, beginning at $100 or $200.
- In most cases, allow twenty-four hours to pass prior to beginning investigation to allow the cage to clear all activity and to ensure there is an actual variance.
- Cage theft ranges from relatively small theft at the cage windows to larger thefts occurring in the main bank.
- Check and rotate chips and cash held in reserve to protect it from pilfering.
- Investigation of the cage begins with comparison of video and paper documentation to the actual transactions.
- Keep in mind that there is a reason for a variance. The money came from or went somewhere. Too many investigators give up before finding what occurred.
- Place surveillance cameras to provide high-quality video of guests, employees and transactions. Overviews of cage areas are highly recommended.
- Extend video retention for all cage areas. A number of thefts and scams aren't detected or reported for thirty days or more. A forty-five-day rotation is recommended.
- Require surveillance to monitor all fills or credits of $10,000 or more.

Best Practices

- Investigate cage variances of $100 or more.
- Inspect and rotate checks stored or held as inventory on a regular basis.
- Monitor table fills and credits of $10,000 or more.
- Monitor slot transactions of $5,000 or more.
- Ensure the cage and its support areas are well covered by cameras and that transactions and operations can be observed clearly.
- Ensure cameras at cage windows provide clear identification of customers conducting transactions at the window. This should include a clear view of the transaction being performed.
- Monitor the drop and count process at all times,
- Surveillance personnel should be rotated frequently when observing the drop and count perspective to maintain alertness.
- Perform audits of the drop and count process on a regular basis to ascertain their adherence to controls, policies and procedure, and to detect suspicious activity.
- Audits should be performed for at least two days to be considered a thorough review.

Chapter 24

Investigations in the Slot Department

The use of ever-improving technology makes slots hard to beat, but not impossible.

Derk J. Boss

Even with the new high-tech slot machines there are ways to take advantage of or cheat the machines or the systems that support them. The slot department has far fewer employees than it did twenty years ago, which has reduced the opportunities for theft and fraud but has also increased dependency on software-based systems to include the slot machines themselves as well as the market and customer loyalty programs associated with them. When these systems are breached untold thousands of dollars can be stolen in a very short period, while being almost undetectable. In this chapter, we discuss the necessary techniques and approaches to detect this activity.

We often believe that because almost all slot machines are now coinless and because of the modern technology used in today's machines, theft and cheating will be prevented. For the most part that is true. The scams and cheating techniques used prior to the entry of coinless machines have disappeared into history. We no longer see the stringers and handle poppers, or the setup of jackpots (although, in our world, old scams seem to come back, so you shouldn't forget them).

However, having said that, that doesn't mean the slot department is theft- and cheating-free. In fact, what occurs in slots today costs much more than what happened years ago. In the old days of slots, a thief may steal a bucket of dollar tokens and get away with $300; today's technology allows employees to steal thousands. Instead of walking out of the casino with hidden tokens or cash, an employee or an outside agent working with an employee can have thousands of points or free play added to their club account, win a promotion set up by their friend, or be paid for a false jackpot set up by a slot tech working from his shop!

We have to change what we look for and how we investigate in slots if we hope to stay on top of the crime that does occur there. In this chapter we'll discuss some of the types of advantage play, theft and cheating that occur in slots today and how to investigate for them. Please keep in mind that we can't predict all the various methods that will be used against us but we can provide techniques that will stand the test of time. Note that this statement is true for all of our departments and for the illicit activity that we've discussed in this book.

Types of Advantage Play, Theft, Fraud and Cheating in Slots

We are now seeing the response from the bad guys to the technological changes we made to slots. I'm sure they've been up to things for a long time it's just that we are becoming more aware of what they're up to.

What we are experiencing now seems to revolve around the following.

Advantage Play

There are individuals and teams of individuals who identify slot machines that they can beat with their play or obtain more than their fair share of redeemable points. In a number of cases they are able to do both.

An example of this activity is video poker machines that are set for a high return to the player. Advantage players who understand the game very well and use an effective strategy can over a period of time beat those machines.

Another example is some of the craps slot machines that are now on the floors of many casinos. There have been a number of cases where the players found that by betting the Pass and Don't Pass line at the same time they wouldn't lose their wager. Now this doesn't sound like a big problem however these players were also earning redeemable points each time they played and were able to obtain a considerable balance before the machines were corrected.

Advantage players are very quick to realize when there is a weakness in a type of machine or individual machines. They often share information with their associates and others on the internet and social media. It's amazing how fast such information gets out. I remember on one occasion when new slot machines were placed on the casino floor and within a few days every one of the new machines was being played 24/7 and losing consistently. Investigation determined that the machines had not been set correctly by the technicians and were accepting quarters as dollars. Of course, the payout was in dollars, also resulting in large losses.

These are just a few actual scenarios where advantage players are able to take advantage of the casino. As we know this type of activity is not illegal, but it can be costly. Usually such activity continues for a good period of time before we catch on to what's happening.

While there are many types of slot advantage play and more developing as new machines, systems and promotions hit the floor there are common tells you can use to detect advantage play activity.

We have discussed throughout this book the necessity for reviewing depart-mental reports, monitoring statistical information and checking exception reports. This remains true for investigations in slots. In fact, a number of reports from the player's club can be used to assist in slots. Such exception reports as those related to point adjustments, free play, top players, top redemptions, etc. can be used to locate illicit activity in the slot department.

Slot statistical information will locate existing or arising issues. It is important to remember that a slot machine, just as a blackjack table, should win (hold) a certain percentage. In fact, a slot machine should hold a determined percentage or *par* (the expected outcome of the game). A slot machine that is operating properly and is played legitimately should hold what it is set for (the PAR). Slot machines do not vary their hold signifi-cantly and are not as volatile as table games. They are subject to large wins and losses but normally recover much more quickly. We should compare the actual win to the PAR to identify issues.

Every casino prepares daily reports that list the activity of each machine including coin-in/coin out, jackpots paid, win/loss and hold percentage. This information is usually shown by day, month and year to date. It is also listed by machine, by banks of machines and by type of machine. As we do in table games we should review the slot report for underperforming or losing devices or banks of devices.

Once we identify slot machines that require observation or review it's an easy matter to place a camera on the machine or review existing coverage to determine the reason for the loss.

We can use this process for advantage play, cheating and internal theft and fraud.

Cheating and Internal Theft and Fraud in Slots

Most of the common cheating methods used on slot machines over the years have disappeared with the advent of coinless machines. However, new scams and/or variations of old ones have been developed and used. These scams usually involve using the new technology to the cheat's advantage.

One example of slot cheating is a method used a few years ago. Three individuals with a long history of cheating slot machines devised a way to place a device into a slot machine that gave $100 in credits for $1 placed in the machine. This worked only on certain machines, forcing the trio to travel the country to locate the machines. The scam was ultimately exposed, the trio identified and apprehended. The first clue to its detection was that one casino that paid attention to their numbers noted the unusual losses on the machines and thought it suspicious enough to report it to their surveillance department.

We must also be concerned with internal theft and fraud. Because there are now no coins or tokens to be stolen, the employee must resort to using the system or machine against itself to steal or collude with others. Some examples are a slot floor person who uses the slot system to locate tickets that haven't yet been redeemed and are near expiration, prints them and redeems them for herself. Another example is the slot technicians who found they could set up false jackpots using a test machine in their shop. They and the friends and family they used to collect the jackpots stole millions before they were caught.

The first scam was caught by a lucky break. One of the ticket owners returned to the property prior to the expiration date to redeem his ticket and it was found to be already been redeemed. The investigation into how the ticket was redeemed led directly down the electronic trail to the slot floor person who redeemed the ticket. See Case History.

These examples illustrate that there is always a way to cheat a slot machine and that we often don't know how it will be done. However, no matter how a machine is cheated or taken advantage of, the loss can be detected and investigated if you know where to look.

Investigating Slot Theft, Fraud, Cheating, and Advantage Play

The first thing we should keep in mind is that slot players, slot machines, slot areas and floor, and the department itself must be monitored on a regular, if not constant, basis. At the very least large wins and jackpots should be reviewed and analyzed. We all tend to spend a lot of time watching table games and forget most of our money is played and made in the slots. In fact, if we treated slots like we do table games we would detect a lot more of the crime and other issues occurring there.

The surveillance department should do the following:

- Perform constant IOU patrols of the slots
- Review large wins and payouts
- Evaluate high action and suspicious players
- Review slot statistical information, operating and exception reports on a regular basis

Each of the above is a form of proactive investigation. We are searching for indicators of illicit activity. We patrol the slots looking for suspect individuals and activities. Large wins and payouts are reviewed to make sure the machine wasn't cheated or compromised. We evaluate high-action players and suspicious players to check for cheating, advantage play or theft. And we review the numbers and reports on a regular basis to pinpoint which machines or areas are not holding as they should and focus our observations on those machines and in those areas.

It is recommended that investigators and surveillance personnel spend some time with the slot director on property going over the reports generated each day to learn what information each provides, and how to interpret it.

Key Slot Reports to Monitor

- Slot Daily Win Report: Lists the win/loss for each individual slot machine and includes handle, jackpots paid and usually daily, month to date and year to date hold percentage. This report will quickly identify slot machines losing consistently.
- Slot PAR Report: Lists what the machine is set to hold and usually will show the variance between the actual hold and PAR. This report will also quickly identify losing slot machines.
- Top Player Win List: This report lists the players by their daily and year-to-date win. Usually the players are listed from top to bottom. The report may also list players by their coin in. This report shows who your top players are by win and handle, and is used by surveillance to check that players listed are, in fact, real. This report may be best suited to determine who is not on the report. A person receiving large amounts of free play, comps or point adjustments should be on the list. If not, it may indicate that the player is receiving benefits without play, an indication of fraud.
- Daily Hit Report: Lists the players who won jackpots and payouts over a certain amount (usually $2500 or more) and the machine that paid it. This report is used to verify that the wins were legitimate and occurred as stated.
- Extended Handle Report: Shows the dollar amount of coin circulated through the machine.
- Bill Validator (BV) Report: Lists variances from individual BV boxes between what was counted by the count team and what was reported by the machine itself. Use this report to identify and investigate suspicious variances.
- Manual Override Report: Some machines and/or jackpots require that in order to be paid completely (due to how the pays on a machine are set up, or possibly due to a malfunction), a manual override of the system must be performed. A manual override can be used to create fraudulent jackpots or payouts.
- Manual Point Adjustment: Points earned by playing slots can be adjusted manually. Adjustments are usually made for customer disputes, complaints or to correct a machine malfunction. These adjustments can also be made fraudulently to award unearned points to outside agents.
- Void Report: Lists any jackpots that were voided and can indicate suspicious activity.

Ideally these reports should be reviewed on a daily basis or at minimum once a week.

When an incident occurs in slots that may involve cheating, advantage play, or internal theft or fraud the investigator should review the reports associated with the involved slot machines and/or the personnel interfacing with the subject machines.

Case History

A player at a casino in Las Vegas had to leave suddenly. He was a firefighter from California who was called to immediate duty to fight fires then out of control in Southern California and threatening homes, property and lives. He left so fast he was unable to redeem his slot winnings but he did keep his TITO voucher.

He returned to Las Vegas almost ninety days later to do some partying and redeem his ticket. It was worth several hundred dollars. When he submitted his ticket to the cashier, she scanned it as required and found it had already been redeemed a few days earlier. The firefighter was adamant that he had not redeemed the ticket and refused to accept the cashier's statement that there was nothing she could do. A supervisor was called, then security, then the slot manager. No one could appease the firefighter; he remained firm and wanted to be paid now!

The slot manager began to believe that the firefighter was telling the truth and decided to give him the benefit of any doubt. He paid the young man the money, apologized for the inconvenience and wished him well. He did not, however, believe that it was just a mistake or malfunction in the system. Something else must have happened and he wanted to know what it was. He called surveillance.

The surveillance department assigned one of their investigators to look into the report. The investigator immediately pulled all the pertinent records and saved video from the cage windows, particularly the window where the ticket was redeemed.

The investigator reviewed the video of the cage window where the ticket was redeemed and found that the person redeeming the ticket was a slot floor person. This was suspicious because if the firefighter had his ticket, where did the ticket redeemed come from, and why was a slot floor person cashing it out?

The investigator set out to answer these questions. He reviewed the paperwork that detailed the history of the ticket. He found the date it was issued originally and the machine that it was printed out from. The next time the ticket number appeared was when it was redeemed by the floor person at the window about two days prior to the date the ticket would have expired.

The investigator reviewed the video of the ticket when it was redeemed. The slot floor person brought the ticket to the window, where the cashier appeared to question the floor person about the ticket. The investigator noted the cashier entered the ticket number manually rather than scanning it into the system.

The investigator obtained the ticket from cage records. He found that the ticket's bar code appeared to have been burned or melted in some fashion, preventing it from being read properly, if at all. The ticket number was handwritten on the ticket. That explained why the cashier had had some questions. He would next speak to the cashier to ask her what had happened.

The cashier stated that the floor person told her that the player was too busy playing a machine and asked her (the floor person) to submit his ticket for payment. The floor person said she was told that he had accidently left his ticket in his pants while they were run through the dryer. The floor person looked up the ticket on the system and had written its number onto the ticket in order to get it redeemed. The cashier said she thought it was odd but had no reason to disbelieve the floor person so she paid the ticket.

The investigator knew that the owner of the ticket had the original ticket in good condition and hadn't attempted to redeem until he returned to property. The floor person had some explaining to do.

The investigator then reviewed the computer records that detailed what files and applications the floor person had accessed in the last few weeks. This review determined that she had continually accessed the file listing tickets that had not as yet been redeemed. This was suspicious because she really had no reason to open or work with this file.

It was time to interview the floor person. She was called in and confronted with the information gathered. She eventually admitted to redeeming tickets that were due to expire and had cashed in a number of them for over a couple of thousand dollars.

She stated that she would access the file listing outstanding tickets with their expiration dates. She would select tickets that were near their expiration and were less likely to be redeemed. Because she was unable to print out such tickets she would write down the ticket identification number. She would then find a ticket that had been thrown away or a machine that had a few credits on it and print out the ticket. Next, she would mutilate the ticket so it wouldn't scan or read. She would do this by placing a heated iron on the bar code of the ticket, crumpling, tearing and cutting the ticket. She would write the number of the ticket due to expire onto the mutilated ticket and take it to a cashier.

Her story was the customer was in the slot area playing and wanted her to redeem the ticket. The ticket itself had accidentally been run through the washer and dryer. She had been able to find it in the system at the player's request and it was a legitimate ticket. No one ever questioned her and the ticket was redeemed. The floor person, of course, kept the money.

The floor person was terminated, and the case reported to the GCB.

This case illustrates that there is always a way to beat any system, and people will find a way to do so. It also illustrates that there is always a trail left behind for the investigator to follow back to the perpetrator.

I would also note that "Murphy's Law" affects criminals too, not just the good guys. The firefighter coming back to redeem his ticket was not expected by the floor person and resulted in her demise.

Key Takeaways

- Slot machines and systems remain vulnerable to advantage play, theft, fraud and cheating.
- The cost of illicit activity occurring in slots can be significant due to the use of technology allowing more to be taken faster.
- Treat the slot department the same as table games and closely monitor employees, key transactions and activities.
- Use technology to catch the misuse of technology (data analysis).
- Review statistical information, operational and exception reports to detect losing machines, and suspicious activities and trends.

Best Practices

- Patrol the slot department regularly and consistently to detect illicit activity.
- Evaluate high-end and winning slot players to ensure play is legitimate.
- Establish a level of win out that shall be reviewed by surveillance for indicators of advantage play, theft, cheating or fraud.
- Assign specific personnel to analyze statistical data and reports, including reports detailing edits made to the slot system, for indication of advantage play, theft, cheating or fraud.

Chapter 25

Investigation of Table Games

Where the protection of the casino began and continues to this day.

Derk J. Boss

Our reason for being and where it all began for gaming surveillance and investigations: a good case can be made that casino security and surveillance were formulated to provide protection of table games. In fact, not too many years ago most surveillance work began and ended in the pit. At that time and to a large extent today table games were scammed and cheated on a regular basis and required that protection. It is the nature of the beast for table games to be attacked. This is due to those who protect the games, who may not be as knowledgeable or as experienced as they should be, attempting to detect a cheater or advantage player who is an expert at their scam or move. Additionally, employees working in collusion with each other or outside agents can go undetected for years. This chapter provides investigative techniques and knowledge to assist you in your detection and investigation of cheating, advantage, play, theft or fraud occurring in the pit.

We see cheating, theft and fraud occur in table games on a regular basis. This has always been so. I think this occurs for a number of reasons: there is always someone out there who is trying to cheat the house; games can be cheated; and our table game staff are usually untrained, unprepared and often fail to enforce game protection procedures.

What this means for the investigator is you will have no shortage of work in this area. Crimes and other issues arise on a regular basis in table games that will require your expertise. Let's start by looking at what types of investigations are necessary.

Cheating and Advantage Play

While cheating at gambling is against the law and advantage play is not, the methods used to investigate are the same. To illustrate this let's review a case involving each.

Cheating

Surveillance detects suspicious play on a blackjack game. Unknown players are exhibiting an unusual hit/stand pattern as compared to basic strategy, and are winning consistently. Surveillance believes the players may have marked the cards. In order to determine if this is true, surveillance must ascertain if the players are receiving and using information not available to other players. This is a key element that must be present to demonstrate that a crime was committed.

It is important to note that when a team of cheaters marks cards it's done to receive information. That is the reason they marked the cards in the first place. In any scam where the cheater's intent is to obtain information, such as in marking cards or hole card play (using a device), the cheater must use the information obtained to attain his/her objective. What that means to the investigator is the use of that information is what will aid us in the identification of the crime and proving that it occurred.

In this case, the surveillance investigator observing play makes note of three plays made by the players that are indicative of knowing the next card to come into play. The player fails to double down on a ten, hits on a nineteen and receives a two, and stands on a fourteen against a ten. Review of these plays determines that on the double down play the next card out was a two that would have lost the hand for the player. When he hit the nineteen the next card was a two and the player needed to hit to win the hand against a dealer's twenty. On the fourteen, the next card would have been a ten and busted his hand.

The above is an example of what we're looking for to prove that the players are using the information they've obtained from marking the cards. Certainly, the more examples we can obtain of the team using the information, the better. This helps us illustrate to law enforcement and ultimately a jury that the way the individual and/or team is playing is not due to a fluke but is due directly to receiving information from the cards that were marked illegally. The investigators should place the play information onto a hard chart or into a player tracking program (such as BJ Survey) for easy reference.

Our next step should be to secure the cards that are suspected of being marked. This is a time-sensitive issue and must be done subtly. In most cases the marks will not be easily apparent and the cards will have to be checked thoroughly. This will require removing the cards from the game at some point, which will obviously alert the individual or team to our suspicions.

If at all possible gaming control or other law enforcement should be contacted as soon as suspicious play is confirmed. This will hopefully allow time for agents or officers to respond and get in place. Ideally, we want to secure the cards and detain the suspects at the same time. However, what usually happens is that when the cards are changed or otherwise removed from the game the suspects will leave the game and cash out their checks at the cage. We must be prepared for this to occur.

It may take some time to determine if the cards are marked and how they are marked. This is evidence we need to have. If we can show that the cards are marked and that certain players marked the cards and took advantage of information provided by the marked cards, we can detain the suspects for the purpose of awaiting gaming control agents.

In some cases, we may not be able to determine the cards are marked before the suspects attempt to leave the casino. If you have enough evidence that the suspects were using information that was unavailable to other players (by reading the marked cards) you may be able to detain them to await gaming agents. Usually, you will get instructions from the responding agents, and/or they will already be stationed on your property and able to make the decisions for themselves. As you can see, it is critical that surveillance quickly develop and gather as much evidence as possible to allow the apprehension of the suspects.

It is possible to delay the suspects at the cage during the redemption of the checks. In other words, a quick call to the cage supervisor requesting that they "slow down" the redemption may assist surveillance by providing some additional time to locate the evidence. Of course this is only a temporary delaying tactic and can only be used for a short period of time.

Regardless of whether surveillance is able to locate the necessary evidence or not to allow an arrest to be made, surveillance must obtain clear identification of each suspect (if they haven't already). This may be the only time you are able to do so. Remember that if you are able to ultimately find that the cards were marked and you have maintained a solid chain of custody of the evidence, charges can be filed after the fact.

It is important to note that individuals and teams that cheat at gambling are usually known. To ply their trade they must hit casinos on a somewhat regular basis. That means they may have already been identified and even arrested at another property. That means they may be listed in a database that you can access to identify your suspects.

Security may be able to obtain identification by requesting it from the suspects. However, it isn't required by law that an individual identify himself or herself to anyone other than law enforcement, and most cheaters know this and will not comply with security's request. It is always best to have law enforcement obtain necessary identification. It is our job to put them in a position to do so.

The more you are able to build your case properly around the facts and evidence, the more probable cause you can provide to law enforcement for their handling of the incident. This will often make the difference in whether the suspects are arrested or even charged.

Remember, in cheating incidents, in order to prevail, you must prove each element of the cheating at gaming statute. Nevada's Revised Statutes are a good example. The pertinent statute is listed below:

Unlawful Acts and Equipment

NRS 465.070 Fraudulent acts. It is unlawful for any person:

1. To alter or misrepresent the outcome of a game or other event on which wagers have been made after the outcome is made sure but before it is revealed to the players.
2. To place, increase or decrease a bet or to determine the course of play after acquiring knowledge, not available to all players, of the outcome of the game or any event that affects the outcome of the game or which is the subject of the bet or to aid anyone in acquiring such knowledge for the purpose of placing, increasing or decreasing a bet or determining the course of play contingent upon that event or outcome.
3. To claim, collect or take, or attempt to claim, collect or take, money or anything of value in or from a gambling game, with intent to defraud, without having made a wager contingent thereon, or to claim, collect or take an amount greater than the amount won.
4. Knowingly to entice or induce another to go to any place where a gambling game is being conducted or operated in violation of the provisions of this chapter, with the intent that the other person play or participate in that gambling game.
5. To place or increase a bet after acquiring knowledge of the outcome of the game or other event which is the subject of the bet, including past-posting and pressing bets.
6. To reduce the amount wagered or cancel the bet after acquiring knowledge of the outcome of the game or other event which is the subject of the bet, including pinching bets.
7. To manipulate, with the intent to cheat, any component of a gaming device in a manner contrary to the designed and normal operational purpose for the component, including, but not limited to, varying the pull of the handle of a slot machine, with knowledge that the manipulation affects the outcome of the game or with knowledge of any event that affects the outcome of the game.
8. To offer, promise or give anything of value to anyone for the purpose of influencing the outcome of a race, sporting event, contest or game upon which a wager may be made, or to place, increase or decrease a wager after acquiring knowledge, not available to the general public, that anyone has been offered, promised or given anything

of value for the purpose of influencing the outcome of the race, sporting event, contest or game upon which the wager is placed, increased or decreased.

9. To change or alter the normal outcome of any game played on an interactive gaming system or a mobile gaming system or the way in which the outcome is reported to any participant in the game.

[1911 C&P § 198; RL § 6463; NCL § 10146] + [1911 C&P § 199; RL § 6464; NCL § 10147] – (NRS A 1967, 587; 1977, 477; 1979, 1476; 1981, 1292; 1987, 414; 1989, 1112; 2001, 3095; 2005, 723) (https://law.justia.com/codes/nevada/2011/chapter-465)

NRS 465.075   Use or possession of device, software or hardware to obtain advantage at playing game prohibited.   It is unlawful for any person to use, possess with the intent to use or assist another person in using or possessing with the intent to use any computerized, electronic, electrical or mechanical device, or any software or hardware, or any combination thereof, which is designed, constructed, altered or programmed to obtain an advantage at playing any game in a licensed gaming establishment or any game that is offered by a licensee or affiliate, including, without limitation, a device that:

1. Projects the outcome of the game;
2. Keeps track of cards played or cards prepared for play in the game;
3. Analyzes the probability of the occurrence of an event relating to the game; or
4. Analyzes the strategy for playing or betting to be used in the game,

except as may be made available as part of an approved game or otherwise permitted by the Commission.

(Added to NRS by 1985, 970; A 2011, 216; 2013, 1317) (www.leg. state.nv.us/law1.cfm)

You will note that, as we've discussed in our marked card scenario, the following is pertinent to our case and should guide our investigation (NRS 465.070, point 2):

To place, increase or decrease a bet or to determine the course of play after acquiring knowledge, not available to all players, of the outcome of the game or any event that affects the outcome of the game or which is the subject of the bet or to aid anyone in acquiring such knowledge for the purpose of placing, increasing or decreasing a bet or determining the course of play contingent upon that event or outcome.

If we can prove that the markings placed on the card were used by the players to place, increase or decrease a bet or to determine the course of play after acquiring knowledge not available to all players, our case will stand a much better chance of being prosecuted.

Another factor to consider in our investigation is the securing of our evidence. In this case it is the video of the play and the cards that were marked. As many of us in surveillance know, when cards are suspected of being marked it seems like every floor person and pit boss on duty must grab the cards and look through them for the marks. We can't allow that to happen. I can tell you that if you're not trained to detect marks on cards (and there are many ways to do so) and don't have the proper equipment to identify the marks, there is only a remote chance you will find the marks. Certainly most floor personnel will not find them, and allowing them to try and do so will only contaminate and possibly destroy the evidence on the cards. Do not allow the cards to be placed back into their boxes or to be rubber banded. It is a best practice to leave the suspect cards on the table or pit podium while you await the arrival of gaming agents or other law enforcement.

The cards should also remain under camera until they are taken into evidence by an authorized person. In the event that gaming agents or law enforcement are unable to take the cards into evidence in a timely manner, surveillance should do so. The card should be placed (unboxed or rubber banded) into a paper or plastic bag or envelope and sealed with date, time, where the cards were obtained, contents within the envelope and name of the individual sealing the envelope.

I will also note that if there isn't anyone available who knows how to find how and where the cards are marked, it may be worth tracking down an expert to do so. The marks on the cards are a critical piece of evidence and it must be established that the marks were placed on the cards by certain individuals in such a manner that they provided information to certain players not available to other players, and that information was used by those players.

It is okay to look at and handle the cards under controlled circumstances, taking extreme care to not remove or alter the marks, provided that proper evidence-handling controls and procedures are followed.

Note that while we are discussing marked cards in this case there are other methods that can be used by cheaters that can result in the same suspicion (players obtaining information) such as nicks, bends, waves etc. Placing such altered cards into a box or wrapping them with a rubber band will destroy the evidence.

We must treat the cards and the game as a crime scene until determined otherwise. We should maintain continuous coverage of the game and the cards. It is a good practice to leave the suspect's cards on the game and/or in the discard tray during the investigation and until they are taken into evidence.

Handling of the cards should be kept to an absolute minimum and, if possible, should await the arrival of law enforcement. If the cards must be handled it should be limited to a minimum and to as few individuals as necessary. Of course, continuous coverage should be maintained. As mentioned previously, it is a best practice to keep the cards on the game or at the podium while the cards are checked. If you treat the table and cards as a crime scene you can usually control the evidence.

Advantage Play

Surveillance detects suspicious play on a blackjack game. Suspect is an individual, "refused name" player who is betting $100 up to $2,500, and is winning consistently. Initial evaluation of the player determines that he is playing near-perfect basic strategy and appears to be wagering with the count. The on-duty surveillance supervisor orders a complete evaluation be performed.

A more thorough evaluation is performed to determine that the player is, in fact, counting and not using any other advantage play system or displaying tells that indicate cheating. At the same time a search of surveillance databases is conducted.

The evaluation of the player determines that he is card counting only. He is also found in the database and is a known card counter who plays at casinos across the country. He normally plays until he is detected and leaves without issue.

The surveillance supervisor on duty now picks up the phone and calls the casino shift manager to report that the player is a confirmed card counter. Because the player is a card counter, is not a regular, is winning consistently and is now ahead several thousand dollars, the casino shift manager decides to back the counter off. The counter is approached and politely told that while he can play on other games he may not play blackjack. The counter cashes out his checks and leaves the property. Surveillance takes a number of identification photos of the counter that will be used to update the database for all casinos to use to identify the player if he visits their property.

Because advantage play is not against the law, telling him he can't play blackjack is as much as we can do in most jurisdictions (other jurisdictions prohibit backing off a player for advantage play but allow countermeasures such as shuffling up or flat betting) but it is effective and will stop the loss.

Note that the table games department normally makes the decision on how such a player will be handled. It is advantage play, not cheating, and does not require any response at all. It really is a business decision. If we think that the player is not a significant threat or we do not believe the player will beat us for a lot of money, then we may allow him to play. Or we stop him from play immediately because we don't want to risk dealing to him. These decisions are made by table games in consultation with surveillance. Developing and maintaining a good rapport between the departments is key to the effective handling of such incidents.

The normal next and final step is for surveillance to complete their report documenting the play, specifically identifying the wagers and card plays that determined the subject was counting cards, his buy-in and what he ended up winning or losing. Photos of the player and any other identifying information should be sent to the surveillance databases used by the surveillance department for the use of others.

It is a best practice to maintain hand charts or computer charts of the advantage player's play and attach them to the incident report. Video of the play should be placed into evidence. While advantage play is not illegal, issues can arise such as: the player claims he was misidentified as an advantage player; the pit believes he is not a counter; or the player claims he was mistreated. It is always wise to maintain the results of your evaluation and investigation.

Collusion in Table Games

Another common type of investigation performed in table games is one that involves collusion between a dealer and a player. Some collusion may involve a floor person, either working with the dealer and the player, or directly with the player. Some scams only require the unwitting assistance of the dealer or floor person, or the player.

One definition of collusion is: "An agreement between two or more people to defraud a person of his or her rights or to obtain something that is prohibited by law. A secret arrangement" (www.dictionary.com/browse/collusion).

There are many ways a dealer and player can collude to steal from the casino. For example, when a dealer agrees to "help" a player win by overpaying winning hands, or paying or pushing losing hands, that is collusion. Or the dealer may provide a player card information by flashing the top card or hole card. A floor person could also be involved with a dealer and/or a player to authorize credit for a certain amount but place more than the authorized amount on the game or even just alter or destroy the records of the transactions.

Such activity is usually reported by a guest or employee, or detected by surveillance. Regardless of how the conspiracy is found, a complete and thorough investigation will be necessary.

When we are looking at a case in which collusion is suspected it is important that we consider the following:

- Who is involved? We will want to identify all individuals involved before we begin responding to the incident. Once employees are interviewed or disciplined the activity will be stopped, at least temporarily, and suspects will disappear or will have time to cover their tracks. We don't want to move on a case before we know everyone who is involved.

- How does the scam work? We must make every effort to understand how the scam is being perpetrated. Hopefully, understanding the scam allows us to follow it, either through observation or video, or by tracing the paper trail from beginning to end, allowing us to see it unfold and observe each suspect's role in the crime. Obviously, the better we understand the scam, the better we are able to investigate it, identify all who are involved and ensure the proper evidence is obtained.

- How long has the scam been perpetrated? Certainly we want to know how long the scam has been in progress. Knowing this will give us a good estimate of how much money or property was stolen. We can use this information to put a cost to the theft in order to charge the suspects correctly and to seek restitution. As the law and legal process varies from state to state in how charges can be filed for a theft or fraud and how each incidence of that crime must be proven, the involvement of legal counsel is highly recommended.

- What can we actually prove? We may "know" a lot of things but knowing and proving are two different things. We may know that the suspect began stealing at a certain date because the paper trail of loss began on that date, however unless we can establish and document that the loss occurred and that the suspect was the one responsible for the loss, we may not be able to prove our case in its entirety. Many district attorneys and prosecutors will only charge suspects with what they feel can be proven beyond a shadow of a doubt and will not include incidences of theft/fraud that do not rise to that level.

Case History

Surveillance received a report from the table games manager that he had a dealer tell him that a floor person had made him pay out an incorrect amount to a player during a buy-in. The dealer stated that the same situation had occurred on at least two other occasions. The dealer, who had started only a few weeks before, at first thought that he had made mistakes when he paid the player that required correction, but the more he thought about it, the more he believed he'd been taken advantage of.

The player involved was a well-known local who owned a car dealership in town. He played blackjack regularly and was considered one of the casino's top players.

The floor man had worked at the property for a number of years. He had never been in trouble before but was known as a smart-ass and a "know it all".

Surveillance began the investigation by reviewing their logs and rating cards to locate recent play for the subject. A number of sessions were found but only two still had video remaining. The others were past the video retention.

Investigators thoroughly reviewed the video and located two buy-ins that were confusing and suspicious. On both occasions the dealer who reported the incidents was present and was being supervised by the floor person he had complained about.

Continued review determined that on both occasions the player bought in with $1,800 in cash. The dealer properly notified the floor person of a cash buy-in, and the floor person then walked over to the game to observe and supervise the transaction. The investigator noted that the dealer properly handled the transaction and placed the correct amount of checks on the game on each occasion. The floor person intervened and directed the dealer to stack the checks differently and ultimately added an additional $500 incorrectly for the player. Although the player bought in for $1,800 he received $2,300 on both occasions.

It was clear on video and backed up by the dealer's statement that the floor person had instructed the dealer to overpay the player.

The floor person was interviewed and claimed he had made a mistake on both occasions. When contacted, the player claimed he never realized he was overpaid although he could be clearly seen on video counting his cash and the checks when he received them.

The word was, in this small casino where everyone knew about everyone else, that the player and floor person were friends outside work. This was probably true but couldn't be proven.

Continued review of the video located no other person involved in the scam. Investigation determined that the floor person made up false information on a rating card to attribute the loss of $500 to a "refused name" player on both occasions.

Surveillance investigators concluded that the new and inexperienced dealer was used as a dupe by the floor person to overpay the player by $500 each time he bought in. The floor person attempted to confuse the dealer on each occasion, however the dealer wasn't fooled and ultimately reported the floor person's actions.

The case was turned over to the gaming commission for their investigation. Only the two incidents that were on video were considered because the one other incident the dealer was aware of could not be substantiated by video. Interestingly, other dealers came forward during and after the investigation to report their own concerns about the actions of the floor person and the player, but as noted no way existed to prove their allegations and these leads were not followed.

The floor person was arrested and ultimately lost his gaming license. The player, due to the efforts of his very good lawyer, was not arrested but was banned from property.

The above case is just an example of what surveillance investigates on a regular basis. Proper investigation and considering all information is always necessary.

Key Takeaways

- Cheating and advantage play should be investigated using criminal investigative protocols.
- In order to prove that cheating at gambling in table games did occur, it is usually necessary to prove that the suspects used the information obtained from marked or altered cards, etc.
- The gathering and securing of evidence including video, witness statements and physical evidence is critical for the success of the investigation.
- The location where the incident occurred should always be treated as a crime scene.
- Detection of cheating and advantage play requires surveillance personnel trained in the recognition of pertinent tells and behavior, and the ability to assess a player's skill/threat level.
- Collusion between employees and/or with outside agents can be very costly and difficult to detect.
- In most cases, only the circumstances of a crime that can be proven in a court of law will be included in charges filed by a district attorney's office.

Best Practices

- Surveillance personnel must be trained to recognize the tells and behavior of table games cheating and advantage play, and possess a thorough knowledge of the games and the ability to evaluate a player's skill level to properly assess their threat to the casino.
- Investigate table games incidents using criminal investigation protocols.
- Gaming equipment such as cards, dice, shoes etc. suspected of being altered or otherwise used to cheat at gaming should only be inspected by trained personnel.
- Until secured properly, evidence should remain on camera and recorded, or otherwise placed where it can't be tampered with or inadvertently damaged.
- Table game play suspected of being cheating or advantage play must be documented by surveillance using hand charts or computer analysis, and included in the surveillance report.
- In suspected cases of collusion the investigator should make every attempt to determine who is involved, how the scam is perpetrated, and secure all existing or potential evidence prior to interviewing witnesses or suspects.

Chapter 26

Investigation of Player's Clubs

Not your Mom and Pop Operation anymore. They're giving away more than toaster ovens and coffee makers.

Derk J. Boss

Every gaming property now has a player's club. These are the frequent flier clubs for our industry. We reward our players for gambling and other spending on our property. By tracking what and where they spend we can design offers and rewards to attract them back to stay and play again. Over the years player's clubs have grown to the point that they really are the central piece of our marketing strategy, or at least the one that is the most used and recognized.

Overall, player's clubs are an excellent tool to attract and retain players. And our comp programs of today are controlled to a much higher level than they used to be in the days of the "golden pen". Some of us still remember comping players because we "thought" they were good players rather than basing the comp on actual numbers such as we have today. I'm still amazed with how little players, who I thought were big players, actually played!

There is no question that we are better off today with player's clubs than we were without them. The clubs allow us to track each player for their time on device, amount wagered and win/loss, thus identifying their value to the casino and specifically determining what is returned to the player in comps.

However, as effective as they are, player's clubs are extremely vulnerable to theft and fraud. And because the club centralizes all marketing programs and promotions, and player information and their value, when fraud does occur the losses can be enormous. It isn't uncommon for a scam to cost a company tens of thousands of dollars and some scams have resulted in the loss of over a million dollars to the victim company.

Usually theft and fraud develops and continues in a club without being detected for a considerable period of time. This is why the loss can be so costly: because of the length of time it is allowed to continue. It is critical that methods to detect theft and fraud are in place.

In this chapter we'll discuss club operation, types of thefts and frauds found within the club, and methods to detect and investigate them.

Player's Clubs Operation

As mentioned previously, player's clubs are based on airline frequent flier programs. The more you play, the more rewards you receive. Your play is tracked whatever game you play (and on-property purchases such as meals, gift shop etc. are now also being tracked and awarded points) and points given for time on device and amount of wager. Play is tracked through the use of the club card that is issued to the player when he/she joins the club. From then on the player should use the card to obtain and redeem rewards.

Slot players insert their card into whatever machine they're playing. Their play, including each wager, is then tracked automatically and stored in their account. Slots, relatively and by far, is the easiest to track.

Table games is a different matter altogether. Floor personnel in the pit track a player's bets, buy-in and win/loss. This is called "rating a player". Usually the time of the playing session is tracked by swiping the player's card into a recording device on the game or by manually listing it on a card. Most casinos today use some type of automated tracking system. There are a number of player tracking systems on the market today. Some track wagers and time, and some just time. Almost all require some human involvement, and there are many casinos that still track players manually.

The speed of a game and skill level of the player is also part of the equation for rating a player. Both of these components are usually set at a default. Speed of the game, while it can vary extremely, is usually left at a medium level (in blackjack I usually see the default at sixty decisions per hour). The skill of a player is usually left at average because few people, besides surveillance, can actually determine it.

Individuals known as pit clerks are used at some properties to input the tracking information into the system in some cases or, as mentioned earlier, it is entered automatically.

As opposed to slots, there is a lot of room for error in table games. This is due to the necessity for human involvement, and the very nature of table games; determining player ratings requires floor personnel to determine an average bet for a player who may change his wager frequently and also often requires the floor person to depend on a dealer to report the player's buy-in and win/loss.

Players get rated for their play on all games: blackjack, craps, roulette, baccarat, poker and all the carnival games. Most player ratings are performed in blackjack and baccarat.

Rating information, once entered into the system, manually or automatically, is then housed in an individual player's account within the club. Each account contains the player's name, birthdate and address, value (points) and other information used to market to the player.

Player Account Security

Security of a player's account is the responsibility of the property. Most of the security is built into the software system itself by its manufacturer. The property and, more specifically, club management should provide additional layers of security to protect the card holder. In fact, several gaming jurisdictions now require minimum controls be established and maintained in order to prevent theft. This was done in response to the massive amounts of theft and fraud occurring within the clubs on a regular basis.

What you will generally see is system security based on access levels for employees requiring access to a player's account to open, close, add, edit, update and maintain the account, and identifiers required from the account owner to access the account such as proper identification and personal identification numbers (PIN).

Employee access levels are based on job title and/or responsibilities. A front line clerk should only have the access required to open or close an account, make simple updates to the account such as address changes, and issue authorized comps.

At the supervisor and manager level, access levels may include edit capability allowing name changes, point adjustments etc. to an account. Access levels for supervisors and managers usually vary by what can be edited and the value of point adjustments.

Player club tracking systems may be made by different manufacturers but they are all essentially the same and perform the same functions. Once you have a good understanding of one you will be able to work with them all.

The key to player's clubs for an investigator is that the controls in place to protect the club actually do work. It is just that they, like other controls and exceptions in the casino, are not normally or consistently monitored as they should be by the people in charge of the area or department. Checking for violations of controls and reviewing is an essential first step for the investigator attempting to uncover theft or fraud within the club.

It's important to note that most of the theft or fraud that occurs in the club is predicated on the necessary bypassing of controls or exceptions to normal operation. We must allow methods to do so in order to operate the club and adjust to changes in an account holder's life and to correct arising issues and problems.

For example, when a club member gets married and wishes to change her name within the system and on her card, there must exist a way for her to do this. An employee, of supervisor level or above, would, upon verifying the member's identification, enter the member's account and edit the account, updating it with the new name for the player.

Another example is when a member forgets their PIN. There must be a process to provide the member with a new PIN. As this occurs quite frequently every club does have such a process in place to assist the member.

Because we must necessarily provide for exceptions that occur, we also expose the club to attack from within and to collusion with outside agents. Again this is a reality we must accept and prepare for. Knowing that, the investigator can detect theft and fraud proactively during and after a crime has occurred through the use of exception reporting.

Table Game Player Rating Inaccuracies and Fraud

Table game ratings require special attention. Because there is some manual input involved in the rating of table game players you will usually find inaccurate information listed for a player's session and/or fraudulent information.

As mentioned previously, table game player ratings are not done automatically as they are in slots. In slots, because the play is tracked by the system, there is little error. In the pit, ratings, or at least some part of them, are done by a floor person who, like all humans, can make a mistake or take advantage of the system for their own benefit or that of their friends and family.

It has been my experience that table game player ratings are done incorrectly for the following reasons:

1. There is not a system/formula in place for determining a player's average bet or for accurate and consistent listing of a player's time for the session, buy-in or win/loss. This results in each floor person completing the rating differently and breeds inaccuracy and fraud.
2. There is a system/formula to be used but not all floor personnel use it properly.
3. Floor personnel often do not see all the players and must try to reconstitute their play.
4. Floor personnel do not approach every player that should be rated.
5. Supervisors fail to check/verify rating cards for accuracy and legitimacy.

Rating inaccuracies occur much more frequently than one would think. In fact, you can almost count on a good percentage of submitted ratings being incorrect in one area or another. This is important to keep in mind because when ratings are inaccurate/incorrect as a rule, it is much easier for a fraudster to cover his/her illicit activity and much more difficult to detect it.

Additionally, most table game operations use rating card information to balance the float using the player's buy-in and win/loss information. For example, a player walks winning $600. The floor person lists that on the rating card and/or inputs that information into the system. The $600 is deducted from the balance of the float, in this case, correctly. At the end of the shift and/or the day the float should balance with what was taken in through buy-ins with checks and the win/loss of players. Taking into account table/fills and credits during the shift/day and the rating card information, table games should know how much the float should have.

However, when the rating card lists a player win of $600 when the win was actually $300 the float is then incorrect. This allows a dealer and floor person working in collusion, for example, to safely remove $300 for themselves yet the float will remain correct as far as the paperwork is concerned.

Experienced surveillance personnel will remember that, in the past, the floor staff would often call surveillance to report that one table or another was short some black checks or even purple, and request surveillance review video to locate what happened to the checks. This call is rarely made these days. That's because floor personnel don't know if cheques are missing or not due to inaccurate player win/loss information. When the rating is wrong, the float is wrong.

The only method to actually verify player ratings in table games is for the surveillance department to compare the rating submitted or input into the system to the actual video of the play. It is a best practice for the surveillance department to conduct regular and frequent audits of player ratings.

Investigating Theft and Fraud

When a surveillance agent patrols through the player's club what he/she usually sees are clerks working on their computers as guests stand in front of them and others wait in line. Even if the agent zoomed in to read a clerk's computer screen it's unlikely he would see anything suspicious, even if the clerk was up to criminal activity. This is because live activity usually looks normal until it is compared to a detailed read-out of the activity or to an exception report.

For example, a surveillance agent watches a clerk as she assists a player in redeeming a coupon for twenty-five dollars of free play for a player. The activity appears normal but the clerk does not cancel the coupon in the system. The clerk appears to hit the right buttons on the computer but she is moving so fast the agent can't see what she's doing. Because the clerk did not cancel the coupon, the player (the clerk's friend) is able to redeem the coupon again and again.

The above example illustrates how fraudulent activity can occur even when the club is being monitored by surveillance. In order to properly monitor and/or investigate the player's club the investigator must compare system and exception reports to video of the activity to identify what actually is being done.

Note that while a number of scams can be perpetrated by employees of the club working on their own, other scams involve colluding with others outside the club. We call this the "friends and family plan" because when an employee must use an agent to receive stolen funds, points, free play or comps, he or she usually uses someone they know as the agent to fulfill that role.

There are two methods to investigate the player's club. Both are based on when the investigation is conducted.

Proactive Investigation

An excellent method to prevent, deter and detect theft and fraud from occurring in the club is to proactively search for red flags that may indicate illicit activity using system reports. There are numerous reports generated routinely by the club computer system to aid club management and the loss prevention team in the protection of the club.

Such reports can and should be used to monitor club activity and search for theft and fraud on a regular basis. Examples of some of these reports are below:

- PIN Change Report: Tracks issuance of and changes made to PINs.
- Name Change Report: Tracks name changes made to individual accounts.
- Merge Report: Tracks account merges (e.g. man and wife decide to merge two accounts into one).
- Transfer Report: Tracks point transfers between accounts and/or to an account (i.e. a points adjustment).
- Point Adjustment Report: Tracks points that are manually added to an account. Often used to resolve a complaint or correct a machine malfunction.
- Redemption Report: Tracks redemption of points.
- Comp Issue Report: Tracks comps issued to account holders.
- Free Play Issue Report: Tracks who is issued free play and how much.
- Top Pointer Earner Report: Identifies who the top point earners are during a specified time period.

Of course, there may be other reports, or other reports may be developed. A thorough understanding of the system and what reports are available is necessary. What investigators should do is review available club reports on a regular basis. As discussed in previous chapters a best practice is to assign an investigator to review these reports each day for indicators of theft or fraud. Such a review usually takes under an hour to perform each day and can save a company from losing many thousands of dollars.

Proactive investigation can detect developing and existing theft and frauds occurring within the player's club and should be used on a regular basis. A good method to assist in doing this is through the assignment of audits.

Reactive Investigation

Reactive investigation means that the criminal activity is already in progress or is fully developed, and has been in operation for a period of time. Usually investigators are made aware of the crime by a tip from another employee and/or a complaint from a guest. The investigator must now obtain the necessary reports and information confidentially and in such a fashion so as not to alert the suspect(s).

As we've discussed in previous chapters, be very careful about who you speak to and obtain reports from. Anyone could be involved in the scam or may mention your interest to the wrong person. The best way to follow up on tips and criminal activity that has been detected is to have access to the reports and information you need already in place.

It is important to remember in club investigation and almost any other gaming investigation that there is almost always some type of paper trail (reports, statistical, exceptions etc.) that can be picked up and followed to the suspect.

Let's take a look at what we've discussed in action.

Case History

A surveillance agent is patrolling through the pit and as he moves his camera past the pit clerk working on her computer in the middle of the pit he sees the clerk hide a piece of paper underneath her keyboard. Thinking this was suspicious activity he zooms his camera in and observes the clerk more closely.

He next observes that the account the clerk is working in is in her name, and that she appears to be editing the account. It isn't unusual for employees of some casinos to gamble on their property or have an account. However, an employee shouldn't be able to access and edit their account.

The surveillance agent continues to monitor the clerk's activities and observes that she keeps referring to the list she has placed under her keyboard. On the list are a number of names. The agent can see that the clerk accesses the accounts of those names listed. As she calls up each name on the list she removes the name of the account owner and replaces it with her own thus taking ownership of the account.

The surveillance agent reports his observation to his supervisor and an investigation is initiated. First the clerk's account is reviewed. It is quickly determined that the clerk has more points in her account than even some of the casino's biggest players! Review of the redemption activity reveals that the clerk consistently redeems her points for gourmet meals, hotel suites and cash back.

Review of her play history shows only minor play and there is no history that relates to earned points. In other words, the system will track and record on what machine(s) a player earned their points. This allows the surveillance to locate a player on video when necessary and observe their activity. In the clerk's case, there wasn't any history to review as she had stolen the points from someone else.

It was noted also that the accounts she had targeted were players who were tourists who visited the property once to twice a year meaning it was unlikely that theft of their points would be reported for a period of time, if at all.

The investigators compared the clerk's address to others in the club database to see if anyone else in her household also had accounts. They found that two additional account holders lived at the same address (they were identified as the clerk's fiancé and their roommate). Both of the accounts were similar to the clerk's; high value with little or no play listed. They also obtained comps and cash back.

The investigators then checked with auditing for any existing reports that may provide further information. They were provided with a report that listed name changes made to any account, who made them and when they were made. These reports were issued every day for review by auditing and the club manager, however no one reviewed these reports. The investigators quickly found that each time the clerk changed an account to her name it was listed on the report. Unfortunately they also determined that she had been doing it for eighteen months!

The reports also uncovered another issue. The clerk was just that, a clerk. According to computer access protocols she should not have had access to the "edit" function. Only a supervisor or above should have the ability to access that function. In this case the clerk was given the access by the club manager to assist the manager when the manager was on her days off or on vacation. This access allowed the clerk to perpetrate her crime.

The investigators determined that the clerk, her fiancé and their roommate took over one hundred and fifty accounts over an eighteen month period and cost the property over $100,000 in cash and expenses for rooms, food and beverages, as well as reimbursements made to victims.

As the points were earned by players from gambling the crime was reported to the Nevada GCB. The clerk was arrested and charged with forty counts of computer fraud.

All of this could and should have been prevented by proactively monitoring the exception reports issued each day.

Key Takeaways

- The player's club is the central database for almost all casino marketing and promotion activity.
- Clubs are extremely vulnerable to theft and fraud and can cost the property hundreds of thousands of dollars if such activity is not detected.
- Almost all theft and fraud occurring in the club is perpetrated by club employees working alone, or by the employee working in collusion with "friends and family".

- Most theft and fraud is perpetrated through the unauthorized use of necessary exceptions and adjustments made to accounts by club employees for the benefit of account holders.
- Investigators can proactively monitor exception reports to detect illicit activity and use such reports to investigate criminal activity within the club.
- Ensure computer access level to key functions within the system is established and issued correctly. Generic logins and passwords should be prohibited. Each club employee should have their own login and password that is changed on a regular basis.
- Assigning one person to monitor a player's club's daily reports and exceptions will detect existing and developing theft and fraud.

Best Practices

- The player's club should be well covered with strategically placed cameras that can observe clearly all activities occurring within the club areas.
- The ability to clearly observe, monitor and record what a clerk is entering into the computer can assist investigations tremendously. There are a number of systems that can be used such as econnect to accomplish this task. Cameras dedicated to each computer in the club can accomplish much the same mission.
- Ensure employee access levels to player's club computer systems and databases are established and controlled. Only supervisors and managers should be able to access higher-level functions.
- Review operating and exception reports regularly to detect suspicious activity, and to investigate reported criminal activity.
- Player ratings in table games should be audited on a regular basis by the surveillance department.

Chapter 27

Investigation of Marketing Scams

I've never seen a marketing promotion not get ripped off.

Derk J. Boss

Marketing programs and promotions are normally not monitored by surveillance or security personnel. In fact, it's probably the last thing we think about. After all, such programs would be hard to rip off because they are usually programs or promotions set up and operated internally by people we know and work with, and we expect that they will be monitored by our audit personnel. Besides, most promotions consist of small payouts or inexpensive gifts. Nothing can be further from the truth. Marketing programs and promotions are easy to rip off with a little collusion between employees and/or an outside agent. Costs of theft or fraud, or even players taking advantage of a poorly designed program, can be in the hundreds of thousands. In my experience I have never seen a marketing program or promotion not get ripped off. These programs and promotions deserve your attention.

It wasn't too long ago that we didn't pay any attention to the marketing department at all. A lot of us figured that they gave away coffee mugs and t-shirts and didn't require our attention. Additionally, we thought that since they designed their marketing programs and promotions they would be responsible for monitoring and protecting them. I think it's safe to say that we've all learned that marketing staff aren't trained in loss prevention and they do need our support.

The protection of marketing is best served by preventing scams from occurring in the first place. Proper design, preparation and planning of a program or promotion allow the installation of fundamental controls to aid in loss prevention, and will assist in an investigation when a scam occurs. Both the marketing and surveillance departments should work together to ensure that loss prevention is considered when developing a new program or promotion.

Working together will reduce the opportunity for theft and fraud, and will increase the likelihood that it will be detected should it develop. However, there will always be individuals who will devise ways to commit theft and fraud, thus we cannot eliminate it entirely. We must always remain vigilant.

As we've discussed throughout this book, in gaming the investigation for theft and fraud has two separate components: looking for indicators of a scam on a routine basis in order to detect it before it becomes a significant loss, and investigating a scam after it has been detected or reported. Both components are critical and must be understood by the investigator.

Proactive surveillance departments should include marketing areas, programs and promotions in their audit rotation to monitor each for any red flags that could indicate the presence of theft or fraud. Unfortunately, we can't always depend, nor should we, on those in marketing to alert us to suspicious activity. It's important to note that marketing executives, managers and supervisors are normally not trained in loss prevention and are usually unaware of what to look for.

Routinely monitoring and auditing marketing programs and promotions for fraud should detect most existing and developing scams. However, we can't prevent all scams from occurring. Some will get through. We must be prepared to investigate those scams that come to light through tips, internal audit, guest complaints etc.

Investigation of marketing theft and fraud is based on identifying the individuals involved and determining the method(s) used to perpetrate the activity. In most cases, a marketing manager or supervisor will report to the investigator a tip received from an employee or a complaint received from a guest. The information received normally involves what an employee has seen another employee do such as giving a free play voucher to someone who doesn't deserve it, or a guest report that something is wrong with their account such as the points they thought they had are not there, or their comps aren't available as they should be. In all such reports an investigation is warranted.

Theft and fraud usually happen when there is value present. As most, if not all, marketing programs and promotions involve earning more points or cash during a specific time period, giving away cash or gifts, or winning a prize, there is always value present, ensuring that every program and promotion is vulnerable to attack.

It has been my experience that every program and promotion does get attacked, whether it is by the employee, players or both working together. I recommend that surveillance and other loss prevention teams keep this in mind and prepare to protect each program and promotion. Of course, due to the number of marketing efforts going on even at one property, you can't be everywhere. You will probably only be able to monitor and protect the programs/promotions with the most value and/or that are the most vulnerable. We will discuss this further later in the chapter.

It is important to note a few things I've learned about marketing over the years that I feel will aid you in protecting yours:

1. Marketing departments don't always know what they are doing when it comes to gaming. They often come up with ideas to market table games or slots that give away the house edge. For example, running a promotion to

increase blackjack play that pays 2 to 1 on a blackjack instead of 3 to 2 not only reduces the house edge but will probably attract only the skilled players and advantage players. You can expect this particular promotion to lose money (and cause surveillance a lot of trouble while it's being run). Marketing should check with knowledgeable people in table games or surveillance to determine if their promotion is mathematically sound.

2. Guests, players and even employees will find the weakness in a program or promotion before we do. I've seen it over and over again. If there is a weakness in what you're putting out there, it will be found and taken advantage of within twenty-four hours of when the program/promotion begins. Believe it or not, there are players out there who study the promotions that are out there just to find where they are vulnerable to attack and will do so immediately. Normal guests will find out about the weakness and will also take advantage of it. You would expect employees to be aware of and report that something is unusual about the promotion. Unfortunately, I've found that employees usually don't pay any attention to such activity, or may not say anything because they are being tipped. Another issue arises if employees are allowed to participate in the promotion: if employees are allowed to do so you can expect that they will also take advantage of the weakness. For example, a marketing department decided to run a promotion on a bank of video poker machines to increase their play. They increased the return to 101 percent payback. They did this knowing that they may lose a little but would make up the difference in handle. The promotion works and the play on that bank increases dramatically. However, surveillance notices that each of these particular machines is constantly in action around the clock, every day. The surveillance director checks the numbers on the machines and finds that they are losing drastically. He then looks into the players and finds that some are known advantage players. Continued investigation determines that the players found that by using a video poker strategy system (readily available in books and on the internet) they could take significant advantage of the machines. Most of the money to play the machines was fronted by a well-known blackjack counter. To add insult to injury the players were earning a tremendous amount of points for cash back and comps. The machines were immediately converted back to their original par. The machines lost tens of thousands of dollars in less than a week.

3. Be extremely wary of a marketing program/promotion that is a tremendous hit (very popular) and obtains considerable attention from players. It may indicate that there is a weakness in the promotion that is being exploited.

4. Every program/promotion gets taken advantage of. It is a best practice to ensure that the security of the programs/promotions be considered in order to prevent unnecessary losses.

Auditing Marketing Programs and Promotions

Audits of marketing programs/promotions should be performed on a regular basis. However, the sheer number of promotions in operation at any given time at any casino can be overwhelming. We can easily tie up our personnel on marketing alone to the neglect of every other department.

It is recommended that audits be focused on those programs and promotions that can result in the largest losses, may be subject to frequent loss and/or would cause damage to the property's reputation should they be taken advantage of or otherwise compromised. Additionally, each program/promotion should be checked on a regular basis to ensure it is performing as expected.

An audit should look at a number of things, most of them paper (expense reports, inventory logs, list of winners etc.) and some video (how do individuals obtain entries, observation of gift redeemers and winners, etc.). The paperwork is readily available from marketing personnel or audit/accounting. If you're working closely with these departments and have developed a good rapport, obtaining such documents shouldn't be a problem. Of course it may not be that easy in some jurisdictions or with some people. In some cases you may have to go over a person's head to get what you need. Working with marketing and auditing beforehand may help avoid this problem.

When reviewing the paper you are looking for the following:

1. Individuals who win promotional contests and drawings frequently.
2. Individuals who redeem or obtain points or free play frequently.
3. Friends or family of employees winning programs/promotions and redeeming points/free play frequently.
4. Missing coupons or certificates from inventory.
5. Expenses for program/promotion over budget.
6. Frequent changes or adjustments to player accounts by the same employee.

Observation and review of video should include the following:

1. Observation of the club to ensure card holders are present when new accounts are opened or changes are made to account.
2. Identification of employees/card holders present when new accounts are opened and account changes are made.
3. Observation and/or review of drawings or contests for consistent winners.

4. Checking of employees responsible for distribution of tickets, points, gifts and free play for suspicious activity.
5. Checking for continuous play or activity of slot machines, table games or other areas such as bingo or poker, indicating the program/promotion is very popular and may have a weakness or vulnerability.

As mentioned in Chapter 26, it is a surveillance best practice to assign one person to monitor the player's club. Because the club is part of the marketing department the person assigned to monitor and audit the club can also monitor marketing programs and promotions.

The club and programs/promotions should be monitored daily and audited at least once per month.

Investigation of Marketing Programs and Promotions

When a scam, theft or fraud does develop and is detected or reported, an investigation will be conducted. As in all investigations we need to determine who is involved, how the scam is perpetrated, the amount of value or property taken, when it occurred and for how long, and where it takes place. Why it occurred is usually determined later in the investigation. There will be personal motives for those involved as well as breakdowns or violations of controls, policies or procedures that allowed the scam to occur.

A marketing investigation normally requires that we identify the person(s) involved and the method used to commit the crime. Usually the person involved will be an employee and the method he/she uses will be associated with the work duties assigned and/or within the work area itself. Because this is so, it is usually easy for the investigator to identify the employee involved and what he/she is doing.

A good first step is to identify and review the transaction records for the program/promotion. Most of what we need to look at will be inventory control sheets, redemption logs and winner lists. Inventory control sheets should list coupons, tickets, gifts etc. issued by employee and location. Redemption logs should list the persons who redeemed their free play, coupon or tickets. Winner's lists include the guests who won the program/promotion. These records may be paper or held electronically.

We review these records to locate suspicious activity such as: inventory variances that indicate missing coupons, tickets or gifts; or too many items issued to one location. This may indicate an employee is giving out unearned coupons, tickets or gifts, stealing the items or both.

In order for coupons or tickets to have value they must be redeemed. Reviewing the redemption lists may tell us who is redeeming an unusual number of coupons or tickets, or has too many entries in a contest/draw.

The list of winners will show us who's been winning the program/promotion. Someone who wins consistently should be investigated. We want to know how it became possible for that person win at all and certainly why it was more than once. It's quite possible they had a helping hand. Now that we have identified that winner as a person of interest we can focus on determining how the wins occurred. This is a matter of pinpointing what a person needs to do in order to win, such as playing a slot machine during a "Hot Seat" promotion. In this type of promotion, a slot player is selected randomly by a computer to win a prize. The question now becomes: how did one player get selected so often?

In the above case, an investigator should look into the situation as it was when the player won. Questions could be asked such as: How many players were in action at the time of the win? Did the winner play regularly or only during the selection period? Is the winner in some way related to an employee in marketing or slots? Answering these questions may lead the investigator to why this player won so often.

Note that "Hot Seat" promotions have been beaten in the past in just such a manner. In an actual investigation of a player who had won the promotion several times, the player was found to be a friend of the employee operating the computer that selected the winner. It was found that although the computer selected a player randomly, the employee could override the selection by starting the selection process over again. The employee overrode the selections until the friend was selected.

Case History

A casino started a promotion in which players would win scratch tickets that would pay different amounts of money (from $5 to $100); if, when scratched, the amounts matched on the ticket, the person won the amount listed. Players received these tickets as they played any game in the casino. Employees being allowed to gamble on this property were also allowed to receive the tickets.

It wasn't long before the cage reported that an unusual number of employees were cashing in tickets and that the ones they did cash in were the higher values ($50 to $100). Surveillance was notified and began an investigation.

Surveillance began by determining how the tickets were distributed, to whom they were given and how they were issued to the players. They found that each gaming department was issued a certain number of new tickets. These were then passed out to players as they gamed. Surveillance decided to monitor the keno department to observe how the tickets were given to employees. Surveillance had selected keno as the number of tickets from keno (determined by serial numbers on the ticket and compared to master distribution list) that were redeemed by employees was significantly higher than usual.

As soon as surveillance began observing the keno department the case was solved. Keno employees were observed opening packets of tickets, removing individual tickets and holding a flashlight under the ticket. The majority of tickets were replaced in the packet; others were removed and set aside.

Further investigation determined that the keno employees had found that by holding a light underneath the ticket the symbols on the ticket could be seen. Thusly, the employee could easily identify winning tickets and isolate the higher paying tickets for themselves. The keno employees soon shared their discovery with other employees and they used the trick as well.

A number of keno employees were terminated for their involvement in the theft. As a result of this incident, a disclaimer was listed on all new programs/promotions prohibiting employees or their immediate family from participating.

This incident, while easily solved, illustrates how marketing scams can be solved.

Key Takeaways

- Deterrence of marketing scams through the coordination of loss prevention and marketing teams and regular audits will prevent most scams from occurring.
- Investigating marketing scams requires a good understanding of how programs/promotions are supposed to operate, and reviewing pertinent reports.
- Most marketing scams are reported by a tip from an employee or a guest.
- Most, if not all, marketing programs/promotions are attacked by employees, guests or both.
- Those who devise marketing programs/promotions may not understand gaming or loss prevention, and may set up a program/promotion that is inherently vulnerable and/or can be taken advantage of.
- Players often find a weakness in the program/promotion before anyone else.
- A marketing program/promotion that is very popular may be so due to the fact that it can be easily beaten or otherwise taken advantage of.

Best Practices

- Surveillance and/or loss prevention should work with marketing to prevent scams from occurring. Implementing a marketing program/promotion protection committee for the protection and monitoring of upcoming promotions is very effective.
- Plan to audit new and ongoing programs/promotions on a regular basis.
- Assign one agent/investigator to monitor programs/promotions.

Chapter 28

Investigation of Keno and Bingo

Rarely monitored areas that can contain long-running employee collusion with outside agents.

Derk J. Boss

Bingo and keno are games that have been played and enjoyed for many years. While bingo remains consistently popular, keno's popularity has declined, although there has been a recent increase in its play across the United States. What hasn't changed for either game is the potential for theft, fraud or cheating. While scams in these areas aren't reported often, the fact is that both games are vulnerable and are attacked, despite the use of technology in recent years to operate and protect these games. The investigator will learn that these games are usually operated without routine observation by surveillance personnel, and that the long-term employees in these areas can work with long-time players to maybe increase their tokes, and perhaps to collude to beat the game.

Bingo games are operated at casinos throughout the country both in tribal and commercial casinos. Keno, although fast disappearing, is still hanging on and it may even make a comeback. For these reasons both games must be considered.

Both of these games are somewhat similar. Each is based on random numbers being selected. In bingo the numbers are selected by a computerized random number generator (RNG) or manual blower or other manual system to select a number, or a ball with a number on it, one at a time, from a pool of 125 balls. As each number or ball is selected, it is called out by an employee. Players who have the number called on their bingo card mark their card. The first player to cover the required number of spots wins a pre-determined prize.

In keno, players select numbers from a keno ticket containing eighty numbers. The number of spots selected, and how they are grouped, determine the payoff if the ticket wins. In keno, as in bingo (seventy-five numbers), the numbers are selected by a RNG or manual system. To win, the numbers selected must match the numbers on the player's tickets and the "way" that is marked.

Both keno and bingo have a significant house edge, about twenty-five to thirty percent for keno and about twenty to forty percent for bingo, making them a great game for the house. I've seen keno hold twenty to twenty-eight percent, and bingo can be anywhere from five to fifteen percent.

When keno or bingo are cheated it usually takes the form of a false jackpot perpetrated by an employee, outside agent or both colluding together. Over the years, lower awards all the way to the maximum win in keno of $50,000 have been targeted.

Like several other departments, theft and cheating occur in keno and bingo primarily because of the lack of a consistent surveillance presence. Surveillance tends to leave these departments alone due to the low amount of money at risk and the infrequent payment of the larger jackpots. We will discuss keno and bingo together as they are so similar in their operations.

Scams and theft that occur in keno and bingo normally revolve around fraudulent payouts. Employees may create a false win or jackpot, increase the amount of a legitimate payout, duplicate a legitimate payout, past post a game to win a payout or jackpot, or manipulate the balls in the drawing device to force a win.

There is no doubt that there are other scams or that new ones will be developed.. However, the majority of scams and/or theft will involve the above. The key to deterring and detecting fraud and theft in keno and bingo is through the consistent review of the pertinent operational reports and paperwork and its associated video.

Auditing Keno and Bingo

As in the other areas we monitor and audit, key transactions are what we want to stay on top of. In keno and bingo those are as follows:

- Ball draw and/or number selection
- The numbers that are entered into the system and displayed on the boards as drawn
- Wins and jackpots
- The individuals winning the larger wins and jackpots
- Employee tokes
- Variances

While there are probably other transactions that bear watching, the above are the most important. As always, it is about following the money. Let's discuss each transaction or activity type:

Ball draw: Whether balls are selected manually or by a RNG, it is important to make sure that the numbers entered into the system are the same as the ones drawn. This is especially important in manual system with blowers and rabbit ears. Over the years such systems have been beaten by failing to clear the rabbit ears of balls from the previous game completely, leaving all or some of the balls in place. This allows the confederates of the employees to bet on the balls still in the tubes and to win illicitly. Another method is for an employee to ignore the numbers drawn and enter their confederate's numbers into the system. We must compare the draw to the system display.

Numbers displayed: The numbers drawn are then entered into the system and displayed on the board for players to see. If the employee enters numbers other than those drawn, illicit payments may be made to outside agents. It is normally required that an employee other than the one entering the numbers verify that those numbers are the ones drawn. However, this control may be bypassed for any number of reasons, including collusion to set up a false jackpot or payment. As mentioned previously, we should check the numbers drawn against the numbers displayed, particularly in larger payments and jackpots.

Wins and jackpots: Verification of payments and jackpots should be made at established levels. It isn't enough to only verify the larger ones. Remember that employees know that large payments and jackpots are verified by surveillance. The lower that surveillance can drop that review level the better keno and bingo are protected. It forces employees and/or outside agents to lower the amount they can take. It is a surveillance best practice to review payments and jackpots at a level that will prevent theft of payments or jackpots at minimum levels. For example, any payment or jackpot of $2,500 or more can be reviewed by surveillance for suspicious activity.

The amount paid out should match the wager made. In both keno and bingo the more you wager on your ticket or the more you pay for your bingo card the more you will be paid when you win. Employees may pay a win for a higher amount that was not wagered. The amount wagered should also be checked.

Individual winners of payouts and jackpots: If an employee is working in collusion with outside agents they will more than likely be friends and family of that employee. Winners should be checked for their relationship with employees. We should also be on the lookout for an individual who wins more than once. It is important to make sure that the individual is winning legitimately and not receiving some type of assistance.

Employee tokes: Of course it is okay for employees to receive tokes, if they are allowed to do so. It should be concerning when employees are making a lot of tokes and/or there is a sudden surge in tokes. Normally, tokes are recorded for tax purposes leaving a paper trail that can be checked and monitored. The reason we do so is that one method to "launder" stolen funds is by placing the funds into tips. Additionally, employees may be receiving extra tips from certain players for services rendered such as free tickets or bingo boards, extra drink or meal tickets, illicit payouts, etc. An individual or department that receives a significant amount of tokes and/or a sudden, dramatic increase in tokes may be signaling the presence of theft or collusion.

Variances: Shortage and overages indicate an employee made a mistake when paying out or receiving cash. It may also indicate theft. A shortage may occur due to a mistake or theft from the employee's cash drawer. An overage may occur due to a mistake or the employee's inability to keep track of what he/she has stolen. It is a surveillance best practice to investigate variances of $100 or more.

If these transactions and activities are monitored on a regular basis the likelihood of being scammed or ripped off will be reduced. However, there is always a way to beat any system and someone will always find a way to do so. We should be prepared to investigate a report or indication of theft or fraud.

Investigation of Theft or Fraud in Keno or Bingo

Most keno or bingo thefts and frauds occur on the payouts and jackpots. This makes sense because that is where the most money is located. As such, there are two categories of theft/fraud we should consider for payouts/jackpots. These are the setup of false payment/jackpots and payment of false payment/jackpots.

Setup of Payment/Jackpots

As discussed previously, one method used to set up false payments/jackpots is to fake the winning combination or draw to allow payment. In other words, the scammer must ensure that the numbers he or she needs to authorize the payout are displayed. There are a couple of ways to do this that have been used over the years.

In a manual system an employee can leave all the balls in the ears from the previous game, or even just a few balls. Doing so allows a confederate to select those numbers and bet accordingly. Very easy to do if no one verifies that the ears were clear before the game started. Yes, the controls require that another employee verify that the ears were cleared, but we all know that controls are bypassed all the time, accidently and on purpose.

Another method used to beat the manual game is to alter the balls or use damaged balls. If you place a brand new ball in with balls that have been in use for a period of time it is likely that new ball may come up more often. That is because it is not as heavy as the others that may be covered in dust from use. Another method used is to put a pinhole or small dent in a ball or a number of balls. Again, doing so may help or hinder that ball in its selection. Either way, the ball selection will be changed to allow the prediction of the numbers selected, and wagers made accordingly.

That is why surveillance must be called whenever the balls are changed and why we require that when one ball is changed, they must all be changed.

Nowadays, most gaming properties use RNGs to draw numbers in keno and bingo. I think that whenever we use technology we have a false sense of security that it can't be beaten. That certainly isn't true. There is always a way to beat anything and that is certainly true for any system that requires employee involvement. An employee that works with a system each and every day knows how the system can be beaten and will use that knowledge when necessary.

An example of this is the case of Ronald Dale Harris. He was a computer programmer that worked for the Nevada GCB whose job was to test slot machine programs and other types of gaming programs for glitches and errors. He went to the dark side and began setting up the programs he was testing to pay jackpots to his accomplices. He set up a RNG for a keno game to hit a $100,000 jackpot in Atlantic City in the early 1990s. His accomplice was caught when attempting to collect the jackpot because he didn't appear to be excited to have won the money, which raised suspicions.

It is important to remember the RNG will do its job by randomly selecting and posting numbers. Once that is done the employee becomes involved and potentially can manipulate or bypass systems controls to create falsified payouts or jackpots. Of course this is where the investigator can catch them through the verification of the numbers and payout.

Another way to manipulate payouts and jackpots is to pay a higher amount than what is authorized, either by fraudulently increasing the amount wagered or altering the type of bet made (ways) on the ticket. In bingo, higher denomination cards may be purchased that increase the amount of a payout or jackpot. Claiming that a player won on a more expensive card than actually purchased is another method used to scam the system.

The above are some of the ways used to falsify and/or manipulate payouts and jackpots in keno and bingo. There are others occurring out there, I'm sure, that we're not even aware of yet. The key to detecting any such scam is verifying the actual wager, win and payout through review of video and documentation. When the investigator follows the audit trail it should take him/her to the point where the payout or jackpot was manipulated.

Fraudulent payouts and jackpots are accomplished more easily through the collusion of employees and/or employees using outside agents. When collusion is involved it is more difficult to catch because the control (verification by more than one employee) designed to prevent one person from committing the act has been breached. It is believed to be more difficult for one individual to convince another individual to conspire to commit an act of dishonesty. In fact, casinos base their entire payout system on the use of more than one person for a payout. Nowadays we also use technology, such as electronic verification from the slot machine involved in the payout, as a separate verification. Unfortunately when collusion is involved this control is easily bypassed.

Such fraudulent activity can be detected and/or investigated by confirming the legitimacy of the wager, the draw and the payout/jackpot.

Variances

Overages and shortages should be investigated. Of course, we can't investigate them all. As we've mentioned previously in this text, it is a surveillance best practice to investigate any variance of $100 or more. This includes overages. Overages may indicate an employee has placed or kept stolen funds in the register or otherwise mixed in with company funds and has lost count of the amount taken. It also may indicate the employee shorted a customer. Both should be resolved.

It is important for the investigator to remember that variances should be accounted for. Many investigators treat variances as minor issues, and give up quickly if the variance isn't found easily. This is a mistake because variances are often the red flag indicating an existing or developing theft or fraud. Not all thefts and frauds are sophisticated; an employee can steal a considerable amount of money right out of the register and may do so until caught.

Because we usually have keno and bingo thoroughly covered with cameras we should usually locate the variance. In fact, it should be rare that we do not locate the variance. As mentioned above we often treat variances as minor issues and don't spend the time to determine why they occurred. If we treat variances for what they are we may detect the underlying scam. At the very least, because it will be apparent that we do treat variances seriously, we send out a strong message to departments and individuals that variances are investigated thoroughly, possibly deterring potential thefts.

Most, if not all, variances will be located in the paperwork. Because casinos do track money very well from the documented issue of funds to a cashier or department, tracking of sales, credits, fills and payouts throughout the shift and the return of the funds/bank at the end of the shift or day, where and when the variance occurred should be located. Continued investigation should locate the individual(s) responsible.

Case History

A casino GM was looking over the daily numbers for the casino when his attention was drawn to the hold in keno for the day and noticed that the win percentage for the day was in the minus. Looking further he noted that there hadn't been a lot of play, at least not enough to account for the loss. Concerned, he called the surveillance director to get his thoughts.

The director agreed that the numbers were odd but reminded the GM that the numbers do jump around day to day. The director said he would look into it immediately and get right back to him.

The director called back within thirty minutes. He told the GM that something was wrong. Not only was the daily number low but it had been low for the last two months, holding twenty percent when it had normally held twenty-five percent. The director told the GM that surveillance would begin a thorough investigation.

It didn't take long at all. Verifying the two largest jackpot ($2,000 and $1,500) paid from the previous evening one thing stood out immediately: the same person won both. Of course, that does happen, but it could be suspicious.

Reviewing the wins, surveillance started with the draw. The numbers drawn and displayed in the rabbit ears were the same. The wins were paid correctly for the ticket and the documentation was completed properly with the proper signatures.

The investigator then noticed that the time stamp on the winning ticket was later than the start of the game by about three minutes. Next he reviewed the video to determine when the bet was placed. He observed that the player arrived at the window and gave the ticket to the clerk before the game was called, as it should have been. However, instead of the ticket being time stamped and placed into the system it was handed back to the supervisor at the main station. The player did not receive a copy of her original ticket of her selections back as required.

The investigator then pulled the video from the supervisor's desk and observed the following. The supervisor held the ticket while the game was called. When the draw was completed the supervisor then marked the ticket and entered it into the system. Of course the ticket won and the player returned to the counter and was then given the ticket and paid for the win. Obviously the supervisor had found a way to past post the system and was working in collusion with the other employee and the player.

The investigator reviewed back as far as he could go (eight days) and found that on six of those days the player won at least twice. On the remaining two days a different crew was in place and the fraudulent payments did not occur.

The investigator had the tickets pulled by auditing. He found that on each ticket a five number combination was played for $5 that, when hit, paid $1,000. However, a good estimate of what had been stolen could be made by identifying (through statistical information and the particular bet that was made) when the losses began occurring (about sixty days prior). It appeared that the casino had lost about $80,000 (two $1,000 jackpots each day, five days a week).

When interviewed the employees readily admitted the fraud. The supervisor had found a glitch in the system that allowed her to enter a bet after the game had already been run. This was accomplished by changing the time of the game to allow her to submit the ticket and then changing the time back. She then convinced the clerk to join her in the theft. The player was the sister of the clerk. They only committed the frauds in amounts under $1,200 to avoid having to complete a tax form. All three individuals were arrested by the GCB.

A critical thing to remember in this and in any other so-called foolproof system: the system can always be beaten!

Key Takeaways

- Fraudulent payouts and jackpots are a common method used to cheat keno and bingo.
- Employees colluding together and/or with outside agents to set up and collect fraudulent payments and jackpots is a primary threat to both keno and bingo.
- Most, if not all, theft and fraud occurring in keno and bingo can be detected and/or investigated through the audit trail.
- The same individuals consistently winning and collecting jackpots may indicate theft or fraud is occurring.
- An increase in employee tokes or variances may be a red flag that theft or fraud is occurring, and should be investigated.

Best Practices

- Surveillance coverage of keno and bingo should include the drawing device, the rabbit ears or other such device containing the drawn balls, the display board, employee and supervisor work stations, customer windows and an overview of the entire keno/bingo area.
- Surveillance should conduct regular patrols and audits of keno and bingo.
- Surveillance should establish a limit when a review of a payment or jackpot is required, such as $2,500 or above.
- Surveillance must be notified whenever the balls are changed.
- Review the activity and wins of consistent winners.

Chapter 29

Investigation of the Race and Sports Book

A little-understood operation with a lot of value that attracts professional players and wise guys.

Derk J. Boss

The race and sports book is not completely understood by most people, and that includes the people charged with protecting it. As we've seen throughout our discussions, we've grown too dependent on our own technology to protect our games and forget the need for regular monitoring. Tremendously large amounts of money can be wagered at a sports book, especially for events such as the Super Bowl or March Madness, which will and do draw the attention of those looking for a score. Of course, as always, the potential for internal theft or collusion with outside agents also exists. With the recent proliferation of sports books around the country the potential for scams to be used against these areas only increases. Investigators be warned!

The race and sports book is probably the least understood gaming operation in the casino. Where allowed to operate, the race and sports book (book) often sits off by itself and is rarely visited by casino executives and managers, or patrolled by surveillance. Most people, including experienced gaming personnel, aren't really sure how the book works and just leave it alone or only enter it to make football bets during their breaks.

Of course, as we've seen with the other gaming operations, such lack of specific knowledge inhibits the deterrence of fraudulent activity (because we don't know what to look for), and there will be a learning curve for any investigator assigned to investigate a case of theft or fraud.

To prevent and detect theft and fraud in the book we should treat the race and sports book as we do every other department by developing a good understanding of how the department operates and its controls, understanding the types of theft and fraud that are common to the book, and conducting regular audits to detect the red flags of illicit activity.

Let's begin with gaining an understanding as to how the book operates.

Sportbook Operation

In their excellent book *Practical Casino Math, Second Edition* (Trace, 2005), Robert C. Hannum and Anthony N. Cabot say:

> In sports wagering, the better is not playing against the casino as in games like blackjack, roulette, or craps. Sporting contests are not governed by the laws of probability theory and so the house has no built-in mathematical edge on sports bets the way it does for other casino games. Instead, a sports book makes money by acting as a middle-man or broker in essence for betters on opposite sides of a proposition and then charging a commission for this service. Simply put, a sports book offers two equally attractive betting options in an attempt to ensure that equal amounts of money will be bet on both sides of the wager. The commission charged on every bet made is known as the *vigorish* or *vig* or *juice*. If the total amount wagered on each side (e.g., on each side) is the same, the book is assured a profit from the commission but if more money is wagered on the winning side, the sports book may incur a loss in paying off the winning wagers. To minimize the risk of incurring such a loss, the book uses a betting *line*, or method of handicapping to make the *underdog* in the sporting contest as attractive to bet as the *favorite*. There are two basic types of betting lines, the *point spread* and the *money line*.

Point Spread

Points are given to the underdog. As mentioned above, point spreads allow the wage to offer attractive betting options on each side of the wager. The bet on the favorite will win if it wins by more points than the point spread. A bet on the underdog wins if the favorite doesn't cover the point spread or if the underdog does not cover the point spread. The bet ties if the favorite wins by exactly the spread amount. Point spreads can also be called the line, the number, the price or the spread.

Other Bets

You will also see over/under bets, which is wagering that the total points scored by both teams will be over or under a predetermined amount.

Another type of bet is the parlay. A parlay is a single bet that a combination of two or more games will win. All games on the parlay must win for the bettor to win. An example of this is the popular football parlay card.

There are several other bets such as the teaser card, which will adjust the spread in the bettor's favor but reduces the payout. The proposition bet can be a wager on anything. A good example is the bets that are made during the Super Bowl, such as how many field goals will be made, or what the score will be at halftime. A future bet is a wager that a team will win the pennant, division, conference, etc.

Middling is a situation where a bettor can take advantage of the difference in point spreads posted at different books that would allow him to win both bets. Such wagering is usually an indicator of a professional player or at least an experienced player.

Money-Line Betting

The money-line also has a favorite and an underdog. The favorite is indicated by the numbers with the minus sign (–150). The underdog is indicated by the plus sign (+110). The negative value tells us how much money we must bet to win $100, the plus value tells us how much money you will win if you bet $100 (–150 Mayweather, +130 Pacquio).

The casino win percentage for the sports book ranges from a minus (due to an event such as the Super Bowl going against the book) to about an average of six to seven percent per type of bet. Parlay bets have a win percentage of thirty to thirty-five percent.

The Race Book

Pari-Mutuel Betting

Essentially the way a race book operates is that a group of bettors pool their money together through the book and the book takes out a cut for themselves; the rest is given back the winning players.

There are various types of bets available. All money bet on a specific kind of wager is pooled together.

Betting Options

There are a number of betting options. Most are listed here. My thanks to the Wizard of Odds for this information from his website (www.wizardofodds.com).

Win: This is that most basic bet that the chosen horse will finish in first place.
Place: This is a bet that the chosen horse will finish first or second.
Show: This is a bet that the chosen horse will finish first, second, or third.
Daily Double: This is a bet on the first place position in two consecutive races, generally the first two of the day. Bettor must correctly pick both races to win.
Daily Triple/Pick Three: This is a bet on the first place position in three consecutive races.
Pick Six: This is a bet on the first place position of six consecutive races, generally the last six. If the event nobody wins the winning pool is split

between those correctly picking five (or less if nobody picked five) and a carryover to the next pick six pool.

Exacta: This bet is on the first and second place horses in a given race in the correct order.

Quinella: This is bet is on the first and second place horse in a given race in any order.

Trifecta: This bet is on the first, second, and third places in a given race in the correct order.

Twin Trifecta: This is a pair of trifecta bets on two races. The winning pool is split between winners of the first trifecta and winners of both of them. After the first race winners of that trifecta should redeem their tickets for winnings from first half of the pool and a ticket for the second half.

Superfecta: This bet is on the first, second, third, and fourth places in a given race in the correct order.

Odd/Even: This is an uncommon bet based on the number of the winning horse.

The race book usually has a win percentage of sixteen to seventeen percent.

Concerns in the Race and Sports Book

Over the years a number of scams have occurred at sports and race books. Because of the amount of money wagered at a book and the time it takes to detect the activity these scams result in the loss of a large amount of money.

One of concerns in the book is the use of messenger bettors. Messenger bettors are individuals hired by betting syndicates and/or professional bettors to place wagers as specified and directed by the entity or person they work for.

The syndicate or professional researches the point spreads and money lines posted by each sports book, searching for situations such as a middling opportunity as described above, or other weaknesses in the spreads or lines that they can exploit. Such weaknesses usually arise due to a book, in an attempt to attract additional bettors, adjusting some or all of their lines to make them more attractive. A book director may also post a line incorrectly or use bad judgement in setting the line. In doing so, the book may draw attention from the professionals. Such professionals can be termed advantage players.

There have been theories advanced that some of the syndicates may be funded by organized crime and even terrorist organizations. I don't know if that's true, however the possibility certainly exists. I can say that it is an area where money can be laundered easily.

Additionally, such professional players and/or syndicates may be privy to inside information about teams or individual athletes that aids in their decision making. Information about who is or isn't playing, or a player that is playing injured, can affect how a team will play, and may change how a player will wager on that game.

The bets made by messenger bettors can be costly to the property if the book director doesn't set the lines properly. Again, favorable spreads are often created when the book attempts to attract additional players and money to their book.

Although there isn't much a surveillance department can do about messenger bettors other than have them removed by security, however, doing so will keep such betters from getting out of control (i.e. using your property as a headquarters or hangout). I also stress their role because they could be a prime reason why a book is losing consistently.

We must also not forget that a book director working in collusion with others can set lines incorrectly or more favorably for his agents to take advantage of. This happens more often than you would think. Sports books, like anywhere else on the property, have their own clientele, players that are there every day and every week. The closer such players get to the employees the more of a chance that preferential treatment will be given. This activity can occur and grow much more easily in the book due to the general lack of understanding of how the book operates, and how lines should be set. In other words, there is usually a lack of accountability for book managers and directors.

Past posting, or wagering after the contest has been decided, has long been an issue in the race and sports book. In fact the term "past posting" originates from horse racing. When the bugler blows "call to the post" that is also the end of betting for the race.

In today's book we use technology to prohibit past posting. Once the computer locks out betting at the start of the game or the race no further bets will be taken (there are some proposition bets that may be taken such as at halftime in the Super Bowl, but conventional bets are off). Of course, as we've learned, there is always a way to beat the system and book employees and/or outside agents have exploited weaknesses in the various systems to allow bets after a game or race has ended and the result known. We've also seen book employees (writers) enter their own tickets into the system and void the ticket if it didn't win.

A few years ago a sports book in Las Vegas was hit by a group consisting of the book manager, a writer and outside agents for a total of $800,000 in a race scam. The manager and writer would allow the agents to bet invalid quinella bets. In a quinella wager the bettor picks the first- and second-place winners without specifying their order. If the two selected horses finish first and second, the bettor wins. Variations of the quinella allow the bettor to pick a combination of three horses to finish first and second. In this scam the agents were allowed to make their wagers in a diminished field, meaning in a race with fewer than six horses, thus increasing their odds of winning. Their winning bets were paid and any losses refunded.

And, of course, there are those robberies occur that at the book itself or during the transport of cash from the book to the cage. Some of those have been inside jobs over the years.

These are some of the methods used to commit theft and fraud within the book and I'm sure there are others. As I mentioned previously, the biggest problem with protecting the book is our lack of knowledge and understanding of how the book operates. When we take the time to learn about the book we find that it isn't that hard to monitor and protect. It just takes our time and our attention to key transactions and reports.

Key Transactions and Reports

Like other departments, the book performs key transactions and issues operational, statistical and exception reports that will aid the investigator in the detection and investigation of developing and existing criminal activity and advantage play.

I think that we should start, as we do with blackjack, with the win percentage. Is the sports and race book holding what it should? Normally, you will find this number on the table games analysis report (the book is usually placed under the numbers for table games). While each book markets and operates differently you should expect to see a win percentage of two to seven percent in the sports book and sixteen to seventeen percent in the race book. Of course, we would expect to see most of our handle generated during football season and major events such as a major boxing match. Wagering on baseball and basketball remain consistent throughout the season until we reach baseball's World Series and in basketball March Madness in particular.

Low win percentages that continue for long periods of time (over sixty days) should be investigated. As noted previously, there should be a reason for a consistent low win. We need to identify where exactly within the book the leak is occurring. Remember, within the book there are a number of different wagers bet on many different sports and will include the race book component of the book.

For example, we may have lost a significant amount of wagers during the football season. If so, these losses may account for the year to date loss. Our next step is to determine if the bets that were made were made properly, and were won and paid legitimately. We can do this by isolating individual wagers and verifying their accuracy. We will check the following at a minimum:

- Did the wager receive the correct point spread and/or money line that was being offered when the bet was made?
- Was the line moved before the wager was made and returned to its original status after the wager was made?

- How was the bet paid and by whom?
- What was the exact time the bet was made (was the bet made before the game started)?
- Was the wager altered in any way after the event was over?
- Are specific individuals or groups of individuals receiving special wagering conditions such as: early wagering, when wager can be placed, favorable point spreads or lines, amount of wager allowed, etc.?
- Does the wager made meet the conditions required for the bet being made? In other words, if a horse race requires a minimum field of six horses to allow a quinella bet, determine if at least six horses ran that particular race.
- Who is winning the money? Determine who is winning the majority of the money.
- Which employees handle the winning wagers?
- Identify what types of bets are losing the most money.

The above is an example of the information needed to conduct an investigation in one aspect of the book. These questions, while not all inclusive, can be used to begin investigation of any type of concern within the book.

There are other reports we can also look at. Within the book itself the director or manager can review a report listing, among other things, the time the bet was made, what the line was at the time of the bet, what the bet was, how much the bet was for and which writer completed the transactions. In other words, most of what we're looking for is on this one report.

Exception reports are also generated to detail point and line changes, changes made to game or event starts, or the amount or type of wager. This information helps us identify collusion, past posting etc.

Book reports are standard but are called by different names at each location. Note: a number of gaming properties are using third party companies to operate the book on their property. Doing so removes the exposure and liability of operating a race and sports book operation while providing the convenience of allowing guests to make wagers on the property. Third party book operations are becoming more popular and are used at a number of properties. I mention this here because, due to the third party companies, the information, statistics, reports and exceptions are becoming more standardized throughout the industry.

Also note that when the book is operated by a third party, the operator of the property must still be involved in the investigation of any indication or actual incidence of illicit activity. While the operator may not be financially responsible, there are reputational and regulatory/licensing concerns that must be considered. The investigator in such cases will work with the third party to investigate the crime and to protect the interests of the property.

Case History

The numbers were too low in the sports book. A number of large wins in football had driven the win percentage down to a point where the GM was asking questions. Not getting good answers from the sports book director, he contacted surveillance.

The surveillance director began checking who the winners were overall, and especially in football. The director was able to determine that there were several winners that stood out and required further review.

Investigation determined that each of the winners was legitimate. They were known players with a career win/loss record in favor of the casino, as it should be.

However, one player, a frequent player, had in the last six months been winning much more than was usual or expected from average players.

When that player was identified, and his play analyzed by investigators, it was determined that his wagers were made with a different point spread not available to others making the exact same bet. In fact, no one other than this individual had made wagers with the same point spread. Continued investigation ascertained that this individual had won each of his substantial wagers only because of the favorable point spread he had obtained from the sports book, which no one else had received.

Review of the records indicated that the point spread for each of the bets made by the individual had been changed by the sports book director, for that one player only.

The surveillance director, having identified the player who had won the money that had reduced the win percentage, and that he was being given a point spread not available to anyone else, realized he had grounds to alert the GCB, as well as human resources, to initiate charges of cheating at gaming, and termination proceedings.

It was later determined that the player, who turned out to be a judge for the county, was the father-in-law of the sports book director and they had been working together to make hundreds of thousands of dollars in ill-gotten gains to supplement their incomes.

Although they weren't arrested because of the judge's reputation and standing in the community, the director lost his job and never worked in a casino again.

Key Takeaways

- The race and sports book is vulnerable to many types of cheating, theft and fraud, and advantage play that can and have resulted in the loss of significant amounts of money. We must operate proactively to deter and detect illicit activity.

- Surveillance and other investigative personnel should be trained in book operations and the tells of cheating, advantage play, theft and fraud that may occur.

Best Practices

- Surveillance cameras should be placed at each window of the race and sports book in such a fashion as to observe and record the employee, the guest and the transaction. Cameras covering the counters and working areas of the book should also be placed to observe and record employee activities and movements. Pan–tilt–zoom cameras (PTZs) should be placed to provide the ability to zoom in on any transaction or activity within the book or in the book area. Any computer terminal that allows access to the book operating system and/or the ability to edit game or wager parameters (game time start/end, void of wager etc.) should be covered by a surveillance camera.
- Surveillance should possess a solid understanding of how the book operates, the various types of bets that can be made, how they are won and lost, and the tells and other indicators of illicit activity.
- Surveillance should patrol the book regularly and conduct audits of its operations frequently to identify violation of controls or procedures, cheating, advantage play, theft and fraud.
- Operational, exception and other key reports should be reviewed on a daily basis to detect suspicious or unusual activity.
- Player wins over certain amounts should be reviewed for legitimacy and accuracy. Amounts will vary by property and the type of action they accept. I recommend any wins of $5,000 or more be reviewed.)
- Security should escort book personnel carrying large amounts of cash and checks to and from the cage to deter robbery. Additionally, surveillance should provide camera coverage of the escort in order to obtain video of any individuals perpetrating a robbery.
- Messenger bettor activity should be discouraged.
- Surveillance should routinely compare the bet offerings and lines provided by his/her casino to that being offered at other properties. Significant variances or differences should be investigated to determine why the difference between the books exists.

Chapter 30

Investigation of Nightclubs and Party Pools

Where the money and alcohol pour freely, so does the potential for graft, corruption and theft.

Derk J. Boss

Nightclubs have long been used as vehicles to launder or move cash and goods simply because there is so much cash and product available. Theft, fraud and corruption exist where there is such value to be found, and that is true in the nightclubs and day clubs found at many gaming resorts. Each of these areas can be extremely profitable for a gaming property, so much so that a little theft and corruption might be overlooked. Some properties have found, to their serious dismay, that regulators frown on the activity and behaviors that occur in these areas, and have reacted accordingly with fines and restrictions, as well as strict regulation. Humans, being who they are, always find a way to make more money for themselves or to take advantage of situations to their benefit. Because, again, areas such as nightclubs and day clubs are not always monitored by engaged and objective personnel, the scams can only grow until they are large enough that they must be stopped.

Investigating resort nightclubs and party pools can be like a general sending his army into the unknown and without intelligence as to what the enemy is up to and in what strength. Unlike gaming and traditional non-gaming departments (hotel, food and beverage, etc.) nightclubs and party pools often operate outside of established policies and procedures, or they don't always follow the ones they do have. While this is changing due to the efforts of the Nevada Gaming Commission and some operators, these areas remain a concern and, for the investigator, a challenge.

There are a number of reasons that these venues are such a challenge. First, there is a considerable amount of money involved. These areas truly are cash-rich environments. Lots of cash breeds greed and corruption. Employees working with these venues can easily supplement their wages by increasing their tips through hustling and/or by providing services to patrons not on the menu (drugs, prostitution, special treatment such as early entry, etc.). Employees may also turn a blind eye to patrons involved in illicit activity so as not to interfere with receiving a tip.

Second, the services that are authorized and provided in nightclubs and pools are very expensive. For example, to sit down in a roped off area with a couch and table for your group can cost, at a minimum $500 for what is called bottle service. Bottle service consists of a personal waitress assigned to your section, as well a security officer to ensure you're not bothered by the minions, and an ample, but limited, supply of alcohol (vodka, rum, tequila, whisky, etc.) and appropriate mixers. Bottle service in Las Vegas is usually much more expensive. Depending on the club or pool you may pay up to $1,500 or even $5,000 or $10,000. Even at these prices you have only a limited amount of time to reserve your section. At some point you must pay more or leave to make room for the next party.

In addition to paying for your bottle service you will also pay for the tips to your waitress (this will already be on your bill). Of course, she won't tell you that and will expect a further tip, as will the security officer guarding your section and anyone else who had anything to do with you getting into the club and obtaining a place to sit and bottle service.

It is the same way at the pool. If you want a lounge chair that will cost you. You must pay a minimum fee for alcohol and food in order to use that chair. And of course party pools have cabanas, and even rooms that can be rented. The cost of the chairs, cabanas and rooms vary from pool to pool but usually are a minimum of five hundred up to tens of thousands. The tip situation is the same. Patrons will charged for tips on their bill and will also be expected to tip further.

I tell you this because it's important to understand the money that is floating about in the clubs and pools, which influences how these areas operate and the actions of employees. There is so much money being made by these venues that even when huge amounts are diverted to employees' pockets it is usually not missed. The venue still makes a tremendous amount of money each day or evening they're open.

Additionally, and more importantly, as far as the host property's gaming license is concerned, employees of these venues make more money by either assisting patrons in obtaining drugs or prostitutes, or allowing a minor to enter and drink alcohol, or turning a blind eye to what illegal or disreputable activities are occurring. It is such activities, among others, that concern the Commission and other local and state agencies and, when these activities are allowed to continue, result in disciplinary fines.

Nightclubs and party pools are set up intentionally to appear that the venue is so popular and busy that patrons must wait in line to get in. In most cases this is a sham. Often after waiting to get in (and paying to do so) a patron may walk in to the club and find it deserted. The line, the security people and the hosts are in place to establish that the venue is worth the wait and to build excitement. Nothing is wrong with that but in some, not all, nightclubs and pools the need for the wait is just an illusion.

The investigator will do well to keep in mind that it is the nightclub and pool's ability to make a patron feel special, privileged and "one of the few" that is able to come into an exclusive club to party, and perhaps see a celebrity or two, that encourages him/her to pay any price to be part of the "in" crowd. This is why these venues can make so much money, and can corrupt employees so easily and absolutely.

Let's discuss the employees, and their positions, that patrons may interact with to obtain entrance into one of these venues.

Hosts

There are two different types of hosts. The first is the host that works directly for the venue and is usually paid a salary plus commission. These hosts usually are positioned in front of or nearby the nightclub or pool. Hosts usually arrange getting your party into the venue and the reserving of a booth, table, cabana, lounge chair etc. The other type of hosts are independent and sell services as a third party to most nightclubs and pools in the local area. They often also arrange limousine services and other entertainment. Independent hosts work on commission. While independent hosts are supposed to work off-property I have seen them be allowed to work on-property with their own booth.

Security

Security personnel are posted at the entry way to the venue. At this point they will check identification of those entering to verify they are of legal age and have proper identification. Most venues will check bags or purses for drugs, alcohol, weapons or other illegal items. Some locations may have patrons walk through a metal detector or even allow a quick pat down to check for weapons. Security will also check patrons for proper attire, and to ensure individuals are not overly intoxicated, or displaying aggressive tendencies.

Security will check those entering to see if they've been prohibited from entering due to prior behavior such as fighting, use or sale of drugs, or prostitution. These individuals will be refused entry.

Within the venue security personnel are posted throughout the club or pool and are prepared to respond to arising issues. They usually communicate with radios and flashlights. When an incident occurs, security will normally attempt to deescalate the issue and remove the involved parties from the area as quickly as possible.

A security officer is usually posted at the entrance to a booth, section, cabana etc. to ensure only those patrons authorized to enter can do so.

In a number of venues medical personnel such as emergency medical technicians are posted within the club to assist with any arising medical issue.

VIP Hosts/Waitresses

Booth/cabana service includes the assignment of a specific VIP host/hostess/ waitress to your party. These individuals are usually pretty young women whose job it is to provide you with the bottle service the patrons purchased. Bottle service can be defined as: a service purchased by a guest, usually in a nightclub or lounge, that provides a reserved area with alcohol and mixers served by staff assigned to that table. Security may also be provided.

As mentioned previously, bottle service can be quite expensive, usually ranging from five hundred up to tens of thousands of dollars.

Nightclub/Pool Manager

A nightclub or pool manager is normally on duty anytime the venue is open to interact with patrons and ensure everything is operating smoothly. They are usually in charge of hosts, VIP bottle hosts, food and beverage personnel, security, pool attendants, lifeguards and clerks.

The managers handle problems or disputes and make the final decision on how the issue or individuals will be handled.

Nightclub/Pool Investigations

I mention the positions above because they are, along with bartenders, usually involved in (or at least aware of) the scams, corruption and reputational concerns that can occur in the nightclubs and pools.

Bartenders often work a scam independently but can also work in collusion with others. Note should be made that when each of these positions work together to commit theft or fraud, and/or allow others to commit illicit activity to obtain increased tips, the result can be disastrous for the venue and its host property. Both can suffer tremendous financial loss, damage to reputation and severe regulatory fines.

It is also important that we take time to put in context and frame what our concerns are for the nightclub and pool venues.

In the late 1990s and continuing through the early 2000s nightclubs began opening at casino resort hotels throughout Las Vegas. Party pools followed shortly thereafter. These venues were and are tremendous money makers for their owners and the host property. In some locations nightlife operations produce considerably more revenue than does the casino. This has resulted in some of those casino resorts reducing their gaming operations in favor of focusing their resources on nightlife operation.

While the nightclubs and party pools were becoming money-making machines, problems began appearing. There was so much cash floating around in the clubs and pools that everyone wanted a piece of it. Employees, for a price, would turn their heads while patrons engaged in sexual activities, bought, sold and ingested drugs, and while minors somehow gained admittance and were able to drink alcohol and do drugs. Prostitutes plied their trade with impunity. Employees at some locations began procuring women and drugs for anyone willing to pay.

As conditions worsened, patrons started turning up outside the clubs overly intoxicated and apparently were "dumped" on the streets to fend for themselves. Some female patrons claimed knockout drugs were placed in their drink and that they had been taken advantage of.

These activities and others got the attention of local police, the Gaming Commission, and other county and state agencies. Both the local police (Metro) and the Commission conducted undercover investigations of a number of clubs and found incidents of illicit activity, employee theft and corruption, employees procuring drugs and prostitutes, as well as health and safety issues. The Commission levied significant fines against the clubs involved.

Conducting investigations within and of nightclubs and pools may involve regulatory issues as discussed above and, of course, our usual lineup of concerns such as theft, fraud and employee misconduct.

Proactive Investigation

Let's begin with the proactive investigation. We can initiate a proactive investigation in two different ways: 1) sending in secret shoppers and/or 2) conducting a surveillance audit.

We highly recommend using competent and experienced (and licensed where necessary) shoppers to visit your nightclub/pool venues to pose as guests to see and get a feel for what really is going on. In fact, in Nevada, it is required that a licensee must use shoppers to perform an independent audit to evaluate the effectiveness of club venue employees in a covert manner and that they specifically audit prevention measures and/or activity in the following areas (Nevada Gaming Control Board, www.gaming.nv.gov):

A. Entry by underage individuals
B. Fraudulent identifications
C. Drug ingestion and sales by patrons and employees
D. Overconsumption of alcohol
E. Prostitution activity/trafficking
F. Physical violence
G. Sexual assault
H. Illegal activity by employees and patrons
 I. Employee facilitation of illegal activity

Please note that the above audit points encompass just about everything we would probably look for and investigate with the exception of hustling for tokes and/or the receipt of tokes for allowing the above activity to occur. Bear in mind that it is the toke itself that is the precursor to the activity and/or allows the activity to occur.

Due to the wide variety of incidents and issues that can arise in the nightclubs and party pools the use of surveillance audits and secret shoppers to detect indicators of illegal activities and employee misconduct is highly recommended.

The surveillance department, or whoever is assigned to monitor the nightclubs and pools such as security or a third party, should conduct audits on a regular basis. These areas should be assessed as having the potential for high threat, high impact and frequently occurring events. Performing regular and frequent audits should detect existing and arising concerns.

In addition to audits, secret shoppers should be used to enter each venue to see and hear what is actually being said and done within. It can be very difficult for surveillance to see with their cameras within the nightclub with its low lighting, and the crowds of people who frequent both the clubs and pools. Part of a shopper's job description is to place themselves in a position to test employees by asking employees to provide them with prostitutes, drugs or other favors, such as not having to stand in line, etc. Of course, if the employee does, that employee will expect payment through a large toke.

Shoppers may also be used to purchase drinks, bottle service, a premium section or a cabana in order to ascertain whether the payments made actually and completely reach the register.

Shoppers, used in conjunction with surveillance (to document observations and incidents, and identify those involved), can be very effect in detecting illicit activity, employee theft and fraud, and violation of controls and/or regulations. In addition, the consistent use of shoppers in nightclubs and party pools may mitigate any regulatory fine by the Commission. Of course, in order for this to be so, the property must be able to prove that the reports submitted by the shoppers were reviewed, and that corrections were made or discipline issued to discourage or eliminate the activity from reoccurring.

It is a surveillance department best practice to monitor and record shopper visits and activities at the venue to provide video documentation of reported events.

Investigations Initiated from a Tip or Report

Hopefully, we will detect most or scams and thefts proactively. When we can do this we can stop losses before they become so large that they may affect company profitability. As we know, most thefts and frauds go on for about sixteen months (ACFE Report to the Nations 2018). The faster we can detect them, the more money we can save the property.

However, in the real world, we know that we can't catch everything. In some cases, especially when the fraud is well hidden, we will have to depend on tips from employees, guests and venders. That's okay; almost in every case where a scam is reported by an employee, guest or vendor the tip turns out to be correct. For investigators that means you should never discount the source of your tip. It should lead you to where you need to go.

Once the investigator receives a tip or report the process for the investigation is the same as we discussed in previous chapters. We must identify suspects and witnesses, ascertain what is occurring and/or being stolen, locate or develop evidence, and build our case. If the activity is still in progress, the investigation can be treated as an active one in which shoppers and surveillance can be used, as well as the securing of the paper trail, if available, to gather evidence of the crime.

In the event that the investigator receives a report of a theft or fraud that occurred in the past, investigating that case may be difficult and, in some cases, impossible. First and foremost, most surveillance operations retain their video for seven days only. Others may retain their video for longer periods of thirty to forty-five days. If the incidents falls within the retention period then all is good. The investigator may use the video to aid in the investigation. If there is no video available (which will likely be the case) it's back to old-fashioned footwork.

In such a case, we must identify and locate the records, suspects and witnesses that would allow us to build the case. We may be able to interview witnesses and suspects that could lead us to further information or evidence (if they can be found and if they are willing to speak).

In the nightclub/pool venues there are or should be documents that record the following:

- Sales (alcohol, cover charges, line passes, food, etc.)
- Exceptions (voids, no sales, splits, etc.)
- Purchases records (bottle service, cabanas, etc.)
- Inventory (liquor, food, lounge chairs, etc.)
- Tips (toke pool list, payroll information)
- Commissions (hosts inside/outside)
- Names of patrons entering venue (from ID scanner)
- List of patrons purchasing services (bottle services, cabana, etc.)
- Reservation lists for section, booth, room, cabana, lounge chair, etc.
- Comps issued (by whom and to whom)

- Banned/eighty-sixed list (individuals removed/barred from venue)
- Security/surveillance incident reports and daily logs

Reviewing such information can aid the investigator in the verification of the information provided by the tip and help compile a case. Information as to whether an individual was present/working on a specific date or during a specific period of time, whether certain items or services were sold or provided to certain patrons, the amount of money paid for such items and services, names of employees working in the venue at time of the incidents, and tokes received/distributed, to mention a few, may provide the elements necessary to identify suspects and witnesses for potential interviews.

As we've discussed throughout, money is tracked very well in the gaming resort environment. If you can follow the money, you can find the crime and those involved.

There are a number of issues, scams, thefts and frauds that routinely occur in these areas that we can be on the lookout for.

Entrance

At the door we need to monitor that security is checking individual identification to ensure each patron is of age and that the identification used is legitimate. Security should also check the arriving patrons are properly attired and not intoxicated.

Normally, patrons are checked for alcohol, bottles, drugs or weapons. Security may pat down male patrons and check backpacks and purses. At other venues a metal detector may be used to locate weapons. Each property differs somewhat in their policy on how this will be handled. Ideally we want patrons to enter without outside alcohol, glass bottles or drugs (including prescription bottles), we want to prevent over-intoxication and ingestion or sale of drugs, and, of course, we want to prevent weapons of any kind entering the premises, including broken glass or bottles used as weapons, guns, knives, brass knuckles etc.

It is at the entrance that we often see our first incidents of employee misconduct. Hosts will, because they've been toked well to do so, attempt to have their "clients" bypass the line and in some cases not checked by security. Some security officers, because they are either intimidated by the host or venue manager or they have been toked to do so, will allow this to happen. Of course there are many problems with such activity: underage minors may gain entrance, weapons or drugs may be brought into the facility, there may be violations of the dress code and, at the very least, other patrons will be angry that others got in before them. Don't get me wrong, some groups and individuals should and will get in ahead of others, but not just because you toked the host or security officer. And no one should ever be allowed to bypass the security check (unless it's been prearranged with security such as in the case of a celebrity).

The above is a violation of policy, procedure, controls and regulations, and is an illustration of corruption and hustling that can occur in these venues.

Auditing the entrance of the venue is a must.

Hosts

There are many ways that a host (whether an independent or house host) can game the system. In fact, it is usually the host position that is central to many of the scams and schemes that can occur in the nightclub/pool venues.

We discussed hosts attempting to bring their clients in ahead of others in line, and/or bypassing the security checkpoint. Other methods hosts can use to take care of their people and/or to increase their take are as follows:

- Discounting the price of bottle service, private lounge chair, section, room, cabana, etc.
- Waiving cover charges
- Procuring drugs
- Procuring prostitutes or escorts
- Claiming fraudulent commissions

It's been my experience that the money earned from entry fees, bottle service and private areas is not tracked well, especially cash. This means that payments, especially cash, can easily be diverted into a host's pocket.

For example, a host escorts an individual or group into the club. He charges the guests the cover charge (or any portion thereof) but pockets the money instead of giving the money to the cashier.

Another example is if an individual or group requests a private booth. The going rate is $1,000. However, it is very slow and the host offers it for $500 if it is paid in cash. The individual or group does pay in cash and the hosts pockets it. The host will usually give some of the cash to the waitress and the security officer assigned to keep their mouths shut.

These scams work with private booths, lounge chairs, cabanas etc. As mentioned previously, the money collected for these sales is not tracked well. The employees responsible for collecting payment and inputting the transaction into the system are usually the same employees that benefit from the fraud, hence the fox watching the hen house.

Hosts may also claim commission for patrons they had nothing to do with. This can happen when non-hosted patrons enter the venue. The host simply claims that they are his clients and the cashier (usually) will list those patrons as his, allowing a small commission to be posted to the host's account.

There are many scams a host working in collusion with others can do. These scams almost always have to do with the sale of services such as early entry or privileged entry, bottle service or the use of private areas. Any service that can be paid in cash and not listed as a sale can be abused.

Cashiers

Cashiers can steal entry fees and cover charges in several ways. As the cashier operates a POS the methods used to steal from this location are the same as at any other POS. Voids, no sales, cancels, comps etc. can be used to skim funds.

As we discussed earlier, the cashier can also work with the hosts to cover the fraudulent sale of services by not listing the service or private area as having been sold or listing it as sold at a reduced cost (or higher cost).

Security

Security officers are central to the entire nightclub and pool operation. They are present to protect the employees, the patrons and the interests of the property. When the security team works diligently to deter and prevent illicit activity from occurring the venue will operate with minimal concerns.

In the event that the security team is corrupted and officers are working for their personal interests only (make as much money as possible), illegal activity and harmful behavior will arise that will cut into the profits of the venue and expose it to regulatory fines and damage to its reputation.

Security is posted at locations to ensure patrons entering the venue are of age, are not in possession of weapons or drugs, are not overly intoxicated and are dressed in the proper attire, and is also posted at private areas and booths to maintain the privacy of the patrons who paid for entry into those locations and/or for the bottle service. It is therefore very easy for them to turn their heads from whatever illegal activity may be occurring in return for a cash payment.

For example, a security officer may allow an individual with fraudulent identification to enter the venue or allow known prostitutes into the venue and allow them to approach patrons to sell their services. An officer assigned to a private booth may allow the patrons to engage in sex or ingest or smoke drugs. In some cases, security officers have been caught procuring and providing women, drugs and alcohol to the patron.

Usually, if illicit activity is occurring in the venue most, if not all, employees working within the venue are aware of or are involved in allowing the activity to occur.

Nightclub/Pool Managers

It stands to reason that if the nightclub/pool manager is effective at his/her job and works diligently to deter and detect the illicit activity, scams and employee misconduct that occur in these areas, most would not happen. Such activity should be obvious to an astute observer. A manager who pays attention to the floor and to the numbers (sales, inventory, profit margins, etc.) should be able to at least suspect something is occurring.

It is important to bear in mind that if illicit activity is occurring in a specific venue and the manager does not report it, he or she is either too inexperienced to know what's going on, or is involved.

Bartenders

Bartenders in nightclubs and pools can commit theft using any of the traditional methods, as well as some that are specific to these venues. Due to the cash flow, pace of business and number of customers it is much easier for a bartender to cover his/her thefts and can make it difficult for management to know that funds are being stolen.

In the nightclub/pool application the bartender can easily switch house blend for premium and pocket the profits from bottle service or at the bar.

Bartenders can easily work with waitresses to steal from the venue or patrons by overcharging, under ringing, resales, voiding tickets, comping cash-paying guests and/or providing services for tokes that should be charged for, to name just a few.

Other Employees

Every position and employee working within the nightclub/pool venue has the potential to commit or be involved in theft or fraud, or to take a toke to look the other way. It is a best practice that every position be checked for indicators of illicit activity or misconduct.

Because nightclubs and pools are a cash-rich environment we can expect that theft and fraud will occur, certain patrons will attempt to sell/ingest drugs and prostitutes will ply their trade. We can also expect that patrons will attempt to encourage our employees to look the other way and/or our employees will provide illegal services. If this is so, and it is, someone in the venue should be reporting it.

It has been my experience that any employee that has anything to do with the nightclub/pool is on the toke list, meaning that everyone gets a cut of the tokes that are made. When an employee receives a regular cut of the tokes, they grow to depend on those tokes and will do just about anything to keep the tokes coming. In other words, it's more than likely that employees will do whatever they can to increase the toke pool. The investigator would do well to keep that in mind: such employees tend not to cooperate unless forced to do so to protect themselves.

Case History

The surveillance director was concerned about the nightclub on his property. He was receiving reports that the hosts were actually running the operation: allowing their clients to enter first and obtain bottle service with comps or minimal payments. He had also been told that security was allowing such "guests" to bypass the security checkpoint, a direct violation of policy and an indication that security was working with the hosts.

Knowing that hosts would take care of guests that way only if they themselves were taken care of, the director knew something was wrong. He decided to send in a shopper team.

A few evening later the shopper team, three young males, was ready to go. One surveillance agent was assigned to stay in contact with them and follow their movements and encounters on video.

The team arrived at the casino property together and approached the host stand. The young lady asked them if they had a host and they informed her that they did not. She called over a young man dressed in a suit, introduced him as Joe and said that he was a host who take care of them.

Joe asked them what they were looking for and they explained that they wanted to get into the club and have a few drinks. Joe said he could do that. He said if they paid him the price for the cover charges he would escort them in. They agreed, paid him the money and were escorted in past security. As they passed the security podium the host told the officers that the group were his guests. The officer nodded and allowed the group to pass without an ID check, or inspection of any kind.

Once in the club, Joe told the group to let him know if they needed anything and left them to party.

The shoppers paid for drinks at the bar and wandered around. There were a number of booths open; it was a quiet night. After about an hour they contacted Joe and asked him about the cost for a booth. Joe told them he could get them into a booth at a discount since it was somewhat quiet. Joe said the normal price for bottle service would be $1,500. But he would get them the booth for $750.

They agreed and were soon sitting at a private booth, with their own waitress and security officer. Before Joe left he recommended that they tip the waitress and guard, and made it clear that he should be tipped too. They tipped him $100 and told him that they would take care of the others.

A short time later the shoppers told the guard that they were looking for some girls and wondered if he could point them in the right direction. A short time later they were joined by three young ladies who can only be described as "working girls". The girls offered their services for $1,000 apiece. The shoppers politely declined.

At this point, having accomplished their objectives, the shoppers made their excuses to the girls, and left the club and the property. They reported all of their observations and conversations to surveillance.

Over the next few days, surveillance reviewed all of the involved video, and gathered all of the documentation from the POS and host records. Investigation determined that Joe had initiated a string of thefts and serious violations of controls, policies and procedures.

First, even though the shoppers approached the host stand Joe claimed a commission for bringing the group to the club.

Second, although he collected a cover charge from each shopper of $25, he did not give the money to the cashier to pay for the entry. He was seen on video pocketing the cash.

Next, he bypassed the security podium in direct violation of the policy requiring that individuals who looked thirty years old or younger must have their identification checked. Additionally the group should have been patted down for weapons or drugs. Security should have insisted that the group be checked or reported the violation. They did neither.

Fourth, the host sold the booth to them at an unauthorized discount. Additionally, sales of any type of services are to be documented as such and entered into a cash register. In this case, the $750 sale of the booth with bottle service was not found. This indicated that Joe had stolen those funds also. It was later found that Joe had comped the bottle service because the shoppers appeared wealthy and Joe hoped that they would take care of him by tipping generously. A clear case of fraud.

And finally, the security officer had procured prostitutes for the shoppers. Obviously, a violation of policy and, in fact, against the law and gaming regulations.

Joe was confronted and terminated, along with the security officer at the podium who allowed the shoppers entry and the officer who procured the prostitutes.

The surveillance director met with senior executives, including the night-club manager. Controls to increase accountability of the host, their sales and comps were updated. Security was directed to perform mandatory checks of anyone thirty or under regardless of who told them to let them pass.

It was also decided to continue undercover investigations on a regular basis to deter and detect such activity in the future.

Key Takeaways

- Nightclubs and party pools are cash-rich environments that often operate without established policy and procedure or fail to follow those that are in place.
- There is ample opportunity for employees and guests to commit theft/fraud and engage in illegal activity.

- Employees may be corrupted by cash payments and tokes to provide or allow prohibited activity such as the ingestion or sale of drugs or the presence of prostitutes, among other illegal activities.
- The gaming license of a casino resort that contains a nightclub or party pool on its property is subject to discipline, including fines, by state regulators when illegal and prohibited activity occurs in those venues, as well as state, county and city laws, statutes and ordinances.
- There are several key positions within the nightclub/pool venues that can manipulate, orchestrate or participate in corruption, theft, fraud or other illegal or prohibited activity.
- Consistent audit, shopping and review of nightclubs and pools should prevent and/or detect most scams or misconduct.
- There are many common methods used to steal from nightclubs and pools.

Best Practices

- Ensure nightclubs and party pools develop and maintain current and effective controls, policies and procedures.
- Ensure staff in nightclubs and party pools are aware of and abide by state gaming regulations, and state, county and city laws, statutes and ordinances.
- Install and operate a surveillance system independent of venue operations, including security. The surveillance system should be operated by the gaming surveillance team.
- A shopper team should perform an independent audit of the nightclubs and party pools on the property at least quarterly.
- Surveillance should work directly with shopper teams to document, verify and retain observations.
- The surveillance department should conduct audits of the nightclubs and party pools on at least a monthly basis to deter and detect theft, fraud, employee corruption and misconduct, as well as other illegal activity.

Glossary of Gaming Terms

ACFE   Association of Certified Fraud Examiners.

ACSM   Assistant casino shift manager.

action   A bet or wager. Amount of money wagered by the player during the playing session.

active shooter   The United States Department of Homeland Security defines an active shooter as "an individual actively engaged in killing or attempting to kill people in a confined and populated area; in most cases, active shooters use firearms and there is no pattern or method to their selection of victims".

add-on   In poker, the facility to buy additional chips in tournaments.

advantage play   any legal skill, system or type of play that takes advantage of a game or game type, or marketing promotion's inherent weakness(s) or uses the poor training or use of game protection procedures of a gaming employee to gain an edge over the casino (i.e. card counting, hole card play, slot teams, etc.).

agent   A player who works in collusion with a dealer or floor person to cheat or steal from the casino. Also a surveillance agent, title for an individual who operates cameras in the surveillance room.

aggregate limit   Total payout liability of a casino during any one game.

all in   Betting the whole bankroll.

AML (anti money laundering)   A term mainly used in the financial and legal industries to describe the legal controls that require financial institutions and other regulated entities to prevent, detect and report money laundering activities.

ante   Required wager to get money into the pot before cards are dealt.

anti-fraud controls   Systems, reporting, controls, practices, audits, and policies and procedures implemented to protect a business from fraud and theft.

asset misappropriation   Asset misappropriation schemes include both the theft of company assets, such as cash or inventory, and the misuse of company assets, such as using a company car for a personal trip.

audit   A surveillance assignment requiring observation of an area or transaction, department or employee(s) in order to detect violation of controls, policies or procedures, or indicators of theft or fraud.

baccarat   Also called punto banco and chemin de fer (similar to baccarat but requires skill). A table game, using six or eight decks of cards, which does not require skill.

back counting   Counting the game and playing only when the count is a plus. Usually jumps into play at such times; can be signaled in by another player on the game.

back of the house   Employee and support areas of the hotel/casino.

backed off   Not allowed to game, usually blackjack.

bad beat   When a great poker hand is beat by a better hand such as: a straight flush is beaten by a higher straight flush.

ball draw   Selection of the individually numbered balls automatically or manually in bingo or keno.

banked game   In a player-banked game, the money wagered by the players is either put against the funds of one other single player who acts as "the bank" (much as in a house-banked game), or it is put into a common pool of funds that is then distributed to the winner (or winners) when the game (hand) is over.

banker   In card games, the dealer. In some card games, each player becomes a banker/dealer in turn.

bankroll   What the player has available to wager with; will determine his wager amounts.

Bank Secrecy Act (BSA)   The Bank Secrecy Act of 1970 (or BSA, or otherwise known as the Currency and Foreign Transactions Reporting Act) requires financial institutions in the United States to assist U.S. government agencies to detect and prevent money laundering. Also known as Title 31.

barred or banned   A person not allowed to enter the casino premises, permanently.

basic strategy   The optimum strategy for twenty-one play. Used by advantage players and cheaters to obtain maximum advantage and/or utilize card or decision information obtained. Used by surveillance to detect advantage players and cheats.

beard   A player who bets for another player. Someone who does not want his identity to be known.

beef   A problem or dispute with a player.

best practice   A method or technique that has been generally accepted as superior to any alternatives because it produces results that are superior to those achieved by other means or because it has become a standard way of doing things, e.g. a standard way of complying with legal or ethical requirements.

betting limits   In a table game, the minimum and maximum amounts of money that a player can wager on one bet. You cannot wager less than the minimum or more than the maximum amount posted. Some casinos, in special cases, may extend the maximum limit at a table on request by the player.

betting line   Point spread.

bet spread   The difference between a player's highest and lowest bet.

bill validator unit (BVU)   The box that contains cash placed into the machine by a player. Also verifies legitimacy of currency.

Biometrica   Company that pioneered facial recognition software used in the gaming industry. Also provides the infrastructure for the national surveillance information network and database.

BJ Survey   A computer-based twenty-one analysis program that aids surveillance and table games personnel in the detection of advantage play, accurate evaluation of a player's knowledge and skill, and that player's advantage or disadvantage against the casino.

Black Book   The list of undesirable people who are forbidden to enter any casino in Nevada.

blind   A required bet before the cards are dealt in poker. See small blind, large blind.

blockout work   Cards that are marked by blocking out areas or portions of the design.

blower   The device used in keno or bingo to blow the balls up for mixing and selection.

BOLO   Be on lookout bulletin from law enforcement or casino security/ surveillance.

bonus game   bonus video slots differ from standard video slots because they feature a bonus game that does not follow the reel slots format. When playing the standard reel game, a certain symbol or combination of symbols will activate the bonus game. These symbols are called bonus symbols, and often come in the form of scatter symbols. Scatter symbols are particular bonus symbols that must appear in any number on the screen – no matter how scattered they are on the screen. If a player gets a certain number of scatters at one time (three, for example), the bonus video slots game is activated. The bonus game follows the theme of the bonus video slots machine.

book   Industry term or slang for race and sports book.

bottle service   Commonly used in nightclubs and party pools as an incentive to purchase a private area or booth, or a cabana in the pool area. Patrons must purchase a designate amount and type of alcohol and associated mixers. Service includes a server and possibly a security officer assigned to you area. Cost ranges from a few hundred to tens of thousands of dollars depending on venue and event.

break-in dealer   A dealer learning to deal at a particular property but already on the clock, new dealer.

bullet   An ace.

burn card   A card discarded by the dealer after cutting the deck.

buy-back   To buy back your marker at the table or cage.

buy-in   Converting cash into chips. The amount of cash used to purchase casino chips before entering a table game (blackjack, poker, craps, roulette etc.).

buy/sell sheet   Cashier checkout sheet.

cabana   Private area within day pool that can be rented by guests.

calls for service   A listing provided by local law enforcement of all police responses made to a specific property for a specific period of time.

capping   Adding a check to wager after the game decision is made.

card counting   Keeping track of the cards dealt in an attempt to determine when the advantage lies with the player or with the house. There are many different systems but they are primarily based on assigning values to individual cards as they are dealt from the deck or the shoe. Advantage play.

card mechanic   A card cheat who manipulates the cards and/or used sleight of hand.

Caribbean stud poker   Also called 'Casino stud poker'; a casino table game based on the standard five-card stud poker game played on a blackjack-type table. Some casinos also offer a progressive jackpot paid to high ranking hands. This table game is played with one deck of cards.

casino advantage   The edge that the house (casino) has over the players.

casino cage   Where all cash, vouchers and checks are redeemed, stored and distributed; used by employees and players.

cheating   Any illegal activity used to alter the course or outcome of a game or to obtain information not available to other players (e.g. marking cards or using a device to obtain hole card information or to cheat a slot machine).

checks   Same as chips. Normally used by surveillance and table games personnel.

cherry squeeze   Cheating method used on reel machines to make the machine pay over and over. See handle popping.

chip cup   A cheating device used to hide higher denomination chips or checks within the hollow center. The cup is made to depict a stack of green or black checks. A dealer working in collusion with a player will insert higher denomination checks during transactions.

chip inventory   All the chips stored in the cage; also used in some table games operations to describe all the chips located on the games and overall.

chips   Items used to denote amounts of money in gambling. Normally in $1, $5, $25, $100, $500 and $1,000 denominations although larger casinos use $5,000 and higher denominations. Chips traditionally used in roulette games.

chip tray   The tray located on gaming tables to hold the chips.

close watch   A surveillance observation of an area or subject requiring that the subject is continuously monitored by the surveillance department. Usually initiated by information or a tip.

club card   Player's card, loyalty card.

CM   Casino manager.

c-note $100 bill.

coin in/out   Method of measurement in slots. Used to determine player's value and machine performance.

collusion   Two or more players secretly working together or with an employee to cheat or steal. A secret agreement, especially for fraudulent or treacherous purposes; conspiracy: Some of his employees were acting in collusion to rob him.

comp, comped   To provide or receive complimentary food, alcohol, rooms etc.

compliance officer   A person who has been authorized to act on behalf of a company, in a capacity of ensuring compliance with applicable control measures, laws and regulations.

cooler   Deck(s) of cards introduced into a game normally through collusion with the dealer and or/floor staff. Decks are stacked and prepared for player wins. So called because are supposedly cool to the touch as compared to the cards that were in use on the game.

cooling off   The process by which a customer voluntarily requests their own account be temporarily locked in order to prevent them from participating in further gambling. The cooling-off period may be anywhere from 24 hours to 6 months. It is not the period of time a customer is required to wait after terminating a self-exclusion period. See self-exclusion.

countermeasure   A response by surveillance or the property to a threat or actual incidence of advantage play or crime; may be a policy such as prohibiting mid-shoe entry, or an action such as securing a door to prevent employee theft.

count room   Room or area where cash from casino drops are delivered, counted and verified by the count team. Normally the most secure area within the casino.

coverage   In surveillance, coverage refers to the video of an incident taken from the cameras recording the event or area.

cover bet   A bet used by advantage players to camouflage their play, usually when a floor person is watching.

covert investigation   Using a hidden camera or undercover operative to conduct an investigation.

critical index   In blackjack, certain strategic plays or adjustments to basic strategy at certain true count totals.

crossroader   An old, traditional term for a cheater. Normally means someone who works or plays legally in one casino but cheats at another when off duty.

CSM   Casino shift manager.

currency transaction report   A report that U.S. financial institutions are required to file with FinCEN for each deposit, withdrawal, exchange of currency or other payment or transfer, by, through or to the financial institution that involves a transaction in currency of more than $10,000.

cut card   Normally a colored card used to cut the deck and to protect the bottom of the deck from exposure.

daily double   A pari-mutuel bet made in horse and dog racing in which the bettor selects the winner of two races (usually consecutive races but not always). It pays at higher odds.

daily hit report   A report maintained by gaming departments such as table games and slots that lists the winners and losers over a designated amount for a particular day.

data mining   The process of reviewing and analyzing data obtained from electronic sources such as POS, slot information systems, patron management systems etc. to locate desired information.

daub   Any substance used by cheats to mark cards.

day club   Pool parties that normally take place at a casino resort hotel during daytime periods, usually Friday, Saturday and Sunday.

dealer/agent   Usually used to refer to collusion between a player and a dealer to steal (dump the game) from the game.

detection   A surveillance term used to describe the observation of an incident of crime, advantage play or policy/procedure violation.

device   Gaming device: slot machine, gaming table, etc.

DOS   Director of surveillance.

draw   Selection of the numbers in keno or bingo, or in poker.

drop cart   The cart used to store and transport drop boxes to and from the casino floor.

dump the game   A dealer dumps the game to a confederate by overpaying wagers, pushing losers, not taking losers, etc. See dealer/agent.

duty of care   A legal obligation imposed on an individual requiring adherence to a standard of reasonable care while performing any acts that could foreseeably harm others. It is the first element that must be established to proceed with an action in negligence.

edge   An advantage. As in, house advantage.

eighty-six   Remove, legally ban from the property, usually permanently.

embezzlement   The fraudulent conversion of another's property by a person who is in a position of trust, such as an agent or employee.

emergency drop   A drop performed, usually in slots, at a time other than the normal drop period. Usually done because the drop box is too full or is malfunctioning.

employee bank   Area within the cage or other are to receive, store and distribute banks used by employees.

evaluation   A surveillance term to describe the analysis of a player (normally a twenty-one player) by the surveillance department. Usually takes into account the player's knowledge of basic strategy, money management and card counting abilities.

evidence   The available body of facts or information indicating whether a belief or proposition is true or valid.

exception report   A report that lists exception to normal procedure. For example, a report listing each void performed for the previous day.

expected win rate   In slot machines, the percentage on the total amount of money wagered that you can expect to win back over time.

eye in the sky   A term used to denote the surveillance department.

fat   Gambler with a large bankroll.

favorite   The horse, individual or team that is expected to win.

fish   Amateur or naïve player.

flashing   Dealer exposing top card or hole card to player, intentionally or unintentionally.

flash work   Marking cards by shading the back of cards except for a small portion to indicate specific values of cards.

flat bet   Countermeasure to advantage players by requiring the player to bet the same amount each hand.

flat betting   A way of betting where the same amount is bet on each wager. For example, if a player always bets $10 on each hand or spin and never raises or lowers their bet, they would be said to be flat betting.

flats   Shaved dice used to hit certain numbers more frequently.

float   Another name for the chip rack on a table game. See rack.

fraud   Theft by deception.

fraud triangle   A premise that illustrates the three components that are usually present in an incident of fraud: opportunity, pressure and rationalization.

fraud unit   A team of investigators that are assigned specifically to investigate theft and fraud.

free play   The participation in games where no deposit was required from the customer and no actual monetary value is attributable to the customer.

friends and family   A common phrase used to express the relationship between a thief or fraudster and the people he or she used to participate in the crime.

full exclusion   The process by which a customer's own account is permanently locked in order to prevent them from further gambling.

gaff   Anything that is made or altered to cheat at gambling.

gambling syndicate   A group of individuals pooling funds to place wagers on targeted games or events, usually in sports.

game speed   The speed of an individual game. Usually based on decisions per hour.

GCB   Gaming Control Board.

Gem-backs   Borderless card back design developed by Gemaco Playing Card Company.

George   Big tipper, term used especially by dealers.

GGR (gross gambling revenue)   Amount wagered minus the winnings returned to players, a true measure of the economic value of gambling.

GGR is the figure used to determine what a casino, racetrack, lottery or other gaming operation earns before taxes, salaries and other expenses are paid – the equivalent of "sales" not "profit".

glim   Shiny object used to reflect value/index of card.

g-note   A $1,000 bill.

golden pen   The ability to comp.

Griffin   Griffin investigations, a service that provides an online service reporting individuals or teams of individuals who were detected cheating or involved in advantage play.

grind   Low action.

handle   The total amount of money wagered or put at risk by a player.

handle popping   Handle manipulation of a mechanical or electro-mechanical machine involving placing in a two-third down position and hitting the handle so as to stick two reels in one position to set up a jackpot.

hand mucker   A card cheat who specializes in switching cards in and out of a game.

hard hand   A blackjack hand without an ace. Hand has only one value, it is what it is.

high roller   Big player, high action for the casino.

hit   In blackjack, to indicate or request another card from the dealer.

hit frequency   The term casinos use to describe how often a machine will stop on a winning combination. For example, if a machine has a hit frequency of eight percent, it means that the machine will stop on a winning combination about eight percent of the time.

holdout machine   Usually a mechanical device used by a card cheat to aid and hold cards switched in and out of game.

holdout man   Card cheat who switches cards in and out of game as needed.

hold percentage   Percentage of money kept by a casino from the wagers made by the player. Usually refers to slot hold.

hole card   In blackjack or stud poker, the hole card is face down.

hole card play   Using the information provided by an exposed hole card, gained legally or illegally, to make playing decisions in blackjack.

hotline   Anonymous and confidential reporting line used by employees and others to report illicit activity, harassment or workplace violence.

imprest   Cashier and/or employee banks or drawers that are issued a specific amount of funds. The bank or drawer must be returned to the set level at the end of the shift or the day.

insurance   In blackjack, a side bet offered to players when the dealer's up card is an ace. Pays 2 to 1 if the dealer has the blackjack, otherwise the bet loses.

integrity check   Used by loss prevention or undercover personnel to check the honesty of an employee as they perform their duties.

internal theft   Employee theft. Cheating, theft or fraud committed by a company's own employees.

IOU An acronym for a surveillance patrol technique: identify, observe, understand.

IOU patrol A basic surveillance technique. Used to identify individuals, the play or activity in that area, and to determine if the player or activity is a threat to the property; provides for the gathering of evidence.

juice Vig; a commission charged by the casino. Usually seen in baccarat and craps. May also refer to the commission owed to a loan shark.

junket Casino junkets or casino complimentary travel are trips offered to gambling customers, called VIP players, to travel to and play at a particular casino. Depending on the player, the hosting casino will pay some or all of the VIP player's travel and accommodation costs in exchange for undertaking to play at the casino during the player's stay. VIP players are usually obliged to agree to a minimum deposit in advance, normally in the region of $5,000, and commit to a number of hours playing at the paying casino.

keno A casino game, played trying to guess some of twenty numbers out of a field of eighty.

lammer A small chip used on a game to designate the amount of a marker issue or buyback, or call bet. Lammers are usually marked with a dollar amount such as $500, $1,000 etc.

larceny A crime involving the unlawful taking of the personal property of another person.

line Point spread, money line.

loss Usually refers to a gaming loss on a particular game or game type: "we had a loss of $50,000 in blackjack last night". May also refer to a loss due to theft or cheating.

loss prevention The techniques, systems and personnel assigned to protecting a business entity from theft, fraud and waste. May refer to a department such as the loss prevention department.

loyalty club Player's club, slot club.

luminous readers A deck that is marked. Marks are invisible to the eye except when viewed through a red filter (such as the card discard tray located on most table games) or red tinted glasses or contact lenses.

main bank The area within the cage that distributes all funds and checks to the casino, and to the bank. Accepts count room funds and transfers to bank.

main banker The cashier on each shift who operates the main bank.

marker Credit instrument issued in a casino.

marks Substances, indentations, pinholes etc. placed on cards by a person or persons to allow the identification of the value of the card marked. See daub.

mechanic A cheat who specializes in sleight of hand; can be a card or dice mechanic.

mechanic's grip A method of holding the deck to allow a variety of card manipulations. Used by card mechanics.

messenger bettor An individual used by others, who wish to remain anonymous, to place large wagers at sports books.

money laundering   The process by which criminals conceal or attempt to conceal the origin of the proceeds of their or others' criminal activities.

money line   A type of bet in the sports book. The money line is composed of two odds, one for the favorite, and one for the underdog.

money management   Any method devised and employed for wagering to purportedly allow maximum win and/or prevent drastic loss.

monitor   A surveillance term, used to describe the observation of an area or person. Used interchangeably with "observe".

muck   A hand maneuver used to conceal and remove/replace a card from the game.

multiple transaction log (MTL)   At a threshold of $3,000 the casino is required to produce an MTL that details the player's description, player account number, social security number if on file and the time of any transactions.

natural   An ace and a ten, blackjack.

negative expectation   The long-run disadvantage or loss of a given situation without reference to any particular outcome; that is, what you figure to lose on average after a considerable time of play, or after a large number of repetitions of the same situation.

negligence   Conduct that falls below the standards of behavior established by law for the protection of others against unreasonable risk of harm. A person has acted negligently if he or she has departed from the conduct expected of a reasonably prudent person acting under similar circumstances.

NGCB   Nevada Gaming Control Board.

NGR (net gaming revenue)   Gross bets less payout.

no sale   A button on a POS that allows the cash drawer to open without a transaction.

number   The point spread. See point spread.

observe   A surveillance term, used to describe the surveillance of an area or person. Used interchangeably with "monitor".

observe and report   The basic function of a surveillance department.

occupational fraud   The clandestine theft of an organization's assets by employees of that organization. The use of one's occupation for personal enrichment through the deliberate misuse or misapplication of the employing organization's resources or assets.

odds   Ratio of probabilities; the casino's view of the chance of a player winning; the figure or fraction by which the casino offers to multiply a bettor's stake, which the bettor is entitled to receive (plus his or her own stake) if they win.

off the top   First bet after a shuffle.

ORG   Organized retail gang.

overhand run-up   A method used to stack the deck(s).

over/under   Game score results will be over or under a specified amount.

palm   As in, palming a card. Any method used to conceal a card or cards in order to switch it in or out, or steal it.

par (percentage)   A par sheet is a document prepared by the slot manufacturer that shows the possible outcomes from the play of a slot machine, the probability of occurrence, and the contribution of each winning outcome to the payback percentage.

pari-mutuel betting   A betting system in which all bets of a particular type are placed together in a pool, taxes and the "house-take" or "vig" are removed, and payoff odds are calculated by sharing the pool among all winning bets.

parlay   A bet on the total points scored by both teams in the contest.

past posting   Placing a bet after the outcome of the game is known.

pat hand   Hand worth at least seventeen points in blackjack.

patrol   A surveillance term describing the movement of cameras through an area or activity.

payline   The line on a slot machine window on which the symbols from each reel must line up. Slot machines can have as many as twenty paylines, although most have only one.

payout percentage   The expected percentage of wagers a specific game will return to the customer in the long run.

peeking   Techniques used to cheat or in advantage play to see the dealer's hole card or top card.

PIN   Personal identification number.

pivot point   The plus or minus count where a bet or strategic decision is altered.

player rating   Player's value to the casino, determined by time played and wagers made.

player's club   Headquarters and administration center for the player reward program. Player signups, account changes and some redemptions are handled here.

point spread   A certain number of points (point spread) given to the underdog for the purpose of deciding the bet.

pot   In a poker game, the amount of money that accumulates in the middle of the table as each player antes, bets and raises. The pot goes to the winner of the hand.

premises liability law   The body of law that makes the person who is in possession of land or premises responsible for certain injuries suffered by persons who are present on the premises.

pressing   A player presses a bet when they let a winning bet ride along with their original bet.

price   Cost of ticket.

probability   A mathematical calculation that establishes the likelihood that an event will occur.

program   In marketing, a plan or strategy designed to attract players and guests.

progressive jackpot   A jackpot (highest payoff) for a gaming machine (usually a slot machine or video poker machine) where the value of the jackpot increases a small amount for every fifteen games played. Normally multiple machines are "linked" together to form one large progressive jackpot that grows more quickly because multiple players are contributing to the jackpot at the same time.

promotion   In marketing, a specific contest, giveaway, drawing etc.

protect the assets   Basic mission of the surveillance department.

proximate cause   In the law, a proximate cause is an event sufficiently related to a legally recognizable injury to be held to be the cause of that injury. There are two types of causation in the law: cause-in-fact, and proximate (or legal) cause.

push   A tie.

quads   Four of a kind in poker.

rabbit ears   Tubes where balls used in keno or bingo are stored after they are selected.

rack   A plastic container to carry table fills. Also can refer to the check tray on table games.

rake   Money removed from the pot by the house in poker.

random number generator (RNG)   See RNG.

rated   Determination by the casino that a player's skill level is above average or on a professional level. A player's rating may be stored on computer and referred to the pit.

rated play   In table games and slots rated players are those frequent players whose play is tracked for comping and rebate purposes.

readers   Cards marked for cheating.

red flag   Indicator of suspicious activity.

reflector   See glim.

refused name player   A player who will not identify himself for rating and comping purposes. Usually considered unusual or suspect by surveillance due to its relative rarity.

response   A surveillance reaction to a threat or observation that requires action.

retail   Venues where goods or services are sold such as hotels, restaurants, bars, tickets etc.

RFB   Free room, food and beverage. Comped for big players.

riffle stacking   Stacking the deck using a riffle shuffle.

riffle test   Used to test a deck of cards for marks. As the cards are held and riffled, the back design of the cards is observed. If the design has been altered by marks, some (not all) can be detected in this manner.

riffling   A shuffle process. Cards are divided in half and "riffled" together.

RNG   Random number generator, commonly used to generate random numbers in games such as video poker, keno, pai gow, etc.

round   In card games a round can be a round of hands (often used in dealer pace audits), or a round of betting.

rubbernecking   The constant looking around by a cheat checking to see if someone is on to them.

rubber stamping The act of a supervisor or manager approving a transaction for a subordinate without actually verifying the transaction was accurate, authorized or legal.

running count Counting each card, adding or subtracting as necessary to create a count of the deck or shoe at the end of each round.

scared money Playing on money you can't afford to lose.

score A large win.

scout Used by cheat teams or advantage play teams to locate weak casinos or dealers than can be taken advantage of.

self-exclusion The process by which a customer voluntarily requests their own account be locked for a minimum period of six months in order to prevent them from further gambling. See cooling off.

session A player's period of play.

shark A good/crafty player often posing as a fish early in the game.

shill A player employed by the casino to get and keep the game going, in poker.

shiner See glim.

shopper Individual posing as a customer or guest to check level of guest service or employee integrity.

shoe Gaming device used to house and deal cards.

shuffle tracking Advantage play, used by an individual player or a team of players to track certain cards through a deck or shoe.

shuffle up Shuffling cards prior to the designated time, usually at the instruction of the pit boss, to inhibit or send a message to a suspected advantage player.

silver mining Looking for coins, credits or tickets left by another player.

SIN Surveillance information network; a general term used to describe a cooperative network of casinos in a jurisdiction or nationally that share information.

skimming Cash and/or other assets stolen prior to the item being accounted for or placed "on the books". For example, theft of cash before it is entered into the register.

sky Another name for surveillance.

slug A cluster of cards; a lead coin used in coin acceptors of older slot machines.

snapper In blackjack, an ace and a ten-value card.

soft hand In blackjack, a hand that contains an ace that can be counted as one or eleven.

sorts Groups of cards that are marked the same or by the same imperfections.

spooking In blackjack, standing behind a dealer to pick up the hole card and signal the value of the card to a cohort.

spread Point or bet spread.

stack A group of cards secretly set in a predetermined order.

stacking Secretly arranging certain cards inside the deck so that they fall to a certain player.

stiff   In blackjack, a hand that may bust if hit once.

strap   Used to wrap cash in the cage by denomination and amount. For example, a strap of $1 bills equals $100.

stringer   Cheating method used in older coin operated slot machines in which a string is attached to a coin and pulled up and down to add coins fraudulently.

stripping   In card shuffling, reverses the sequential order of the cards.

surrender   In blackjack, to give up half your bet in order to not complete the hand.

suspicious activity report for casino (SARC)   A report made by a casino about suspicious or potentially suspicious activity.

surveillance agent   An individual who works the cameras in the surveillance room.

table hold   The amount of money won by a casino during a particular shift or day.

team play   Using two or more players in advantage play such as back counting, hole card etc.

tell   Any indicator or behavior by a person/player that telegraphs a cheating move or technique, is indicative of advantage play or provides information of how a player will bet or play in a particular situation.

tell play   Playing the game and adjusting strategic plays based on the observation of other players to detect body language or other behavior or tendencies that give away information.

threat   A potential risk to the property by an employee, player, visitor or guest. As in, an advantage player who poses the risk of loss, or an employee who may obtain access to a sensitive area for illicit activity.

Title 31   See Bank Secrecy Act.

TITO   Acronym for ticket in ticket out; slot redemption tickets.

toke   A tip for the dealer or any employee in the casino.

tort   A wrongful act, not including a breach of contract or trust, that results in injury to another's person, property, reputation or the like, and for which the injured party is entitled to compensation.

trip wire   Type, level of activity or wager requiring surveillance be notified. For example, the pit must report a player betting $100 or more.

tri-shot   A basic and minimum surveillance camera set-up used to provide the necessary information and evidence.

true count   An adjusted running count to further determine the balance of cards remaining in the deck or shoe. Calculated by dividing the running count by the number of decks remaining.

true odds   Real odds, actual odds. The ratio of number of times one event will occur to the number of times it will not.

undercover   Individual working covertly to detect illicit activity or gauge service levels. See shopper.

underdog   Team or individual expected to lose in a contest or event.

union   Employee bargaining unit. For example the UAW.

units   Normally refers to betting units, used to denote wager amounts made by individual players. For example, a player betting one $25 check up to four $25 checks can be said to spreading up to four units. The unit in this case equals $25.

upcard   In blackjack, the dealer's card that is seen and played to. Used to determine proper play with basic strategy.

variance   Over or short for bank assigned.

verification   To verify a jackpot or other payment or transaction. To approve.

vig   Juice; commission charged by the casino.

VIP   Very important person, high roller.

void   To eliminate/remove a transaction from a sale or activity.

ways   In keno. Type of bet made and played.

whale   A huge player, often bets the maximum bets a casino will allow. Can make or break a casino's profit for the year.

white-on-white   Card marking method using some type of white substance on the white border on the backs of cards. The marks can be seen at certain angles.

wise guy   Individual believed to be involved with organized crime.

wong, wonging   In blackjack, to join play only when count is advantageous.

writer   Employee who accepts and enters tickets into the system in keno or sports and race book.

wrongful act   Any act that will damage the rights of another, unless it is done in the exercise of another equal or superior right. For that reason, the scope of wrongful acts is not limited to illegal acts, but includes acts that are immoral, anti-social, or libel to result in a civil suit.

x-ray   Often used as the radio call sign for the surveillance department.

z-out   Close out the cash register to determine sales; used in retail.

Surveillance Tradecraft

IOU Patrol

We recommend the IOU patrol as the fundamental patrol to be used by surveillance personnel. IOU is an acronym for identify, observe, understand.
These three components of a patrol accomplish everything that is needed for
detection, response, investigation and the gathering of evidence for any situation. Each investigator should patrol a different area of the property. It is suggested that you break down your patrols as follows: one investigator assigned
to the pit and another to slots; additional investigators assigned to back of the
house or parking lots and garages, and other out buildings. Another setup is
to assign one person to gaming and another to non-gaming, or front of house
and back of house. Again, if you have more than two investigators you can
break it down further. The point is to patrol all aspects of the property. Many
properties have only one investigator on duty. The IOU patrol may and still
should be carried out. The patrol is the most effective method to detect crime
regardless of the number of investigators on duty. You will find that if the
IOU patrol is done properly, it will consistently detect situations or individuals
that should be followed through further observation and investigation.

An IOU patrol is conducted as follows: Begin the patrol at a standard reference point such as blackjack table 1 or slot section 1. At the first table (or
machine, or area):

Identify: Using your camera, identify each person at the table, including
players and employees. Also include individuals standing next to the game or
in the immediate area. It is necessary to identify the game number and the
status of the game, such as the denominations and amounts of checks in the
tray or the face of the slot machine (i.e. payout meters, etc.). When you
have identified the game, company funds or property, employees and players, you can move on to the next step. If you are performing the IOU
patrol in the back of the house area or at a POS, use the same method by
observing and recording all the employees in the area and the condition of
the area at the time, or in the case of a POS located at a bar, you must
record everything in and around the cash register and those seated at the
bar, including the lounge area, bar backs and waitresses in service areas.

Again, everything should be recorded that may be important in the event you must review for a specific individual or incident that occurred or may occur in that area.

Observe: Observe the play or activity for indicators or tells of advantage play, cheating or theft. These indicators include violation of internal controls, policies or procedures. Remember, almost every case of cheating or internal theft (and, frequently, advantage play, such as hole card play) is due directly or indirectly to a weak control or poorly trained employee, not to mention those employees deliberately ignoring or violating a control for their own purposes. In table games, also observe the play for size of wagers, players' knowledge of basic strategy and overall skill level, players' wins/ losses, and so forth. This is the period of time you will use to establish your priorities. For example, while observing players at a particular game, you should be able to eliminate quickly those players who are known, and who are losing, wagering small amounts, betting flat or making consistent basic strategy mistakes. Doing so will help you quickly focus on higher action players moving their bets, playing strong basic strategy or displaying tells of advantage play or cheating.

Understand: The final component of the IOU patrol is to "understand" the activity or action. What this means is that you must determine if it is legitimate play or if it is suspicious. If the play is legitimate (no violation of policy, procedure or controls by employees, no tells of advantage play, cheating or theft, etc.), the operator can move on to the next player, game or area in the patrol. If the play or activity is suspicious for any reason, further observation and investigation are necessary and, in fact, required in order to protect the property properly. Think about it: you may have spent hours looking at normal activity and now you finally find something, no matter how small or insignificant, that is suspicious or outside normal parameters: you're in the right place at the right time! An IOU patrol on a specific game is not complete until the investigator "understands" the action on the table or in the area. This often will mean that the investigator can confidently say that the activity is normal, the action is not unusual, and policy and procedures are being followed. I usually use the guideline in blackjack of being able to predict the amount of a player's next wager. When you can correctly predict what a player will wager on an upcoming hand, you can safely say you understand his or her play and make the decision as to whether further observation is warranted. You can also apply this premise to any area – slots, POS, warehouse – when you can "understand" that procedures are being followed and that the activity is normal, you can then move on. By the way, understanding the game is often where investigators, especially new ones, get tripped up. They don't know when to say they "understand" and often continue to look at a game far longer than they need to. The same can be said of those investigators who haven't taken the time to learn the skills they need or they just don't care. Either one requires a supervisor to step in to help or discipline the investigator as needed. Please note that an IOU patrol on a specific game, slot machine or area may take anywhere from two minutes to eight hours. Of course, eight hours would be an extremely long period of time to evaluate a game or area; however, the point is that the operator, when he or she has determined the play is normal, should move on as quickly as possible. On the other hand, if the operator remains suspicious or uncomfortable with the play or the player(s), then this is the action to observe, and the place the operator should be and, in fact, is paid to be. The operator must stay with the action for as long as it takes until it is "understood" what the action is and what the proper response to it should be. We can't stress enough the importance of speed, knowledge and skill for an operator. You must always keep in mind that someone is out there on your property cheating, stealing or otherwise harming your fellow employees or the guests of your property. If it is not occurring on the table, machine or area that you're looking at, it's occurring somewhere else, and you must detect (find out) where that is. See Appendix 2, Surveillance Patrol Flow Chart.

Tri-Shot Coverage

During the IOU patrol the investigator will frequently find individuals or activities that appear suspicious. Upon detecting a suspicious or unusual situation, tri-shot coverage is placed to obtain the information necessary to make an informed decision about the event or activity or to gather appropriate evidence to prosecute individuals involved, if necessary. You would think that this is something most surveillance personnel would do naturally. After all, we work with cameras all day long! But we often do not do this well. A lot of agents, when covering an incident or when trying to determine what's going on, will often use one camera only or will zoom in so tight that they can't see (and neither will a future jury) what is happening out of camera view, which usually turns out to be important. The requirement of tri-shot coverage is critical for the success of a surveillance room. It really is all for nothing if you detect a crime and apprehend the suspect, only to later see him or her released based on a lack of evidence, not to mention the embarrassment of having to do so. Tri-shot coverage consists of a minimum of three specific camera angles or "shots". Each of these shots is important, not only allowing coverage of suspicious activity, but also providing the ability to gather necessary evidence in the event the suspicious activity becomes an actual incident. Tri-shot coverage consists of the following shots:

Overview: Camera overview of a game, such as a twenty-one game or a slot machine. The overview should provide an unobstructed view of the game device and related equipment used to play or operate the game.

For example, a twenty-one game should be covered by an overview shot in the following manner:

- View of layout to include the chip tray, card dealing shoe (if used), discard rack and shuffle machine (if used)
- Dealer's cards
- Players' cards and bets
- Players' hands
- Table layout to at least the rail

Specific or bet shot: This shot is used to monitor a specific area of the game such as the wager, players' hands or players' cards (or all of these at once). In the case of a slot machine, the specific shot should cover coin or credit meters and other displays on the front of the machine. This particular angle provides close-up observation and recording of a player's hands that he or she may use to alter or manipulate the cards, increase or decrease his or her bet, or insert a device into a slot machine.

The identification or ID shot: This shot is placed to obtain identification of the players on the game, individuals on or around the game, and employees on or around the game or area. This shot shows "who did what" and who was present during, before and after the activity.

Timely establishment of the identification shot and, in fact, establishment of the tri-shot at the onset of an event or suspicion nearly always provides the evidence or information necessary to appropriately stop the event or to investigate after the event. Operators who place their cameras properly will not fall prey to the all-too-common situation of not having enough cameras in place prior to the player or suspect leaving the game or area. The tri-shot also works for those occasions when you initially thought a player was suspicious, set up a tri-shot, but later felt everything was okay and moved on in your patrol. Later, when you determine that your initial suspicion was correct, you can go back on the video and obtain quality video of the play, table conditions and the all-important "ID" of the player.

Audits

One of the single most powerful weapons surveillance can use to detect and prevent crime is an operational audit. This technique catches more violations of controls, policies, procedures, theft and cheating than any other technique I'm aware of. I believe in audits strongly, as anyone who has ever worked for me will tell you. It is one of the reasons our teams were successful. I don't know why other surveillance directors don't use them. They always provide information or catch something somebody shouldn't be doing.

I recommend to you here that if you want to increase your department's detections and to operate proactively, set your team to doing audits. If your staff diligently perform the audit you've assigned, you will soon see a turnaround.

Most surveillance teams do not perform audits effectively for two reasons: 1) they don't use the information at hand to select the right area for audit and 2) personnel assigned to the task don't audit, they monitor.

Recently, I was assigned to assist in the turnaround of a surveillance department that over the years had not been able to catch crime events. It wasn't the fault of the agents; they wanted to succeed but they just hadn't been shown how to do it.

I would say here that in surveillance we often set up our surveillance rooms with all the equipment needed and then we expect the agents to catch things without providing the necessary guidance and training they need to succeed. Nowadays, with the proliferation of gaming across the country and around the world, we often have surveillance rooms staffed with personnel who've never been in a casino!

In the above case, my fix was to immediately set up an audit of the bars on the property. While we didn't catch any theft, we were able to report that not one bartender at any bar ever issued a receipt to any customer. This was significant information to both the GM and the beverage director, who were amazed. Not giving receipts can result in many forms of internal theft and is not a sound business practice.

We then did an audit of the snack bar. In about twenty-four hours we caught every employee working in the snack bar making food without paying for it, giving away food to other employees, and taking meats and product home, again without any payment. We also reported many health code violations. It was apparent that these activities had been going on for a long time and were certainly the primary reasons that the food costs in this area were always higher than they were supposed to be. The food and beverage director immediately made adjustments to personnel and to policy and procedure.

Of course, it amazed everyone that a quiet surveillance room was now catching things seemingly left and right. It also showed the surveillance personnel that they could catch thefts and they could be a force in the protection of the property. All this in about forty-eight hours of well-chosen and well-done audits by a team who had never done one before!

Let's take reason number one: not using the information at hand to select the right area. By information, I mean operating statistics, crime trends, exception reports, violations of internal controls, policies or procedures, and so forth. This type of information and more, when reviewed, will lead you to the proper area to audit.

A thorough and consistent audit schedule will generate numerous leads and detections for the department and for the operator performing the audits. Audits are used to monitor key areas, transactions and processes used within the casino.

Examples of key or critical areas, transactions and processes include, but are not limited to:

- Main cage
- Slot jackpots and fills
- Table game player rating cards
- Credit or "marker" transactions
- POS

Surveillance audits are normally set up as described below:

1. The surveillance director selects an area or transaction type to monitor and establishes the audit's objective, for example, to detect criminal activity or ensure employees are following rules, policies and procedures.
2. Information, documentation, controls, policies and procedures used by the department or area to be audited or to complete the transaction are gathered. Personnel assigned to the audit, including supervision, should review all such information prior to commencing the audit.
3. Photos of employees, subjects of interest or suspects may be included in the case file, as well as work schedules and any other pertinent information.
4. The parameters of the audit are established: time and date to start and end audit, who is assigned specifically to audit each shift, person responsible (case manager), types of notes to be made and who is authorized to know about the audit. This information is used to open the case file and is maintained in the case file at all times. Each person assigned to the audit must read this memo.
5. The audit is initiated as detailed in the case file.

A common audit instruction specifies that only exceptions to policy and procedure, or suspicious activity are logged into the case file. This prevents the file from becoming overloaded with unnecessary information and allows the case manager to quickly locate significant events.

Let's also discuss the second reason audits fail: personnel don't audit, they monitor. Audits require an involved agent. The agent must observe closely what is occurring and understand each transaction or activity performed by those being audited. Remember, individuals who are committing or involved in theft or fraud will do their utmost to hide their theft. It will require an astute and involved investigator to unravel the mystery.

Agents who only monitor activity and who are waiting for an obvious theft to occur will never locate anything except in the rarest of circumstances. Nowadays, employee theft and fraud doesn't always require the thief to place cash directly and obviously into their pocket. The assigned agent must look deeply into each activity and take the time to understand what is being done if he/she expects to be successful. Agents who fail to do so will fail.

It is necessary to keep in mind that an audit of any area or individual should find something, whether it be theft or a procedure violation. An audit that located nothing should be reviewed by the supervisor or manager to determine if the agent was only monitoring the area and missed key tells or activities.

Close Watches

There are three basic observation techniques used by surveillance. We've discussed IOU patrols and surveillance audits; the last one normally used is the surveillance close watch. This observation is usually performed because of a specific observation made or specific information received concerning suspicious or actual criminal activity perpetrated by specific individual(s) and/or occurring in a specific area. The close watch observation is used in these cases to specifically (in other words, closely) monitor the reported individual's every move while on the property or any and all activity in the subject area.

A number of close watches are implemented at the request of a GM, gaming enforcement agents, law enforcement, department heads, employees or the director of surveillance. Such requests are almost always based on a tip from an employee or informant or generated by unexplained losses or consistently lower than expected win percentages.

Whatever the reason for the close watch, it has been my experience that such information received is usually pretty good. Almost all of it has some basis in fact and should always be developed as much as possible. Information received from employees is especially good. Remember, employees working with an individual or a group of individuals usually have at least an idea or suspicion of what's going on. Employees don't like to tell on other employees, but sometimes they do, and the information is usually right on the mark. The key point about close watches is: when such information is received, make sure you follow it up. There is an excellent chance the information is solid and when investigated will result in an effective arrest.

This is usually where surveillance rooms go wrong: they either discount the source of information or disregard it entirely; or, because they don't watch the person or area long or well enough, they don't see the crime.

One property I worked at kept receiving anonymous calls reporting that the purchasing manager was up to something with a supplier. We did watch the individual a number of times, but never saw him do anything wrong. We later found that he was awarding contracts to the same supplier and was getting kickbacks. While we wouldn't have seen something on camera, a proper investigation would have located that information. In this case we dropped the ball too soon.

In another case, we received information from the payroll manager that one of her employees was suspected of stealing money from the purses of her fellow employees when they were out of the room. We set up a hidden camera over one employee's desk where her purse was kept, gave her money to put into the purse, and told her to leave both when she went on break. As we were waiting for things to develop, I went into my office and left the close watch in the hands of one of our agents with the explicit instructions "Don't take your eyes off that purse". I happened to glance up at the monitor in my office where the hidden camera was also displayed and immediately saw the suspect place her hand into the purse and take the cash. I waited to hear the agent yell out something like "I caught her" or "she took it", but I heard nothing. I ran out to the room and saw the agent talking to one of the other agents. He had taken his eyes off the purse and missed the theft. By the time we dispatched security, the suspect had made it out to her car with the cash. Luckily she admitted to everything and gave up the money.

The above is a typical close watch situation. Unless you assign the right person with explicit instructions, it will fail.

Tips for Successful Close Watches

- Obtain as much of the necessary and relevant information to the case as you can at the beginning. You may never get another chance. Get everything you can.
- Never, ever, take received information lightly, no matter how unlikely it seems. I have seen this type of information turn out to be correct more often than not.
- Assign close watches to your best people. You can't take the chance that the signature event will be missed.
- Take the time to put in writing the facts and beliefs of the case as you know them. Put this in a case file along with everything your investigators may need for the case. Include photos of suspects, schedules, pertinent policy and procedures, and so forth. Your people shouldn't have to hunt for anything. It should be at their fingertips.
- Assign a case manager to supervise the case. You need one person you can call and get updates from (and hold accountable).
- Ask for results daily. Close watches tend to start off strong, then slowly lose momentum. Keep your people focused on this critical task.
- Be patient! Close watches are notorious for how long they can take. Don't get discouraged or let your people get discouraged. Usually you will find what you're looking for.

Surveillance Patrol Flow Chart

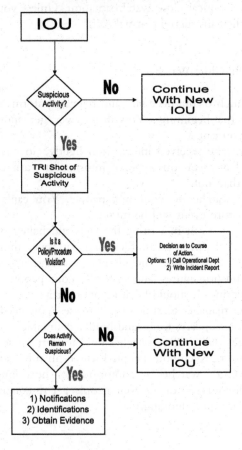

Surveillance Patrol Flow Chart

IOU

Suspicious Activity? — **No** → Continue With New IOU

Yes

TRI Shot of Suspicious Activity

Is it a Policy/Procedure Violation? — **Yes** → Decision as to Course of Action. Options: 1) Call Operational Dept 2) Write Incident Report

No

Does Activity Remain Suspicious? — **No** → Continue With New IOU

Yes

1) Notifications
2) Identifications
3) Obtain Evidence

Common Tells of Cheating and Theft

Tells to a Number of Common Scams or Indicators of Advantage Play Used in Blackjack

Card Counting

- Bet variation
- Strategy variation
- Taking or not taking insurance at certain times
- Player watching all cards
- Non-drinker or doesn't drink beer or cocktail ordered
- Places bets after all cards picked up

Card Mucking

- Player touching cards or bets twice
- Player picking up cards with one hand, replacing with the other hand
- One or both hands going off the table
- Unusual hand movements
- Both hands handling the cards
- Distractions on the game

Card Switching

- Players sitting close together, arms in folded position
- Hands on/off game
- Touching cards or bets twice
- Big money next to small money
- Distractions on the game

Daubing

- Hands off game
- Minimum bets, maximum hands
- Hand movements to body, face or hair
- Handles cards unusually, fingers may not touch all cards
- Rechecks cards frequently

Dealer/Agent

- Frequent player buy-in and color changes
- Dealer favoring player
- Incorrect pay-offs
- Pay-off not clear
- Total of hands not clear
- Tipping hole card or flashing of top cards by dealer
- Unusual hit/stand pattern (receiving information)
- Dealer holding deck unusually
- Rubbernecking

Dealing Seconds

- Unusual deck hand movements (peeking moves)
- Audible snap of cards
- "Dead Thumb"

(Continued)

(Cont).

Chip Cup

- Frequent buy-ins and/or color changes by same player(s)
- Dealer pays frequent attention to and manipulates checks in tray
- Player bets small denomination checks but has larger denomination checks in front or in pockets
- Ratholes checks

Computer Play

- Unusual hit/stand pattern
- Hesitation prior to strategy decisions
- Bet variations
- Unusual physical movements

Cooler Deck or Shoe

- Distraction during cut or placement of cards into shoe
- Player wearing jacket/coat
- Sudden increase in bets
- Game locked up
- Players receiving unusual number of naturals, double downs, splits or strong hands not requiring a decision
- Dealer extends cards for cut farther than normal
- No cut of cards

Marked Cards in Play

- Unusual hit/stand pattern (receiving information)
- Sudden increase in bets to table maximum
- Game locked up
- Signal pattern from other player(s)
- Big money next to small money
- Dealer not dealing as per procedure

Pinching/Pressing

- Movements to bets when dealer is facing away
- Touching cards or bets twice
- Hands moving over bets
- Hands close to bets
- Distractions on the game

Dealer Stealing Checks

- Hands moving/touching body or face without clearing hands
- Unusual pick up of checks
- Frequent manipulation of checks, and/ or straightening checks in tray
- Rubbernecking

False Shuffle

- Incorrect house shuffle
- No squaring of deck
- Sudden increase in bets
- Game locked up
- Players receiving unusual number of naturals, double downs, splits or strong hands not requiring a decision
- No cut of cards

Hole Card Play

- Unusual hit/stand pattern (receiving information)
- Placement of arm or device in a stationary position on the game
- Player(s) slumping
- Signal pattern from other player(s)
- Incorrect hole card placement by dealer

Shuffle Tracking

- Large bets at top of shoe
- Large bets from outside game
- Sudden increase in bets
- When offered cut player takes a long time placing cut card
- Players at game often refuse cut, allowing one specific player to cut cards

Common to Most or Cause for Further Investigation

- Procedure break or violation (intentional or not)
- Unusual hit/stand pattern
- Larger or maximum bets (follow the money)
- Rubbernecking
- Distractions on the game

Tells Indicative of Slot Cheating, Slot Advantage Play or Employee Theft

Counterfeit Bills Placed in Validator Units

- Frequent input of cash, frequent cash out of credits
- Minimal or brief play
- Player or associate continuously cashes out
- Unknown/new player
- Rubbernecking
- Bills rejected often, suspect tries same bill repeatedly
- Counterfeit and good money kept separate, bills into validator from one location and from cash out to another

Counterfeit Bills

- Maximum bills in, then cash out of credits
- Minimal play
- On and off play
- Unknown/new players
- Rubbernecking

Distract and Grab (Purse/TITO Theft)

- Individuals who enter casino together, then split up and move about in different directions in slot area
- Individual(s) roam slot areas without playing
- Often carrying bills, wallet, purse or TITO ticket to throw on floor
- Individual approaches slot players and engages them in conversation or to toss an item on the floor

Injecting Slot Machine RAM with False Information

- Unknown/new player
- Blockers/distracters in use, blocking camera angles, usually must open machine to access RAM (random access memory)
- Playing machine or linked machines for substantial jackpot (usually a progressive) for cash or high-value prizes (cars, boats, etc.)

Manipulation of Machine or Malfunction

- Rubbernecking
- Player attempting to disguise/camouflage or cover up method of play or readouts of the machine
- Payout does not match combination or display on machine or screen
- Wings consistently and cashes out frequently
- Machine in constant play by individuals using same method of play
- Abnormal amount of fills
- Unusual and consistent method of play
- Expert input of coin or use of play/credit buttons
- Items observed that could be used as tools such as bobby pins, drink or cocktail straws, etc.

Professional/Advantage Players

- All machines of type in constant play
- Players are extremely adept at playing machines
- Players familiar with casino rules, procedures and operations
- Players appear to be locals

(Continued)

(Cont).

Devices Used to Disrupt Coin Readers

- Coin payout meter does not match coin paid out
- Payout does not match symbols on reels or on screen
- Player reaches into payout chute or other area of machine to place and retrieve device
- Hoppers found empty or near empty without players present
- Rubbernecking
- Usually occurs on higher denomination machines
- Player may sit with legs up on each side of machine
- Unknown/new player

Drop Door Breaking/Entering – Theft of Bill Validator

- Illegal drop door or drop door open signal/alarms at unusual time of day and/or without prior notification
- Suspicious individuals loitering about during drop or during quiet periods
- Unsecured and/or broken drop door or lock (internal/collusion)
- Drop crew leaves behind drop bucket or validator (internal/collusion)

Theft from Slot Machine

- Floor person or slot technician enters machine for no apparent reason and/or a player not present
- Hands to body without clearing hands after entering machine
- Does not sign entry card and/or use card system

False Jackpots

- Required number of employees not present at jackpot
- Jackpot not locate at machine listed on slot system and/or paperwork
- Signatures of verifying employees not legible or identifiable
- Jackpot paperwork not signed at location of jackpot

Slot/Casino Employee Impersonator

- Dresses as or similar to other casino employee
- Roams slot areas without playing
- Approaches players, obtains cash (pretending he/she will get their change for them) and immediately leaves the property

Tells Indicative of Employee Theft in POS Positions (Retail and/or Food and Beverage)

Discounts

- Tender type
- Timing of discount
- Terminal transactions/patterns
  - Low cash sales
  - Excessive check duration times
  - Excessive tip %
  - Cash drawer log on/log off
  - No sale

Voids

- Tender type
- Access
- Authorizer
- Terminal transactions/patterns
  - Low cash sales
  - Cash drawer log on/log off
  - No sale

Comps

- Tender type
- Timing of comp
- Terminal transactions/patterns
  - Low cash sales
  - Excessive check duration times
  - Cash drawer log on/log off
  - No sales

Splits/Combines

- One pass or multi pass
- Tender type
- Access/authorization
- Terminal transactions/patterns
  - Low cash sales
  - Excessive check duration times
  - Reprint last receipt
  - Cash drawer log on/log off
  - No sale

Overs/Shorts

- Timing of variance
- Washing variance
- Impressment

Print Last Receipt

- Tender type
- Requirement for accounting
- Access/authorization
- Terminal transactions/patterns
  - Low cash sales
  - Excessive check duration times
  - Cash drawer log on/log off
  - No sale

Cash Drawer Log On/Log Off

- Tender type before and after
- Terminal transactions/patterns
  - Low cash sales
  - Pass cancel
  - Print last receipt
  - Discounts
  - Voids
  - Comps
  - Splits/combines

No Sales

- Tender type before and after
- In addition to terminal transactions
- Access/authorization
- Terminal transactions/patterns
  - Low cash sales
  - Pass cancel
  - Print last receipt
  - Comps
  - Voids

Excessive Tip %

- Tip on cash
- Identification of guest
- Compare tip to check
- Access/authorization
- Terminal transactions/patterns
  - Credit card settlements
  - Excessive sale of low-value item(s)
  - Discounts

(Continued)

(Cont).

Credit Card Settlements

- Card decline
- Known customer
- Refunds
- Terminal transactions/patterns
  ○ Excessive tip %

Zero Cash

- Access/authorization
- Terminal transactions/patterns
  ○ Low cash sales

Tells for Other Types of Fraud and Theft

General

- Living beyond one's means
- Excessive gambling habits, use of alcohol or use of drugs
- Financial pressures
- Failure to follow required controls, policies and procedures
- Highly trusted employee with high level of access/responsibility with ability to authorize transactions
- No segregation of duties

Player's Club

- Same individuals win promotions/prizes consistently
- Promotion extremely popular with employees/guests
- Frequent redemption of free play or other coupons by employees/guests
- Friends or family of club employees or other key employees loitering at the club
- Friends or family of club employees possess accounts with unusual activity
- Frequent point adjustments made to certain accounts by the same employee
- Editing of a player's account without guest present
- Frequent name changes made to accounts performed by same employee
- Frequent PIN changes made to accounts performed by same employee

Bingo/Keno

- Wins/jackpots paid to same players
- Rabbit ears not cleared completely or only partially cleared prior to game
- High level of tokes or significant increase in tokes
- Frequent variances
- Same employees consistently verify wins/jackpots

Race and Sports Book

- Early lines offered to a select group of bettors
- Frequent wagers by messenger bettors
- Frequent void activity by writer
- Writer makes personal wagers while on duty

Appendix 4

Case Management Tracking Log

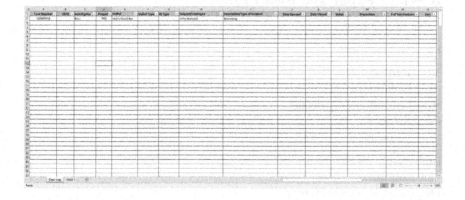

International Association of Certified Surveillance Professionals

Video Review, Investigation, and Retention in Gaming Environments

---

A White Paper and Best Practice

Table of Contents

Position Statement

Purpose

In Gaming environments, the use of Closed Circuit
Television (CCTV) Systems is not only recommended for the protection of people and assets, it is typically mandated by the regulators of the jurisdiction where the gaming property is located. There are two basic areas of CCTV which are gaming and non-gaming at any facility also typically defined by regulations. Gaming areas are highly regulated where non-gaming areas are not depending on the jurisdiction.

CCTV in gaming facilities provide some deterrence to internal and external theft, fraud and other criminal events merely by the obvious cameras located throughout a casino and mounted in ceilings or on walls in the regulated gaming areas. Non-gaming area CCTV cameras are manned and operated either by the physical security department or included in the surveillance function. Non-gaming areas include parking lots or garages, back of house areas, hotel and associated facilities, convention and meeting spaces, entertainment venues, food and beverage outlets and retail spaces.

In most jurisdictions surveillance is staffed by personnel (agents) who monitor gaming operations and money sensitive activity, using video monitors and other technology in a secure location with highly restricted access. Hotel, retail and back of house may be monitored by either the surveillance or security departments. This monitoring is done live with the agent having access to hundreds or even thousands of camera views. The agents are looking for unusual or suspicious behavior that is not routine for the environment. Agents watch for illegal activity, procedural violations, and regulatory compliance. The agents also conduct specialized investigations or review of recorder video.

A good portion of what a surveillance agent or security officer assigned to a monitor location does is to review previously recorded video. Most gaming environments record on a one to one format or every camera in a facility is recorded to either analog or digital video recorders, or a combination of both. Not all camera views are monitored live by surveillance agents.

From a regulatory standpoint, at most casinos and gaming facilities the surveillance department will report to a commission or a higher-level company executive independent of the physical security department. Based on the sensitivity of the gaming area, observations and compliance audits may include observation of the physical security department. The security department will typically report to a high-level executive at the property level independently of the surveillance department.

Using recorded video to review an incident or event that has already occurred for the purposes of investigation to determine what occurred and what persons were involved is a critical skill for a gaming or security surveillance agent, gaming regulators, or law enforcement investigators.

The review of video is also a necessary skill that should be taught, developed, used consistently and professionally by all appropriate personnel to ensure the review is completed according to industry common practices and specific to the property. It is also critical to document the process of review through surveillance or security logs and to secure the video in tape or digital media using a formal chain of custody for criminal prosecution and civil litigation.

In almost all cases of video review, the end result will be used to affect someone's life in a substantial manner; to provide information as to what actually occurred in an infinite variety of situations or to defend against litigation and claims. The result of the review can be anything from loss of employment, other disciplinary action or arrest, prosecution, and incarceration if convicted. The result could also be used to defend in civil litigation.

While the review of video is a serious matter, it is also one of those skills that receive little, if any, attention in formal surveillance training programs. In many cases the lack of video, lack of complete or thorough retention of video and/or lack of documentation in the form of review logs or reports can cause the case under review to fail in formal application for action.

It is the intent of this paper to recommend best practices and protocols for the review of surveillance video, and the securing of video evidence for use when necessary in gaming facilities.

Definitions

Agents: Personnel assigned to a secure monitor room who conduct live observation and video review of prerecorded video.

Back of House: All non-gaming areas where there is not some form of gaming device, table or activity.

CCTV: Closed Circuit Television system utilized in gaming environments.

Cheques: A house negotiable item used on gaming tables with a specific value.

Claim: A legal process that involves some form of allegation and demand for some remuneration.

Commission: A regulatory agency that oversees and assures compliance with gaming activity.

Compilation Video: Also known as a composite of various views of an incident used for criminal prosecution or internal presentation.

Digital Media: Digitized content that can be transmitted over the internet or computer networks. This can include text, audio, video, and graphics.

Digital Video Receiver (DVR): A device that records audio and video input, typically from a television signal, on to a hard disk.

Documentation: Material that provides official information or evidence or that serves as a record.

Network Video Recorder (NVR): A software program that records video in a digital format to a disk drive, USB flash drive, SD memory card or other mass storage device. An NVR contains no dedicated video capture hardware.

Physical Security: The protection of personnel, hardware, programs, networks, and data from physical circumstances and events that could cause serious losses or damage to an enterprise, agency, or institution. This includes protection from fire, natural disasters, burglary, theft, vandalism, and terrorism.

Plot Map: A drawing, diagram or print of the area where an incident or event occurred such as the casino floor or a parking facility, that depicts the location and views of surveillance cameras. It may also include positions of employees such as security officers.

Review: The systematic review of recorded video by security or law enforcement personnel to locate an individual to ascertain his or her activities in a work or public environment, or an incident or event to determine its nature, time of occurrence and duration, those involved, how it evolved, and was managed and resolved by responding personnel.

Review Log: A log documenting components or clips of video depicting certain activities, actions, or movements of a subject, incident or event.

TITO: Ticket In-Ticket Out, a voucher received from a slot machine as payment for credits won or purchased.

Video: A sequence of images processed electronically into an analog or digital format and displayed on a screen with sufficient rapidity to form a moving picture.

Video Analytics: The capability of automatically analyzing video to detect and determine temporal and spatial events.

Video Cassette Recorder (VCR): Video recording device used prior to the introduction of digital video recorders. Some VCRs are still in use today.

Video Review: A review as defined previously. Performed to locate a specific incident, occurrence, individual, witnesses or suspects.

Operational Challenge

Those protective personnel responsible for reviewing video with a need to locate an incident, individual, vehicle, or any other type of issue, including a criminal event, do not always receive adequate training in how to do so nor is there typically a written guideline or procedure to follow other than to review the video from one point in time to another.

While this approach may suffice in capturing the significant event it does not take into account the concerns and issues that may arise as the information or case is reviewed by others for its merit, accuracy, its ability to prevail in a court of law or in arbitration with an outside state or federal agency, or union representatives.

A practical, effective, accountable, and verifiable system that can be used by surveillance and security practitioners to conduct video reviews properly and thoroughly should be utilized. The system should allow for consideration of potential concerns and future litigation, provide documentation of how the review was performed, and preserve the essential video evidence.

Solution

It is the IACSP's recommendation that surveillance and security professionals reviewing video perform the following:

First Step

The first step is to determine the nature of the review and investigation. The theft of a TITO (Slot machine jackpot slip) does not rise to the same level of review of a homicide in a hotel or parking garage. The time and resources applied to the investigation of a minor theft should differ considerably from what is used in a serious criminal event. Each incident should be reviewed; however the depth and scope of that review should be considered prior to a review. The decision for review category is a property level decision and should be commensurate with the event being investigated.

Minimum Level Review

Minor incidents or events (such as: a TITO theft, or a lost item) or requests from other departments (such as: a guest service complaint or theft of an employee's tokes) may only require a minimum level review. A minimum level review is one that is purposely limited to the location of the subject, item or issue involved with the intent to report findings for response by other departments or for later response by the surveillance department (for example: the suspect has left the property, a photo will be taken of the suspect to assist in his apprehension when he returns).

A minimum level review will not usually attempt to determine all of the movements, activities, and whereabouts of the subjects involved. Additionally, reviewing and retaining video preceding and after the event is usually not necessary. Should there be any questions or concerns about the incident these steps should be considered.

Medium Level Review

When reviewing an incident or event that may rise to the level of severe discipline (written warning, suspension and/or termination) misdemeanor arrest, arbitration or litigation, begin at least one hour prior to the event and continue through to at least one hour after the event.

Taking the time to see how an incident developed, progressed and ended may provide new or additional information, make a determination of a behavioral pattern, or identify witnesses or suspects not previously known. Additionally, the extended video may assist in countering potential challenges to the investigation by the subject or his/her defenders. It may also rid you of a confirmation bias or preconceived idea about how the incident happened and who was or wasn't involved. Examples of such incidents/events are employee policy or procedure violations, petty theft, employee misconduct and guest or employee medical issues or claims.

Consideration should be given to demonstrate a security officer presence prior to a fight or disturbance to show a security presence in the area and mitigate allegations of inadequate security in civil litigation.

Comprehensive Level Review

Serious or potentially serious incidents will usually require a comprehensive review. These incidents could be cheating at gaming, felony crimes, deaths or serious injury, or significant loss, guest (or employee) injury, events that could cause significant damage to company reputation, or a disaster affecting the lives and/or health of employees and guests.

A comprehensive review begins with a thorough and comprehensive assessment and review of all cameras in any area that may provide any coverage of the event or of those individuals involved. In such incidents, enough personnel, time, and other resources should be used to accomplish the full review.

By their very nature, serious incidents/events require strict attention and special handling. How the incident/event is reviewed and investigated immediately after its occurrence will determine its final result, identification of those involved, their arrest and prosecution, if applicable, and the extent of liability, if any, to the property and its ability mitigate that liability.

The components of a comprehensive review are:

Identify and review all cameras within a one-hundred- foot radius of the event for pertinent information or activity associated with the event.

Within the one-hundred-foot radius review all ancillary cameras such as those placed in kiosks, ATMs, and those positioned in other areas or departments that may provide potential evidence or information.

Continue the review of all cameras, including ancillary cameras, within a one-hundred-foot radius as those involved and/or the incident itself shifts locations, changes, or progresses, and/or involved subjects enter or exit the area. The one-hundred-foot radius moves with the incident and those involved as the incident moves

Review at least eight hours of video from each camera, including ancillary cameras to obtain potential information/evidence that may pertain to the incident.

Be cognizant that it may be necessary to expand the review and investigation in time, by camera, by area, and those determined to be involved and/ or due to information received.

The video review should include the entire response of personnel including any agency (e.g. Fire, ambulance, EMT, Security officers, police, gaming regulators). This response should include all the way through until they leave the premises.

As an example, it is important to document through video the presence of uniformed security personnel in instances of assaults, serious injury or death. The frequency of their presence will prove beneficial in any potential civil litigation involving a charge of inadequate security. The video may also discover pertinent other information as to the cause of an extended event.

Second Step

A review should include all camera angles available that may pertain to the incident. Video from each camera in the area should be reviewed for the recommended time period and saved. Such review may provide additional pertinent information or may determine that a particular camera and angle does not provide any further information. Both are important and should be saved for potential litigation regardless if it contains specific incident content. This will mitigate accusations of negligence in saving video or spoliation of video claims.

Third Step

Identify, collect or cause to collect (as applicable) and secure physical evidence. Items touched, damaged or discarded by persons of interest could be valuable to the investigation. Close-up photos of environment/ elements that may have caused (or been stated to have caused) injury in civil claims.

Fourth Step

Video from all pertinent cameras and camera angles should be retained until well beyond the end of the pertinent statute of limitations, or as stated in the company's retention policy or as defined by regulation. Whichever policy is used to retain video should be followed consistently in every case.

The industry common practice and most state gaming regulations mandate for retention the video is to be maintained for at least 7 full days and the video should be saved and maintained in the custody of the surveillance or security department. A chain of custody log is utilized to enter the incident, report number, who placed it into secure storage, the date and time, and any other pertinent information for easy identification at a later date when needed. If the video is not collected from the surveillance system and saved within the retention period, permanent loss of that video will occur.

Fifth Step

Review video of the entire incident. This includes the arrival on property or general area of the involved individuals or vehicles, and all activity before the incident and continuing through the incident to its termination. You should provide or be able to provide the entire story of the event. There should not be any surprises nor any questions that you can't answer or haven't attempted to answer.

Sixth Step

When reviewing video to locate an incident, person, or item in which little is known as to where it occurred, when it occurred, or who was involved, it is best to begin your review using one of two methods: outside and work in, or inside and work out. Think of the review in concentric circles. The target or incident is the common center.

In most cases the common center will be the source of the review. For example, when cheating at gaming occurs at Blackjack (BJ) No. 1, the video review would begin at the logical common center, BJ 1. From that point the investigator can work their way out through concentric circles of cameras to locate when each suspect arrived at the game, whether individually or as a group, how the suspects arrived at the property, and using what mode of travel. Additionally, the investigator can then work their way out to determine when the suspects left the game, how much in cash or cheques did they leave with, in what direction, singly or in groups, and what mode of travel was used.

In other cases, the suspect or subject will be the only thing known to the agent and should be used as the common center. In such a case, locating that person(s) entering the property, or an area (outside/in) and tracking him/her to the event or issue.

For example, if an elderly man was beaten in his hotel room and robbed, it is suspected that someone had observed him cashing out and had followed him to his room. Because there is no camera coverage in the hotel areas and room corridors and the man couldn't describe his assailants nor could he remember where he had played, the victim had to be first located on the casino floor and then his movements and interactions could be tracked during the review process.

Using this method to follow the victim through the video review of his activity and movements the suspects who followed him to his room are ultimately found, followed as they exited the hotel and as they left the property in their vehicle. Because of the video, the suspects are identified and arrested by the police the same day.

Seventh Step

A video review log should be completed for any review involving more than five minutes of subject activity or for any video of a significant nature. A recommended practice is to use a video review log for any incident or event that will be reviewed by another person, department, or agency. The video review log should be a standard pre-printed document with appropriate places to list:

a.   Date of review and time initiated
b.   Name or identification number of agent performing the review

c. Applicable internal report number, incident subject, or name of subject
d. Time period reviewed
e. Camera numbers being reviewed, DVR or NVR number and sequence times
f. Monitor numbers of cameras, if applicable
g. Location of digital media storage, DVR or VCR, if applicable
h. Results/notes from review of the camera/area
i. When the video from a camera/area/review provides nothing that pertains to the case it should be described as such using "nothing pertinent to case". A photo of the scene that does not pertain to the case may be taken and combined with the plot map to illustrate that cameras view. Video from such cameras should be saved.
j. Video review logs should be summarized and included in the case file for later reference. Personal opinions or comments should not be included in the review log or in any formal report or summation.
k. Incidents that may require considerable time to review should be assigned to one individual who would serve as a case manager responsible for ensuring all pertinent video, reports, witness statements and other evidence is identified, reviewed, and secured. The case manager should also manage the assignment of reviews to individuals on each shift and that all information is passed on to each shift and detailed in the video review log.

Eighth Step

Resources such as time, personnel, and equipment, etc., should be considered and documented. Intermediate and full reviews can be time consuming and will remove personnel from other duties and responsibilities, and should be only be performed after careful thought, and for the appropriate level of review. It is also suggested that in arrest situations or criminal prosecution, the surveillance function of review should be documented and submitted to the prosecutor for possible restitution and reimbursement of personnel time and resources.

Ninth Step

Video reviewed should be retained as described in section 4. Pertinent video may be copied and compiled into a summation, compilation or "Presentation video" for the purposes of presenting the case to internal departments and executives, law enforcement or other outside individuals or agencies. Original video used to compile the presentation video evidence should always be retained.

A presentation, summation or compilation video is used to present the event and/or evidence in a timely, convenient and easily understood form. Only video that is directly related to the case is used in the presentation video for prosecution purposes. Video that does not provide information for the case is not placed so as to allow easy review of the key elements of the case.

Civil cases should not use a presentation, summation or compilation video as it can be used by a plaintiff to only demonstrate the negative events that help their case. Presentation, summation or compilation video should be clearly labeled or titled as being intended only for the purposes of criminal investigation.

For example, video from a garage camera that depicts a suspect vehicle entering and leaving a garage before and after an incident, may be presented to show the vehicle entering and exiting the garage only, and not the elapsed time between the two occurrences. This is to allow ease of review only. Video used to compile the presentation video should be saved in its entirety as evidence.

Tenth Step

Securing video that may be needed for evidentiary purposes is of utmost importance. It should be properly stored and maintained for potentially long periods of time, be easily retrieved, and in its original format when needed. Additionally, a formal and demonstrable chain of custody of the evidence secured and its handling is necessary.

Presently there are two types of video in use today within the gaming industry: analog and digital. While the majority of surveillance departments have converted to digital systems there are still a number of properties that continue to use analog systems that record video using video cassette recorders (VCRs). There are some fundamental differences for the securing of these different types of video that should be considered.

Video evidence obtained through an analog system using VCRs as the recording medium require the videotapes of the activity to be removed from the VCR and/or from the tape rotation. Any video that is to be saved should be pulled and retained in its original form. For example, an incident occurring on the casino floor may, during the course of the incident, involve many locations and different cameras. Based on the type of incident, it may be necessary to save each videotape that pertains to the incident. If each of the involved cameras is recorded on an individual VCR (or on any type of multi-input recording device) the number of videotapes to be saved can be significant, but it is necessary to retain each of the videotapes that may be used as evidence as stated in Section 4.

Video obtained from digital cameras and their recording systems should be isolated from active recording, saved, and stored. Video media being retained should be placed onto a separate storage drive used exclusively for video storage.

Digital media when released internally, to outside agencies or individuals should be placed on appropriate recording discs, flash drives or other portable devices. Source operating and encryption code should be embedded onto the disc or storage device. All original video should be retained.

Conclusion

Surveillance personnel should use a standard system to review video when conducting an investigation of an event, incident or person. The recommended best practices to use when performing a review are:

- Determine priority of review: minimum, medium, or comprehensive.
- Consider necessary resources to complete review.
- Review all angles and cameras that are present in a one-hundred-foot radius or that may have coverage of the event, incident, or person before, during, or after the occurrence. Video from all pertinent cameras and camera angles should be retained for a defined time period or as stated in the company's retention policy or as determined by legal action.
- Utilize a plot map that can be attached to the review log or report that identifies camera locations in relation the subject or object of review. Drawing in the path taken or specific locations is very helpful during criminal or civil litigation.
- Ensure you obtain and review the entire set of circumstances and those individuals involved that tells the story of the occurrence. This may require you to ascertain the locations, movements, and activities of suspects and victims, other significant persons, or items, for the entire period of time each is on the property.
- Review in concentric circles from a common center (Inside/Out) or to a common center (Outside/In). Concentric circles with a perimeter of one hundred foot should be reviewed one at a time. Review cameras within the one-hundred-foot perimeters, each in turn, as one circle is completed and another initiated, until all pertinent video is located, reviewed, and documented.
- List all pertinent details of observations onto a video review form. Include time, location, monitor/camera, subject(s), and a description.
- Memorialize the contents of the video review log in the formal investigation report in a complete and concise manner without listing any opinions or conclusions.
- Establish chain of custody for all involved video, maintain video in a secure location, and release only with proper authorization and in the proper format.

We encourage surveillance directors and others responsible for the training of surveillance agents and investigators to incorporate the above best practices and guidelines into their video review process.

Bibliography

Boss, Derk J. and Zajic, Alan W., *Casino Security and Gaming Surveillance*, 2010

Original Contributors

Derk J. Boss, CFE, CPE, CSP
DJ Boss Associates
Alan W. Zajic, CPP, CSP
AWZ Consulting
Jen Boss, CSP
DJ Boss Associates

Additional Contributors

Chuck Barry
Randy Boynton
Ron Buono
Kevin Cheeseman
Ron Flores
Abe Martin
Stephanie Wallace
David Norcutt
Darrin Hoke

Document Revision History

Completed by original authors on October 14, 2015
Sent out to International Association of Certified Surveillance Professionals (IACSP) Board of Directors on October 17, 2015
Returned to original authors with input from IACSP Board on November 2, 2015
Final white paper sent back out to IACSP Board for approval on March 16, 2016 and returned on March 31, 2016
Final edits and formatting sent out to IACSP membership and selected industry professionals, add references and footnotes December 15, 2016
Return to original authors, addition of contributor's names, final edit and formatting on June 2017.
Published September of 2017

About IACSP

Founded in 2001, the International Association of Certified Surveillance Professionals (IACSP) is a growing organization established by your peers and colleagues throughout the industry to develop and provide training to prepare surveillance personnel for the future. Our mission is to train existing and future surveillance agents in the core skills of their profession and also to develop the next generation of surveillance agents, supervisors, managers and directors. As you know, surveillance departments are continuously being challenged to protect our properties more effectively. The need for highly trained personnel has never been greater. The IACSP addressed this issue through training; a certification program developed by surveillance directors. For more information, to contact an IACSP member, or to become a member of the association, visit www.iacsp.org.

Index

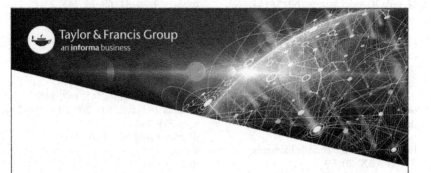